INVITATION TO
THE PALACE

INVITATION TO THE PALACE

How Royalty Entertains

BRIAN HOEY

GRAFTON BOOKS

A Division of the Collins Publishing Group

LONDON GLASGOW
TORONTO SYDNEY AUCKLAND

Grafton Books
A Division of the Collins Publishing Group
8 Grafton Street, London W1X 3LA

Published by Grafton Books 1989

British Library Cataloguing in Publication Data

Hoey, Brian
    Invitation to the palace: How royalty entertains
    1. Household management. Entertaining by British
    royal families
    I. Title
    642'.4'0922

ISBN 0-246-13413-5

Printed in Great Britain by
Butler & Tanner Ltd, Frome and London

Contents

Acknowledgements

I am most fortunate in receiving The Queen's permission to examine and quote from papers in the Royal Archives.

It would be impossible to write an accurate account of how the Royal Family entertains without the co-operation and assistance of members and former members of the Royal Household. I am therefore delighted to be able to place on record my appreciation to those ladies and gentlemen who, although bound by the rules governing all who work for The Queen and her family, were able to advise me when I started out on this undertaking.

It is to Sir Peter Ashmore, former Master of the Household, that I owe the greatest debt. Without his guidance the chapters on State entertaining and the domestic side of life at Buckingham Palace and the other Royal homes would have lacked the authority and insight I hope they now contain. John Haslam, Deputy Press Secretary to The Queen, has been equally helpful. In spite of hundreds of telephone calls, dozens of other personal queries and many visits to his office at Buckingham Palace, he has always been unfailingly courteous and acted as a splendid conduit between the various Household departments and myself. In the Royal Archives at Windsor Castle, Oliver Everett, Librarian, Elizabeth Cuthbert, former Registrar, Lady Sheila de Bellaigue, the present Registrar, and Frances Dimond, Photographic Curator, have been a delight to work with. The former Comptroller of the Lord Chamberlain's Office, Sir John Johnston, and Lady Johnston shared their unique knowledge of the workings of the Royal Household – past and present – and Air Vice Marshal John Severne, former Captain of The Queen's Flight, gave me much valuable information about his command. There are many others in the Royal Household who prefer not to be acknowledged by name; I am glad of this opportunity to thank them.

Mr Chris Paschalides of the Stafford Hotel has been very helpful regarding royal menus and recipes.

As far as the production of the book is concerned, my thanks go to Rachel Stewart for her help with the manuscript, Janice Robertson, whose editing has improved my text considerably, Katherine Everett, who is responsible for the illustrations, and, of course, my publisher, Richard Johnson of Grafton Books. Finally, Mike Shaw, my agent, whose expertise has made the original idea of the book into an economic reality.

BRIAN HOEY

Introduction

Her Majesty The Queen is the heir to a long-standing tradition of royal hospitality. For centuries British monarchs have enjoyed reputations as generous hosts to their fellow monarchs, and also to presidents and other Heads of State. When Queen Victoria was on the throne almost every royal family in Europe was related to her and she took a great delight in inviting them to stay with her at Buckingham Palace and her other homes. Her successors have continued the tradition, and even today, when the remnants of Europe's royalty are spread thinly across a continent which once boasted twenty reigning sovereigns, royal visitors are welcomed frequently to Windsor Castle and The Queen's London home.

As the country's official hostess, Her Majesty entertains on behalf of her people, so royal hospitality has an important political aspect in developing a feeling of goodwill and friendship in the minds of visiting Heads of State.

Hospitality at Buckingham Palace or Windsor Castle could so easily be simply a cold and formal affair. The fact that it has become a warm, human activity enjoyed by hostess and guest alike is due to the obvious pleasure The Queen and the Duke of Edinburgh take in sharing their homes with their guests.

Royal visits vary in the amount of formality they require. A State Visit is a formal declaration of friendship and certain matters of protocol have to be observed. Its length never varies – always four days whether the guest is the Emperor of Japan or a prince of a tiny

principality. In London, the visit begins with a State drive through the decorated streets to Buckingham Palace. A State Banquet in honour of the guest is held; and a further banquet hosted by the Lord Mayor of London takes place at Guildhall. The guest then acts as host himself at a return banquet held either in his country's embassy or in a leading hotel. Members of the Corps Diplomatique are presented to him, and the British Court surrounds him with all the pageantry and ritual at its command.

Much more frequent are the informal 'private visits' of foreign royalty. Although King Olaf of Norway is a regular visitor to Britain, he has made State Visits only twice; at other times he slips into the country unannounced to stay with friends or family. On these occasions he will not be greeted formally, nor will there be a State Banquet in his honour. But The Queen will usually welcome His Majesty to Buckingham Palace and invite him to an informal luncheon. Similarly King Hussein of Jordan, who was educated in Britain and maintains a home near Windsor, comes and goes at regular intervals throughout the year. He prefers, and The Queen respects his wish, little or no publicity to be given to his visits. But he is always welcomed on behalf of Her Majesty by a senior member of the Royal Household, and he is often a guest at quiet private lunches and dinners.

Britain has long understood the subtle art of playing host to the great and famous. If the visitors wish to remain incognito the British are only too happy to pay them this special courtesy. Yet when the occasion demands, few can equal the splendour with which the British can surround them.

In the twenties and thirties, the days between the two world wars, entertaining in London was carried out on a prodigious scale. Hostesses vied with each other as to who could attract the most sparkling guests to her table; and to see which of them could spend the most money on food, drink, decorations and diversions. It was an age of extravagance and splendour, when one of the more common complaints concerned the number of red carpets worn through in a single season.

The great mansions of Belgravia and Mayfair would be ablaze

A formal line-up at a State Banquet held at Buckingham Palace for the Sultan of Oman. Prince Philip is wearing full Court Dress, including knee breeches, with the garter worn below his left knee. In the background the Lord Chamberlain waits carrying his white wand of office.

with lights from early evening until dawn; armies of servants would toil throughout the day and late into the night to ensure that the hostess and her guests wanted for nothing. The leading politicians of the day would arrive from the House of Commons with the latest world news and gossip; artists and musicians fresh from triumphs at the Royal Albert Hall would mingle with the glittering stars of the theatre, and for every hostess, to entertain royalty was the biggest catch of all.

In the thirties the most dazzling royals were the Prince of Wales (later Duke of Windsor), the Duke and Duchess of York (later King George VI and Queen Elizabeth) and the glamorous Kents, Prince George, Duke of Kent, and his Greek bride Princess Marina. Any party that included their names on the guest list was assured of success – and the envy of the rest of London society.

The protocol when a member of the Royal Family was expected was extremely detailed and had to be followed to the letter. The proposed guest list was submitted to the appropriate Private Secretary, who would then return it either approved or with certain names deleted. It was almost impossible to add any names once the list had been agreed. Sir Henry 'Chips' Channon, an old friend of King Edward VIII, was once host at a dinner party attended by His Majesty, at his house at number 5 Belgrave Square. When The King arrived he noticed an unfamiliar face in the gathering. Turning to his host, he said, 'Who is that man? Is he on your list?' On being informed that this was a friend who had only recently turned up in London, after the list had been submitted, The King considered for a moment, and then, somewhat reluctantly, agreed that the extra guest could stay.

The King also insisted on being consulted about the menu and choice of wines, even though he was not a gourmet and frequently left his food untouched. He placed great emphasis on the seating plan and, until the advent of Mrs Simpson, made sure that the prettiest women were always placed next to him.

Another of his little foibles was that he liked to decide what the dress for the evening would be, and would telephone his host a few hours before dinner and decree that 'white tie, tails and decorations will be worn'. There was then a frantic scramble by telephone and messenger to make sure all the other guests were informed. If a dinner jacket was the order of the day, The King would dictate whether soft shirts or boiled fronts were to be worn and on one occasion complained in a loud voice when he saw a fellow guest with the wrong sort of cuff-links.

However, His Majesty was in many ways a contradiction. For instance it was expected that at any function he would always occupy first place in a procession and be the first to be served. But when he went to a private dinner he insisted that the ladies should precede him into the dining room and that the hostess should be served before him. When the ladies left the room after dinner, leaving the gentlemen to their port and cigars, they would all curtsey before the sovereign – and he was the first to notice if a curtsey wasn't deep enough to satisfy the royal honour. He would then take charge of the seating arrangements, once more ordering each of the male guests to a particular place, fully aware that in society proximity to the sovereign signified power and achievement.

Conversation has always been an important part of entertaining, particularly in royal circles. When a member of the Royal Family was expected for luncheon or dinner he or she would frequently decree in advance what subjects would be discussed. In the days immediately prior to the Second World War this practice took on a new and significant meaning, as the leaders of society and industry were canvassed for their attitudes to Germany and the possibility of war. King Edward VIII himself frequently used the 'politics of the dining-table' not only to air his own views but to find out what others felt about world affairs at a time when his official advisers told him only what they felt he should know – which was often not very much. These dinner parties were therefore held in an atmosphere of authority and responsibility, even though the settings might be frivolous in the extreme and hostesses who, in addition to unlimited funds, were required to possess also acquiescent husbands and unbounded energy, used every trick they knew to persuade royalty to grace their homes. Even lesser royals were always welcome, and this was partly because friendship with them might be an avenue to the Court itself.

But one had to be careful not to court favour from one particular personality. Sir Henry Channon recorded in his diaries that on the day following the abdication of King Edward VIII (with whom he had been very friendly for many years) he saw his own royal connections disappearing 'because I backed the wrong horse'. Indeed most of those who had made up the 'Prince of Wales' Set' found that they were excluded from palace functions for some time after the accession of George VI. For those who had prided themselves on being part of the royal 'inner circle' it seemed tantamount to annihilation when their invitations were returned by the new 'in set' now enjoying royal favour.

Today such entertaining has disappeared for ever. The salons and drawing-rooms of a bygone age have vanished. The great houses of Grosvenor Square and Park Lane are now office blocks or are divided into apartments. The money to provide the best food, wine, orchestras and decorations night after night, day after day, is no longer available. The late Duchess of Kent once complained to a friend that she didn't have a single free day for lunch or dinner for five months. Dinner for thirty-six and a ball for 300 were commonplace in the twenties and thirties. Today such gatherings are the exception rather than the rule. Perhaps the biggest change of all is in the absence of formality in social functions. Matters of precedence, social etiquette and good manners are now less significant than the size of a wallet or the fame or notoriety of those attending. In pre-war days it would have been unthinkable for The Queen's photographer or dress designer to be included in the same guest list as their royal patron. Today it is perfectly acceptable.

However, there was an occasion recently when the Princess Royal (or Princess Anne as she was then) subtly showed that she still likes things to be as they should. She and her husband Captain Mark Phillips were having lunch in Sydney, Australia, with the television personality Michael Parkinson and his wife, prior to recording an interview, and Mrs Parkinson had gone to enormous lengths to get everything just right for her first royal guest. However, when they were having a pre-lunch drink the subject of finger bowls arose and Princess Anne said how much she disliked the slices of lemon in them. Mrs Parkinson made an excuse to leave the room and rushed into the dining room to dispose of the offending slices in her finger

The Prince and Princess of Wales meet Their Majesties King Juan Carlos and Queen Sylvia of Spain at the start of their first State visit to Britain. The King and Queen are frequent visitors to London on an informal basis, but on this occasion they received the full formal treatment – including the obligatory curtsey to a visiting monarch.

bowls. Her husband said later that he hoped the royal guests hadn't noticed the slices of lemon lying on the lawn outside the dining-room window when they left; if they did, they were too polite to mention it.

Gone too are the armies of servants who were needed to provide all the services a good hostess thought indispensable to an evening's entertainment. In fact The Queen is probably the only person left in Britain who can entertain on the scale of her predecessors. She is the last of the great hostesses, and it is to her entertaining that we now turn.

1

State Banquets

Buckingham Palace is a blaze of light. Above the East Front façade, illuminated from the forecourt, the Royal Standard proudly signifies that The Queen is in residence. At eight o'clock in the evening a procession of gleaming limousines drives slowly towards the arch that leads into the Quadrangle, drawing up at the Grand Entrance. The privileged passengers are arriving to attend a State Banquet, the grandest of all grand occasions when The Queen plays host to a visiting Head of State.

The ladies are all wearing long evening dresses; most are also decked out in the family jewels and those who can beg, borrow or otherwise obtain them are wearing tiaras. The gentlemen are clad in full, formal evening wear: white tie, tail coat, sashes and decorations, wearing, as the former Marshal of the Diplomatic Corps, Major General Lord Michael Fitzalan-Howard, remarks, 'every rock in the book'. A few guests from foreign countries are dressed in their national costumes and the entire scene is a riot of colour and elegance.

Among the early arrivals is the Archbishop of Canterbury, tall, slim and scholarly, clad in ecclesiastical purple. He will join the other guests for a pre-dinner drink but then, after they have all been presented to The Queen and the visiting Head of State, will wait in the Music Room, as he is to be part of the Royal Procession. The 'ordinary' guests, about half of whom have been invited by virtue of the position they hold – Lord Chancellor, Speaker of the House of Commons, Prime Minister, Leader of the Opposition, Lord

Queen Victoria made every and any formal dinner into an occasion. This was a special mid-summer banquet held at Buckingham Palace in 1887.

Lord Latham
(Lord Chamberlain)

Baron von Pawel
Rammingen

Prince Victor
of Hohenlohe

Prince Christian

Prince Philip of
Saxe-Coburg-Gotha

Duchess of
Buccleuch (Mistress
of the Robes)

Prince Henry
of Prussia

Princess Louise
of Wales

Duke of Connaught

Princess Beatrice

Infante Antonio

Duchess of Albany

Hereditary Grand
Duke of Saxe-Weimar

Princess Sophie
of Prussia

Grand Duke of Hesse

Hereditary Grand Duchess
of Mecklenburg-Strelitz

Prince of Wales

Infanta Eulalia

King of Denmark

QUEEN VICTORIA

Duke of Sparta

Grand Duchess of
Mecklenburg-Strelitz

Crown Prince
Rudolph

Crown Princess
of Germany

King of the
Belgians

Grand Duchess
Elizabeth

Duke of Aosta

Princess Louise

Prince William
of Prussia

Duchess of
Edinburgh

Hereditary Grand Duke
of Mecklenburg-Strelitz

Lord Mount Edgcumbe
(Lord Steward)

Prince Louis of
Battenberg

Marquis of Lorne

Prince George
of Wales

Princess Victor
of Hohenlohe

Prince Louis
of Baden

Princess of
Leiningen

Hereditary Prince
of Saxe-Meiningen

Princess Irene
of Hesse

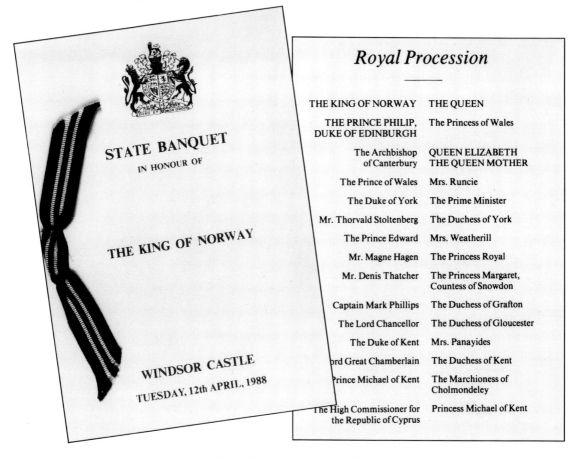

STATE BANQUET

IN HONOUR OF

THE KING OF NORWAY

WINDSOR CASTLE

TUESDAY, 12th APRIL, 1988

Royal Procession

THE KING OF NORWAY	THE QUEEN
THE PRINCE PHILIP, DUKE OF EDINBURGH	The Princess of Wales
The Archbishop of Canterbury	QUEEN ELIZABETH THE QUEEN MOTHER
The Prince of Wales	Mrs. Runcie
The Duke of York	The Prime Minister
Mr. Thorvald Stoltenberg	The Duchess of York
The Prince Edward	Mrs. Weatherill
Mr. Magne Hagen	The Princess Royal
Mr. Denis Thatcher	The Princess Margaret, Countess of Snowdon
Captain Mark Phillips	The Duchess of Grafton
The Lord Chancellor	The Duchess of Gloucester
The Duke of Kent	Mrs. Panayides
Lord Great Chamberlain	The Duchess of Kent
Prince Michael of Kent	The Marchioness of Cholmondeley
The High Commissioner for the Republic of Cyprus	Princess Michael of Kent

His Majesty King Olaf of Norway has been given the rare honour of two State visits. The more recent, in April 1988, saw nearly every member of the Royal Family turn up to attend his State Banquet at Windsor Castle.

Mayor of London – are greeted by liveried footmen waiting at the steps of the Grand Entrance. They are invited to leave overcoats or cloaks in one of the cloakrooms on either side of the Grand Entrance before being ushered up the Grand Staircase towards the Green Drawing Room. Those who are entering Buckingham Palace for the first time usually linger a little as they climb the staircase. It is a magnificent double construction designed in 1825 by John Nash of Carrara marble, with superb bronze balustrades, the work of Samuel Parker. The carpet is deep red and the two sides of the staircase meet at the top before the Guard Chamber where the central figure is a statue of Prince Albert, Queen Victoria's consort, depicted as a Roman general.

The Guard Chamber opens on to the Green Drawing Room, which really is green – walls as well as furniture. It is the central room on the west side of the Quadrangle and guests at State Banquets all pass through it. It contains three mirrored doors which open on to the Picture Gallery, where State Banquets used to be held before the days of Queen Victoria. When the palace was extended during her reign, she decided that the State Ballroom was a more suitable setting and the custom of holding State Banquets in this elegant room has continued ever since.

Once a guest has entered Buckingham Palace he or she becomes the responsibility of a member of the Royal Household. Each Private Secretary, Equerry and Lady-in-Waiting is allocated a guest to look after throughout the evening. If he or she wants to use the bathroom, meet one of the fellow guests or learn something about the palace, the 'host for the evening' will be on hand with every scrap of information. The Household member will have been fully briefed on his 'charge' long before the evening begins. He knows what the man or woman looks like (it sometimes comes as a surprise, on entering Buckingham Palace or Windsor Castle for the first time, to be greeted by name by someone who obviously knows exactly who you are) and he will have learnt your likes and dislikes, your particular interests and the reason you have been invited. If the visiting Head of State is known to be keen on ornithology, for example, the President of the Royal Society for the Protection of Birds might be invited. If a company is carrying out work in his country, a representative of the firm could well find himself on the guest list. It all depends on the Guest of Honour. In recent years The Queen has decided she would prefer to have more 'outsiders' present so the rules have been altered slightly. Previously a Private Secretary, Equerry or Lady-in-Waiting of every member of the Royal Family could expect to be 'commanded' to attend every State Banquet. But in recent years so many staff have become attached to different members of the Royal Family that Household threatened to outnumber guests; these days only one member of the Household of each royal guest is invited – and as we have seen they have duties to perform throughout the evening.

Space is at a premium at State Banquets. At Buckingham Palace 170 can be seated, at Windsor Castle 162, in St George's Hall. The responsibility for issuing the invitations rests with the Master of the Household and around 180 will have been sent out approximately four weeks before the event. Through long experience the Master of the Household knows that some ten per cent of those invited will decline, so ten extra names from the 'reserve' list are added to the original and all the invitations are sent out at the same time. What would happen if everyone accepted is anybody's guess – it hasn't happened yet!

In Queen Victoria's and, later, Edward VII's time, a royal invitation was virtually a Royal Command; nobody ever refused. These days, however, politicians and businessmen do, just occasionally, find they are unable to accept what most of us would regard as a unique social invitation from The Queen.

In the Picture Gallery the guests are offered drinks and cigarettes. Gin and tonic seems to be the favourite aperitif, but there is also sherry, Campari or anything else you care to order. The palace wine steward, whose title is Yeoman of the Cellars, has yet to be caught out but a request for one of the more exotic cocktails would not be welcomed – simply on grounds of lack of time. It is here that the table plan is prominently displayed so everyone can discover exactly where he or she is sitting.

While the guests are mingling and admiring the many treasures in the State Apartments – and all wondering, some rather nervously, when the royal party will emerge – the members of the Royal Family have been arriving at the Garden Entrance. This is a side door set in the North Front of the Palace overlooking Constitution Hill which cannot be seen from outside. It is also the entrance normally used by The Queen herself. The royal guests are escorted to the White Drawing Room. In her bedroom on the first floor Her Majesty, with the help of her dresser, is adjusting the decorations appropriate to this evening. She always wears any honour that has been presented to her by the visiting Head of State. If there is none, the most senior decoration she possesses, the Order of the Garter, will be worn.

Next door the Duke of Edinburgh is making similar final arrangements. He is wearing Court Dress: tail coat, knee breeches and black silk stockings, with the Garter, the symbol of the most senior Order of Chivalry, worn below the left knee.

When The Queen indicates that she is ready the visiting Head of State is collected from the Belgian Suite by the Duke of Edinburgh and the small party moves through the Royal Closet to the White Drawing Room. Despite its previous use as a royal dressing room, the Royal Closet is a splendidly elegant apartment with crimson damask walls and a large, ornate fireplace.

Meanwhile the Royal Family has gathered for pre-dinner drinks in the White Drawing Room. The Queen may enjoy a weak gin and tonic and the Duke of Edinburgh a dry sherry. Queen Elizabeth the Queen Mother likes her spirits somewhat stronger while the Princess Royal sticks to mineral water or her favourite Coca-Cola. The Prince of Wales is practically teetotal these days but occasionally likes a glass of dry white wine. The Princess of Wales is another non-drinker apart from the odd glass of champagne while Princess Margaret is the only person present who ever smokes.

The door from the Royal Closet to the White Drawing Room is concealed in a section of the wall behind a mirror and table, both of which swing open, a device which allows a dramatic entrance and occasionally takes first-time visitors completely by surprise. One minute they are looking perhaps at themselves in the mirror – the next they are face to face with The Queen.

The main colour in the White Drawing Room is not in fact white but yellow, and indeed, it used to be called the Yellow Drawing Room. The furniture is upholstered in yellow damask and this colour is reflected by the giant twelve-foot (3.7m) high mirror doors which open on to the Picture Gallery. There is one single chandelier of mammoth proportions and an ornate, gilded grand piano which was bought by Queen Victoria at the Great Exhibition of 1851. The floor is covered by a large Axminster carpet of crimson and blue which measures some 1025 square feet (95.7m).

The Queen and the Royal Family wait in the White Drawing Room for only a few minutes while the remainder of the guests prepare to file through the Music Room from the Picture Gallery. A receiving line has been formed to enable Her Majesty and her principal guests to meet all their fellow diners for the first time. Each guest is conducted to The Queen by the Lord Steward and, having shaken hands with her, the visiting Head of State, Prince Philip and the Head of State's spouse, is guided through the Blue Drawing Room and State Dining Room to the State Ballroom. Those who will be taking part in the Royal Procession stay in the Music Room, waiting discreetly to one side.

Because State Banquets, like all other royal events, run to a strict timetable, this section of the evening is never allowed to over-run. The guests are gently but firmly ushered into the State Ballroom while the royal party must wait for one more formality before they can sit down. Photographs have to be taken as a record of the occasion, and these are always arranged before the meal is served. With its eighteen columns of blue scagliola the Music Room is the perfect setting for formal photographs and has been used for every royal christening since the Second World War. (The Chapel at Buckingham Palace was destroyed by bombs in 1942.) Its oval shape corresponds exactly to that of the Bow Room beneath, and even though these days it is rarely used solely as a Music Room, it does contain a fine walnut piano from the days of the Prince Regent which is still played occasionally by Princess Margaret and more recently the Princess of Wales.

The Chapel at Buckingham Palace decorated for a Royal wedding in 1896. The chapel was destroyed by enemy bombs in 1942 and never replaced. The Queen's Gallery now occupies the site on which the chapel stood.

By the time the photographs have been taken the rest of the guests have found their allocated places and when all are in position the Royal Procession is ready to enter. This usually consists of twenty-eight people, and the State Banquet held in honour of King Fahd of Saudi Arabia on Tuesday, 24 March 1987 illustrates how they lined up:

KING FAHD OF SAUDI ARABIA	THE QUEEN
THE PRINCE PHILIP, DUKE OF EDINBURGH	The Princess of Wales
The Prince of Wales	QUEEN ELIZABETH, THE QUEEN MOTHER
The Duke of York	The Prime Minister
The Archbishop of Canterbury	The Duchess of York
Prince Saud Al-Faisal	The Princess Margaret, Countess of Snowdon
The Duke of Gloucester	Mrs Runcie
Prince Abdulaziz bin Fahd Al-Saud	The Duchess of Gloucester
The Duke of Kent	The Duchess of Grafton
The Lord Chancellor	The Duchess of Kent
Prince Michael of Kent	The Lady Hailsham of St Marylebone
Mr Denis Thatcher	Princess Michael of Kent
The Lord President of the Council	Princess Alexandra, the Hon. Mrs Angus Ogilvy
The Hon. Angus Ogilvy	The Viscountess Whitelaw

The Royal Procession also provides the Lord Chamberlain and the Lord Steward with what can at times be a slightly tricky problem. These two senior courtiers always precede the procession into the

State Ballroom – walking backwards. Lord Maclean was Lord Chamberlain for thirteen years. He says there are three rules to follow when you have to walk backwards in front of The Queen: 'The first is to practise as often as you can. It's no good thinking, "I've done it before so it will be all right this time." The Lord Steward and I used to spend a lot of time actually rehearsing the walk before each occasion. Second, the patterns on the carpets are seldom altered either at Buckingham Palace or Windsor Castle, so we got to know them rather well and knew which seam to follow. The third rule is to remember to watch The Queen. I was only a few feet in front of her all the time and if I started to wobble a bit, she would gently motion with her eyes, left or right, to put me back on the right track.' It is easier at Buckingham Palace than Windsor Castle, because at the palace the Lord Steward and the Lord Chamberlain walk side by side, while at Windsor they are either side of the huge dining table. At Buckingham Palace the table for a State Banquet is arranged in a horseshoe shape, while at Windsor everyone sits at one long single table. (It is believed to be the longest single table in the world, measuring 167 by 8 feet (51×2.4m), and is carved of solid mahogany.) At Windsor problems do sometimes occur. Lord Maclean recalls the occasion when President Reagan was being given a State Banquet (even though officially President Reagan's was not a State Visit). The Lord Chamberlain was proceeding backwards on his side of the table when The Queen noticed he was in advance of the Lord Steward on the other side. To slow him down Her Majesty muttered under her breath, 'You're going to win by a short head.'

Another point which has to be considered during the Royal Procession is how long it will take the participants to reach their appointed places. The National Anthem is always played when The Queen enters the banqueting hall and must be timed to finish exactly as she reaches her chair. The distance between the entrance and The Queen's chair is further at Buckingham Palace than it is at Windsor, so it's two verses at the Palace and just one at Windsor.

In addition to the seating plan, there is a card bearing the name of the guest before each place (except for The Queen – as hostess she has none). The principal guest always sits next to Her Majesty, with, at Buckingham Palace, the Duke of Edinburgh and the other members of the Royal Family on either side; at Windsor, where they all sit at one single table, the Duke of Edinburgh sits opposite The Queen with the spouse of the principal guest next to him. This is because at eight feet (2.4m) wide the table is too broad to allow conversation across it. At Windsor, the male members of the Royal Family wear the distinctive Windsor Coat which is blue with scarlet collar and cuffs.

Once The Queen and her guests are seated the band provided by one of the regiments of the Household Division (this evening it's the Scots Guards) plays discreetly in the background. The choice of music has been decided by the Director of Music in consultation with the Master of the Household and The Queen.

The chairs are gilt, upholstered in crimson, and only one guest has a chair that is at all different. It is not The Queen but Queen Elizabeth the Queen Mother, whose chair has arms to make it a little more comfortable. Her Majesty is also provided with a footstool as she is not very tall. Princess Margaret also uses a footstool at State Banquets, by special permission of The Queen.

The moment when Her Majesty finally sits down is the climax to many hours of work which began at around 7.30 that morning. The procedure never changes. No matter whether the guest of honour is the president of the most powerful country in the world or the ruler of the smallest independency, the ceremonial remains the same. The Queen makes no distinction, treating every visiting Head of State as an honoured guest in her home.

In the early part of the day the kitchens are the centre of much of the activity as delivery vans arrive on schedule with their cargoes of fresh vegetables, bread rolls, flowers and all the other ingredients required. The kitchen porters working under the supervision of the Head Chef carry their loads to the appropriate station. The catering staff in the royal kitchens, normally around twenty, will have been supplemented by as many as the same number again to cope with the extra demands.

The menu will have been chosen by The Queen many weeks before. It is then communicated to the Lord Mayor of London, No. 10 Downing Street and the Head of State's ambassador, all of whom will be entertaining the distinguished visitor, and must avoid duplicating the main dishes.

The kitchens at Buckingham Palace are in the oldest part of the building but their equipment is entirely up to date. Where once small armies of skivvies were employed for menial tasks, labour saving devices now do the jobs in less than half the time – and at a considerable saving in cost. It has meant a slimming down of the catering staff and the disappearance of a few ancient, quaint-sounding job titles such as Pot-Scourer, Boiler Stoker and the like. The entire catering operation at Buckingham Palace is now computerised and this has meant enormous savings in the supplies of food, drink and equipment as well as improved quality control. However, it has also seen the end of fresh, home-baked bread from their own bakery. The palace staff still have fresh bread of course, but now it comes from the ovens of J. Lyons & Company and is delivered shortly after dawn via the side entrance of the palace in Buckingham Palace Road.

The State Ballroom is conveniently situated two floors immediately above the kitchens, and while the frenzied but controlled activity is going on below, an equal amount of work is taking place to prepare the Ballroom for the evening's function.

The Ballroom was one of Queen Victoria's additions to Buckingham Palace. She claimed, in a letter to Sir Robert Peel, that she needed the extra space because of the 'growing up of our little family'. In reality, a larger State Apartment was required to cope with the increased numbers who were being invited to the many magnificent functions held in the early years of Victoria's reign. The State Ballroom measures 120 by 60 feet (37 × 18m) and is 45 feet (14m) high. It was designed by James Pennethorne, a nephew of John Nash who was responsible for much of Buckingham Palace as it is today. The Ballroom was finished in 1856, and when the decorations by Ludwig Grunner were complete – crimson silk panelling, inlaid polished floor and an organ taken from the Pavilion at Brighton – the total cost was £250,000 for this room alone. It has been estimated that in terms of today's values that would be about £25,000,000. Most of this evening's guests will think it money well spent.

By mid-morning the horseshoe-shaped mahogany dining table will have been assembled and on it can be seen the fairly unusual sight of three or four footmen, in stockinged feet, gliding about as they set out the royal plate. If the visiting Head of State has presented The Queen with a suitable gift it too will be displayed prominently on the table or on one of the sideboards around the room. This was the case when King Fahd of Saudi Arabia dined at Buckingham Palace. His Majesty had given The Queen a gold tray and gold falcon, studded with amethysts, and two gold goblets, during her State Visit to Saudi Arabia in 1979. The gifts were placed in front of the places to be occupied by The Queen and King Fahd.

Also on the table were the following:

1 Ice pails by Paul Storr, Benjamin Smith and John Sharpe 1808–9.

An ice-pail by Paul Storr 1808–9 which is frequently displayed among the Royal plate on show at State Banquets at Buckingham Palace.

   2 Candelabra of the Grand Service founded by George IV made by Benjamin Smith and John Sharpe, 1807–9, Philip Rundell, 1819 and Paul Storr and John Bridge, 1816–28.

   3 Two round plateaux mirrors, made by Philip Rundell, 1819. Two square mirrors made by Paul Storr, 1815.

On the walls and sideboards a large collection of pieces was displayed, including:

   1 Four large Sconces with chased marine figures in high relief. In the centre is the cypher of George IV surmounted by the Crown. Maker: John Bridge of London, circa 1829–30.

   2 Two pairs of Sconces with the cypher of William and Mary surmounted by the Crown – a representation of the Judgement of Solomon. Height $20\frac{1}{2}$ inches (52 cms). Maker: Charles Shelley, circa 1689–94.

   3 A 31-inch (79-cm) circular dish 'The Triumph of Bacchus and Ariadne'. Maker: Paul Storr, 1814.

   4 Two large Wine Flagons with Satyr-head handles and large curb chains. Maker: George Garthorne, 1690.

   5 Two richly chased Wine Flagons with Emblems of the Kingdoms of England, Scotland, Ireland and Hanover engraved with compartments and chains. Maker: John Bridge, 1828.

The most remarkable pieces in the royal collection are the Salts and Wine Fountain given to Charles II by the Corporation of the City of Plymouth. The Great Salt of State is the most magnificent. It is in the shape of a castle and was presented to Charles II by the City of Exeter in 1660, to mark his restoration to the throne. Once the candelabra and plate are on the table, the flowers are placed. Those on the table will be kept simple and low, so that The Queen is able to see and be seen by all her guests. As the State Banquet is taking place in April, the theme is spring flowers in shades of yellow, cream and white, using daffodils, lilies, mimosa, roses and anemones. Around the rest of the State Ballroom are more elaborate arrangements which are not there purely for decoration. They have been

A large wine flagon, part of a pair, with satyr-head handles and large curb chains, made by George Garthorne in 1690. The flagons form part of the collection displayed on sideboards during a State Banquet.

cunningly designed to conceal what are known throughout the palace as the 'traffic-lights': a set of lights operated by the Palace Steward to signal the staff when each course has finished and the next is ready to be served. Rumour has it that The Queen herself works the switch that controls the lights. It's a nice story – but just that! Once Her Majesty sits down at the table she has no duties until it is time for her speech. The actual mechanics of the banquet are left in the very capable hands of the Palace Steward, Mr Cyril Dickman, the palace's senior domestic servant, whose expert eyes miss nothing from his position behind The Queen's chair.

After the gold plate and floral arrangements have been finalized, it is time to lay the table.

Almost as valuable as her collection of gold and silver plate is The Queen's collection of glass and china, and the man responsible for every cup, saucer, plate, tureen, soup bowl and piece of glassware is the Yeoman of the Glass and China Pantry. Together with his colleague, the Yeoman of the Gold and Silver Pantry, it is his duty to make sure that everything required for the banquet is in perfect condition – and that every single piece is accounted for afterwards. Cutlery is stored in the pantries in padded, leather cases and brought out the day before a banquet for a final polish. The main courses are always served on gold plate, of which there are twenty-four dozen. Nor has anybody to ask for the salt to be passed; each guest has his own salt cellar.

The china used for the sweet and fruit courses can vary; there is a wide choice. On this occasion Her Majesty has decided to use for the sweet course a Sèvres service purchased by King George IV circa 1802. It is turquoise blue, painted with flowers and fruit, and The Queen has an interesting little story to tell her chief guest about its origin. It was an official present from Louis XVI to the Duchess of Manchester, wife of the 4th Duke, the man who had signed the treaty bringing the War of American Independence to an end in 1783. The Queen knows something of the history of every article in the palace and can usually find an appropriate or amusing anecdote to suit the occasion.

This evening the fruit will be eaten from a Minton service made for Queen Victoria. Again turquoise is the main colour, with panels of flowers and rich gilding. The centre is painted with a crown and surmounted by the royal monogram: VR, 1877.

Each piece of china is complemented by a set of cutlery of matching design. The Yeoman of the Gold and Silver Pantry has plenty of patterns to choose from and there are up to eighteen dozen of each single item.

More than 800 glasses are polished before being placed on the

This cut glass decanter and wine glasses bearing the Prince of Wales feathers was commissioned by George IV in 1810 and has since graced many Royal tables.

table, a minimum of five for each person: sherry, white wine, red wine, champagne and water (port glasses are added later). Tonight they will be English cut crystal in a fluted style made for the Coronation in 1953 by the firm of Stourbridge. Each is hand engraved with the cypher E II R.

Once the table has been set, the distance between each setting measured with a ruler, the menu cards and place-names are put out. On arrival each guest has been given a booklet measuring 4 by 6 inches (10 by 15cms), so easily slipped into a pocket or handbag. It lists the order of the Royal Procession, then the menu and wine list, followed by the music to be played during the meal and the pipe programme which invariably follows. There are five pages of all the guests who have been invited and on the inside of the back page a pull-out of the seating plan. Not only do you know where you are sitting and who is next to you, but you are able to identify everybody else as well.

All is ready by five o'clock in the afternoon and at six The Queen, as the perfect hostess, joins the Master of the Household for a personal tour of inspection. She will check that the flowers are as she ordered, and that the right china and cutlery are being used. There is rarely any cause for complaint but her presence also has another and equally important purpose. Her Majesty knows only too well how hard her staff have worked to prepare for the evening's entertainment, and by visiting the State Ballroom when some of them are still putting the final touches, she shows that she is aware of all their efforts. She will usually have a word or two with the footmen and maids on duty and when she leaves the room they know – and she knows they know – that she is pleased with what they have done. Sir Peter Ashmore, who used to be Master of the Household, says it is because The Queen is so appreciative that the staff work so well.

The State Ballroom when it is set out for a State Banquet looks truly magnificent, the two thrones on their raised dais immediately behind The Queen's place at table providing a majestic background to the royal function. It is a background of imperial red, the colour of the draperies which came from India, where they were first used during the Delhi Coronation Durbar of 1911 by King George V and Queen Mary, The Queen's grandparents.

The Ballroom has no pictures on its walls, probably the only room in the entire palace where this is the case. Instead two massive tapestries on the longer walls somehow lend the room a warm atmosphere. And the six huge crystal chandeliers spread a shimmering light over the proceedings below, reflected in the thousands of diamonds worn by the ladies.

The staff who wait at table will all be men, and all those on duty will be required to wear State Livery. For senior staff this means black and gold braid livery with fine white wool cloth breeches, stockings and black pumps with gilt buckles. The footmen wear scarlet livery decorated with gold braid, scarlet plush knee breeches, pink stockings and black buckle shoes. Until The Queen came to the Throne in 1952, they would also have been required to wear powdered wigs, but Her Majesty decided that this was an outmoded custom and today all the domestic servants are bare-headed.

The livery is cumbersome and very heavy to wear. The gold braid is as thick as three fingers put together. When footmen are recruited to the staff at Buckingham Palace they are not provided with new livery but are fitted into one of the existing uniforms, some of which are more than a hundred years old. With eighty full sets of livery needed at any one time, and a new one costing a thousand pounds, perhaps it is not surprising that one of the prime qualifications for obtaining domestic work in the Royal Household is to be of the right height and build, which is absolutely average.

By 7.45 pm all those on duty will have assembled at their prescribed locations, where they are inspected by senior members of the Household Staff and given a twenty-two point briefing on their duties for the evening. It rarely varies. State Banquets follow exactly the same format year after year and the staff could probably carry out their tasks blindfold if required. But at Buckingham Palace nothing is ever left to chance and it is this attention to the minutest detail that has earned the palace the reputation for excellence it enjoys today.

Another reason why the briefing has to be done every time is because not all those on duty are regular members of the Buckingham Palace staff. Of the nearly 200 full-time staff employed at the palace only a small proportion work as pages, footmen and in the kitchens, so part-timers are brought in for great occasions. These are sometimes former employees, or friends of employees, all fully trained and experienced and specially vetted for security. In addition it is a long-standing tradition at the palace that the washing-up after State Banquets is looked after by men and women from the Fulham Road branch of the Royal British Legion. As they have all served in one of the branches of Her Majesty's armed forces, it is perhaps felt that they can be trusted with the priceless china, glassware and cutlery.

Service Arrangements for the State Banquet

1 All staff are to be in position in their correct location by 8 pm.

2 The Royal Service will be Number 1.

3 PAGES (senior staff), assisted by FOOTMEN (junior staff), serve each course.

4 PAGES on wine to ladle out soup on their Service.

5 WINE-BUTLERS will serve the gravy.

6 UNDER-BUTLERS will serve potatoes only.

7 UNDER-BUTLERS will bring in all food from the Ballroom Annexe.

8 UNDER-BUTLERS to remove food dishes and cutlery to the Cross Gallery.

9 FOOTMEN enter with clean gilt-plates and leave with all dirty plates (including china) at the East Gallery Door.

10 WINE-BUTLERS will bring in wine from the Ball Supper Room.

11 PANTRY ASSISTANTS take away dirty dishes and cutlery through the East Gallery Silk Tapestry Room and Service Lift.

12 PLATE PANTRY YEOMAN will instruct UNDER-BUTLER to warn PALACE STEWARD that food is up.

13 PALACE STEWARD will instruct YEOMAN for plates to enter by the Green Light signal in Ball Supper Room.

14 PALACE STEWARD will instruct YEOMAN for food to enter by the Green Light signal in the Annexe.

15 On the Amber Light signal in the Ballroom, plates are brought forward and on the Green Light signal are placed in front of guests.
The above procedure is repeated for the service of food. Green Light only for soup.
BE SURE TO WATCH THESE LIGHTS.

16 PAGES on food, after handling sweet dish, to take Petits Fours.

17 Port must be handed clockwise. WINE PAGES are to report

to the YEOMAN OF THE ROYAL CELLARS in the State Dining Room after Port has been handed.

18 Menu Booklets and Gilt Cruets are to be left on the table.

19 When Dessert has been handed, the PALACE STEWARD will see that PAGES and FOOTMEN leave the Banqueting Room and go to the Picture Gallery.

20 STRICT SILENCE MUST BE KEPT IN THE AREA OUTSIDE THE BALLROOM WHILST HER MAJESTY AND THE VISITING HEAD OF STATE ARE SPEAKING.

21 PAGES will be instructed when they are to return to the Banqueting Room to draw chairs back. FOOTMEN remain in the Picture Gallery ready for other duties.

22 Coffee will be served by PAGES and FOOTMEN in the White Drawing Room, Music Room, Blue Drawing Room and State Dining Room.

Every one of these points has to be strictly observed by all staff on duty. The Palace Steward, who has worked his way up through the ranks of the domestic staff, knows each and every job – and the way in which he wants it done. Any page, footman or butler who does not carry out his instructions to the letter had better start looking for another job.

With close to 170 guests arriving at 7.30 pm, the logistics of getting them out of their vehicles, up the Grand Staircase and safely into the State Apartments takes the combined efforts of nearly 50 pages, under-butlers and footmen. Cars are parked in the Quadrangle and the Forecourt of the palace, and each person is received individually at the Grand Entrance before being conducted to the Green Drawing Room. This is the roster for staff on duty before the meal begins.

DUTY	STAFF
To see guests in at the Grand Entrance	8
To direct guests up the Grand Staircase to the Green Drawing Room	1
To be in position at the door leading from the Picture Gallery into the Music Room	1

To be in position in the Blue Drawing Room to direct guests to the Ballroom	2
To direct guests from the Silk Tapestry Room to the State Ballroom	1
To see guests in at the Garden Entrance 4.45 pm (Royal Family only)	2
Top of the lift	1
To prepare drinks in the Throne Room from 7.00 pm	7
To dispense pre-dinner drinks at 7.15 pm	3
To hand pre-dinner drinks from the Throne Room into the Picture Gallery at 7.30 pm	9
To hand cigarettes	2

Sir Peter Ashmore says that guests are never quite sure whether or not they should smoke during the reception before a State Banquet; but cigarettes are always available and many a nervous puff is gratefully taken as visitors wait for the Royal Party to emerge.

The serving of the meal itself goes like a well-oiled machine, each 'service' of three men, looking after nine guests – the maximum number that can be looked after efficiently by one group. Around the table there are nineteen stations, and around the room, keeping a watchful eye on the proceedings, are members of the oldest bodyguard in the world, the Yeomen of the Guard.

This evening the menu is comparatively simple, but exquisitely prepared and appropriate to the guest of honour's taste. It begins with Consommé Royale, the clearest of soups, accompanied by the driest Fine Old Amontillado sherry. There is always a soup course to start a Royal Banquet, and until comparatively recently (at least at Windsor Castle) this has meant that some guests received theirs far from hot while others were in danger of burning their tongues. The problem was that all the food was served from one end. It would be brought up from the kitchens below in a service lift, then carried, at a suitably stately pace, to the far end of the table. By the time the person sitting at the farthest point from the lift received his soup it was usually stone cold. To try and resolve this little

The Green Drawing Room is the first of the State Apartments seen by guests at formal functions. It has three windows opening onto the loggia over the Grand Entrance and three mirror-doors leading to the Picture Gallery.

culinary problem the chefs would heat the soup practically to boiling point, and as the soup was served on gold plate, which of course held the heat very well, those sitting nearest the service lift had to chat politely for five minutes or so while their soup cooled.

Happily, that is now all in the past. A 'back-stage' wall was demolished and a second service station equipped at the opposite end of St George's Hall. Everyone is now served at more or less the same time, with food at exactly the correct temperature.

The fish course is Darne de Saumon Balmoral, fresh salmon from The Queen's own Scottish home on the banks of the River Dee. For the fish course the Yeoman of the Cellars has offered Wiltingen Gottesfuss Spätlese 1979, the lightest of Mosels.

The Queen has her own particular favourites when it comes to the main course and Selle d'Agneau Windsor is a frequent choice: saddle of lamb brought up to London from the Home Farm at Windsor to be eaten with braised celery, glazed broccoli and sweet potatoes. There is one of the truly great Burgundies to go with the main course. Tonight it's Chassagne-Montrachet Morgeots 1978.

This evening, there are no unfortunate dramas, such as when, at a previous State Banquet, the lift carrying the food from the basement to the Ballroom broke down between floors. It had to be wound down by hand and the main coursé transferred to a trolley and brought up in a passenger lift.

Between the main course and the dessert a salad is always served in order to refresh the palate. In the days of Queen Victoria and Edward VII, sorbets would be served, not only after the main course but between each course; but banquets in those days would frequently last six or seven hours. These days tastes, even – or perhaps, especially – those of the Royal Family, are much simpler and ices are kept for the dessert. Champagne – Lanson 1976 – is served with the dessert, which this evening is Crême Brulée and Compôte d'Oranges Sandringham.

Throughout the evening the regimental band of the Scots Guards under their Director of Music Major David Carson (his supper will be served in a private room at 11 o'clock) has been entertaining The Queen and her guests with selections from some of the most popular musicals: *Oklahoma* and *Annie Get Your Gun*, with a little Scott

Joplin thrown in for good measure, together with Robert Farnon's 'Westminster', the film theme from *Gone with the Wind* and ending with the march 'Good Old Vienna' by Schrammel. The music is chosen to blend with the conversation. Nobody pays much attention to it and it is all pleasantly conventional. It would be noticed only if it were not there. The final musical offering of the evening is provided by the bagpipes played by Pipers of the 1st Battalion, Scots Guards under their Pipe Major, Ian Rodgers.

The Queen loves the music of the pipes (a lone piper plays on the terrace beneath her window every morning) and in her eyes no State Banquet would be complete without the stirring wail of Scotland's national instrument. (Musicians from the Irish Guards frequently play the bagpipes too.) In full Highland dress uniform, proudly sporting the tartan of their regiment, the Pipers march into the State Ballroom playing 'The Young MacGregor'. They parade around the dining table as they continue their programme with 'Inverary Castle' and the reel 'The Blackberry Bush', before closing and marching out to the sounds of 'The MacNeils of Ugadale'. Her Majesty knows every one of the tunes they play and even if some of her guests are at times a little puzzled by the choice of instrument to accompany their sumptuous meal, most appear to enjoy the experience – The Queen certainly does.

After dessert, the port is handed in readiness for the toasts. This evening it is Quinta do Noval 1966 and the Archbishop of Canterbury remarks on its quality. Cheese does not appear. For some reason cheese is never on the menu at any official royal meal. Nobody knows the reason – or if they do are not telling.

There are only two speeches – both remarkable for their brevity. The Queen reaches down for her handbag to find her spectacles and her notes. She switches on the microphone located near her place, rises and speaks for seven minutes. It is sometimes slightly less but never longer. The speech, which has been drafted by her Private Secretary Sir William Heseltine, has been rewritten in her own words and concludes with the toast to His Majesty King Fahd of Saudi Arabia. He then rises and makes a slightly longer speech of thanks and offers his own toast – with a soft drink because of course his religion prohibits the drinking of alcohol. His Majesty speaks in

Arabic and written translations have been provided for non-Arabic-speaking guests. The Queen's speech has also been translated into Arabic, by the Foreign Office. It is not the custom at royal banquets for interpreters to be used. There is no smoking at the table. The Queen is prepared to allow cigarettes and cigars in the drawing rooms once the meal has ended, but never permits smoking at the dinner table – no matter how exalted the guest of honour. Once the speeches have ended The Queen and her principal guests leave the Ballroom, again preceded by the Lord Chamberlain and Lord Steward, walking backwards and carrying their wands of office.

At this point in the evening the guests are able to mix completely informally with members of the Royal Family. Everybody moves back into the State Apartments and senior courtiers such as the Comptroller of the Lord Chamberlain's Office, the Master of the Household and The Queen's Private Secretary bring certain guests to be introduced to The Queen and King Fahd; people they particularly want to meet.

For some of the guests this is an opportunity to see at close quarters State Apartments which are used only rarely and are never open to the public. There's the Blue Drawing Room which has been described as the most beautiful room in Buckingham Palace. It is elegant and large enough to be used as a ballroom, which it frequently was before the present State Ballroom was built. One of its most outstanding features is the richly carved ceiling supported by towering columns of pure Carrara marble. There are four magnificent crystal chandeliers and the heavy silk curtains and gilt chairs are all in the coolest shade of ice blue. The room is dominated by a massive Chinese carpet whose main colour is crimson, but the blue from which the room takes its name is woven into the intricate patterns. Every visitor likes to linger as long as possible in the Blue Drawing Room as there are few rooms in this building to rival its style and grace. It is situated between the State Dining Room and the Music Room. The State Dining Room contains a huge portrait of King George IV in his coronation robes and he looks down on a mahogany table around which some sixty guests can be seated.

Meanwhile, Princess Margaret is chatting with the Governor of

The middle window of the centre room, east front of Buckingham Palace. It is from here that the Royal Family step onto the balcony to wave to the crowds below on occasions of national rejoicing. The first sovereign to make use of the balcony was Queen Victoria, when she waved farewell to a Guards battalion as they left for the Crimea in 1854.

the Bank of England and Princess Alexandra and her husband the Hon. (now Sir) Angus Ogilvy are deep in conversation with Geoffrey Owen, Editor of the *Financial Times*, and his wife. The Duchess of York sips a glass of champagne as she joins a group consisting of His Royal Highness, Prince Abdulaziz bin Fahd Al-Saud, the Commander of the Royal Guard of Saudi Arabia, Stephen Egerton, the British Ambassador at Riyadh (who has been specially brought over from Saudi Arabia to be attached to the Royal Suite), and Neil Kinnock, Leader of the Opposition.

Queen Elizabeth the Queen Mother holds court before an admiring throng which includes Lord Hailsham, at that time Lord Chancellor, Dr David Owen (the then Leader of the Social Democratic Party) and David Steel, then Leader of the Liberals. You can be sure of one thing. They will not be discussing politics! It's much more likely to be horse-racing, Her Majesty's passion.

The Chairman of the BBC, Mr Marmaduke Hussey, is on the guest list this evening – in his official capacity. He is here with his wife Lady Susan Hussey, to whom tonight's banquet is just the latest in a long line of functions she attends with The Queen. She has been a Lady-in-Waiting for more than twenty years, but tonight she is not on duty, she is here as a guest.

Sir John Miller, shortly to retire as Crown Equerry after more than a quarter of a century of royal service, has been summoned to the royal presence. He is one of the world's foremost authorities on equestrian matters and the Saudi Royal Family is well known for its love of anything to do with horses.

This informal gathering continues for nearly an hour and then King Fahd indicates that he wishes to retire. The Queen escorts him to the Belgian Suite and she and the Duke of Edinburgh do not return to the Music Room. The Queen Mother remains until after midnight, showing no sign of fatigue – or of her eighty-six years! Eventually she too leaves and with her the other members of the Royal Family. There are still nearly 150 people drinking and smoking in the State Apartments because of course nobody leaves before the Royal Family has departed.

Finally, guests start to drift away. Cars are called to the Grand Entrance and reluctantly coats and cloaks are collected; the precious souvenir menus are stowed carefully away as a reminder of a magical evening.

Back in the State Ballroom the staff have already started to clear the table. The priceless centrepieces are gently removed; the china and cutlery are taken to the kitchens to be carefully washed and polished, then counted and each returned to its leather case. The Yeomen of the Gold and Silver Pantry and the China and Glass Pantry meticulously check every item and, at long last, several hours after the last guest has left, heave a sigh of relief that everything is as it should be, back in its own place.

For the Palace Steward it is a time to reflect on yet another piece of royal theatre that has worked as planned. The Queen has provided the venue and acted as hostess – the Foreign Office picks up the bill, which for each State Banquet is approximately £8,000.

2

Hostess to the World

Her Majesty Queen Elizabeth II is the world's most lavish and generous hostess. No other king, queen, sheik, president or Head of State entertains on the same grand scale, or in so many different places, be it royal palace, royal castle, private home or royal yacht. At Buckingham Palace alone more than eighty functions are held every year. They range from the three Garden Parties, to each of which some 9,000 people are invited, to the small, intimate, informal lunches held every two months when the guest list is restricted to eight, or perhaps a dozen may be asked to dinner. The most glittering State Occasion, the annual Diplomatic Reception, is held at the end of November when 1,200 members of the Diplomatic Corps in London join Her Majesty and other members of the Royal Family for cocktails and canapés from nine o'clock until midnight.

In addition to State Banquets The Queen will host official dinners, State lunches and receptions for visiting Heads of State throughout the year. At Windsor Castle there is a large continuous house-party throughout Royal Ascot week and more than forty close relations join The Queen and the Duke of Edinburgh to spend Christmas in the castle.

When the Court moves to the Palace of Holyroodhouse in Edinburgh for a week in July, another round of parties begins. There is an official dinner every evening for the leaders of Scottish society, and a Garden Party in one of the most attractive settings in the world is attended by a further 6,000 guests from all walks of life.

At the Ghillies' Ball which takes place at Balmoral, the Queen enjoys highland dancing with a variety of partners. She is carrying on a tradition begun by King Edward VII and maintained by every monarch since.

Even when The Queen and her family take up residence at Balmoral, their private holiday home in the Highlands, there is no let-up.

A Ghillies' Ball is held for all the staff who work on the royal estates; the Prime Minister of the day always spends at least one week-end as a guest of The Queen, and shooting parties are organised several days in the week. The New Year is always celebrated at Sandringham, the second of The Queen's private residences, in the quiet Norfolk countryside. Until 1964 the Royal Family always spent Christmas at Sandringham, but the party grew so large they had to move to Windsor – which is, after all, the biggest castle in the world. Nowadays when the festivities at Windsor are over, The Queen and the Duke of Edinburgh go to Sandringham, where close members of the family continue the Christmas holiday, and where friends are asked to stay for a few days' shooting.

Altogether, in a normal year – that is, without a royal wedding, anniversary or jubilee to celebrate – The Queen entertains in her own homes up to 40,000 guests. They come from every race and social background, from all walks of life, from princes to plumbers' mates, and reflect every interest. Nowhere else could you find such a varied group. And nowhere else would you find so many prime ministers and presidents willing, indeed anxious, to accept the gracious hospitality of a hostess who means something special to each of them individually. And one of the most important elements in The Queen's role as hostess is the part she plays in entertaining the leaders of Commonwealth countries.

Since she acceded to the Throne in 1952, Her Majesty has realised the importance of maintaining her home as an impartial meeting place for all the Commonwealth's disparate views and interests. She never takes sides. Every Commonwealth leader is equal in her eyes, and each as welcome as his neighbour. They regard an invitation to Buckingham Palace or Windsor Castle as an honour and a pleasure, and Her Majesty is wise enough, and by now experienced enough, to place her guests where new friendships can be made or old ones renewed. If she is aware, as she usually is, that two of her Commonwealth guests have a mutual problem, she will see each of them individually, before making sure that they have the opportunity of getting together in a relaxed atmosphere to discuss their

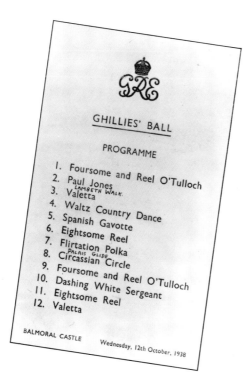

GHILLIES' BALL

PROGRAMME

1. Foursome and Reel O'Tulloch
2. Paul Jones LAMBETH WALK.
3. Valetta
4. Waltz Country Dance
5. Spanish Gavotte
6. Eightsome Reel
7. Flirtation Polka
8. Circassian Circle PALAIS GLIDE.
9. Foursome and Reel O'Tulloch
10. Dashing White Sergeant
11. Eightsome Reel
12. Valetta

BALMORAL CASTLE   Wednesday, 12th October, 1938

King George VI continued the custom of giving a Ghillies' Ball whenever he took up residence at Balmoral. All the servants and tenants were invited with the Queen dancing with as many as she could.

difficulties. She knows how much more conducive to good relations an informal, perhaps intimate, chat around a friendly dining table can be, than the more formal discussions which are conducted in the conference chamber.

The Queen has another advantage when she is the hostess to statesmen and politicians. She is very well read and knowledgeable about the varied problems of Britain and the Commonwealth, and in her thirty-seven years' experience has travelled more widely than any of her subjects. She is a skilled practitioner in the art of conversation so that without appearing to do so, she is always able to direct the talk the way she wants it to go. And she is equally adept at avoiding embarrassing confrontations – situations which so easily occur when people with widely differing views are present at a function.

A great deal of The Queen's entertaining is done on board the Royal Yacht *Britannia*, which in 1987 completed a £19 million refit. It cost only £3 million to build in 1953, which is just about what it costs to run her each year today. *Britannia* is perhaps the most romantic and glamorous of all the royal residences – truly a palace afloat. An invitation to dine on board is highly sought after whenever she puts into a foreign port.

The State Dining Room on board can accommodate just over fifty guests for dinner, but when a reception is held the numbers swell to around 250. As one experienced British diplomat put it, 'There aren't too many countries these days where you can offer your guests something new. Dinner on board *Britannia*, plus the spectacle of the Royal Marines' Band Beating Retreat, makes even the most blasé of world travellers sit up and take notice.'

The man responsible for all catering at all Royal residences – even on board *Britannia* – is the Master of the Household, arguably the most exalted major-domo in the world.

Sir Peter Ashmore held this position for thirteen years and he says that, even though most things run like clockwork, The Queen personally checks every detail herself. When visitors are invited to stay The Queen inspects their rooms before they arrive, to see that everything is in order.

At Buckingham Palace all Heads of State are offered accommodation in the Belgian Suite, which is situated on the ground floor, with French windows opening on to a terrace facing southwest across the palace gardens. It was named after King Leopold I of the Belgians – an uncle and close friend of Queen Victoria – who always used it during his frequent stays at the palace. It also has close associations with our present Royal Family, as The Queen and the Duke of Edinburgh occupied it immediately after King George VI's death in 1952, and both the Duke of York and Prince Edward were born in the Belgian Suite. In the past 150 years it has seen many different royal characters; some with unusual culinary tastes. King Alfonso XIII of Spain (1886–1941) liked a rare steak for breakfast, while Gustaf VI, King of Sweden from 1950 to 1973, enjoyed a large plate of pancakes flavoured with brandy. But the palace chef drew the line at allowing him to cook them himself.

Most of the furniture and all the porcelain in the three large rooms of the Belgian Suite were acquired by King George IV, who reigned from 1820 to 1830. The remainder was bought by Queen Mary, our present Queen's grandmother. In addition there are many personal reminders of previous occupants. In its undoubted grandeur, the suite gives visiting Heads of State some idea of the Royal Family's history.

The main room is called the Eighteenth Century Room. Its walls are hung with yellow linen; the curtains are of French embroidered silk and there is an early nineteenth-century floral Axminster carpet. The furniture is a mixture of English and French and includes a settee and chairs upholstered in silk to match the curtains, a Carlton House writing table and an unusual small round needlework box in rosewood with the signs of the Zodiac worked in ivory around its circumference. Between the windows is a mahogany cabinet made by the eighteenth-century English craftsman William Vile, containing a number of beautiful pieces of Sèvres and Chelsea porcelain. The work of William Vile is also seen in the two smaller chests which stand on either side of the fireplace. Above this hangs a large mirror balanced on each side by three-quarter-length portraits of King George III and Queen Charlotte, both commissions by the King from Zoffany. Other paintings in the room include works by Zuccarelli, Virentini, Canaletto and Gainsborough's famous painting of Diana and Actaeon.

The Spanish Room is the smallest of the three main rooms in the Belgian Suite. Generally used as a dressing room, it can be utilised as an extra bedroom if required, as it contains a small mahogany couch. One of its outstanding features is the beautiful Sèvres porcelain clock flanked by more Sèvres vases and candle-holders.

The Orléans Bedroom, part of the Belgian Suite where visiting heads of State are accommodated at Buckingham Palace. The colour scheme is blue with nineteenth-century hand-blocked, blue wallpaper matched by blue silk taffeta curtains. The chandelier is eighteenth century.

Alongside the Eighteenth Century Room is the Orléans Bedroom, the main bedroom of the Belgian Suite. The colour scheme is blue; nineteenth-century hand-blocked, blue printed wallpaper is matched by blue silk taffeta curtains. An English eighteenth-century chandelier hangs from the centre of the ceiling. The bedroom contains three pictures of Queen Victoria, two of them completed before she ascended the throne and the third, the famous portrait painted by Von Angeli in 1899, barely two years before she died. The two other pictures are by Queen Victoria's drawing master Richard Westall; the first shows a pencil and crayon sketch of her head and was drawn in 1829, and the other is a full-length portrait of the future Queen with a dog at her feet, completed in 1830. The two beds in the room are canopied and there is a settee and chairs which were designed by a refugee from the French revolution.

The third and smallest of the main rooms in the suite is the Spanish Room, which is generally used as a dressing room, but a mahogany bed or couch enables it to be converted to an extra bedroom if required. Easily the finest items in the Spanish Room are the superb Sèvres porcelain vases and candle holders flanking a Sèvres porcelain clock which stands above the fireplace. The two most interesting pictures are by Paul Delaroche, showing Napoleon Bonaparte crossing the Alps and on the island of St Helena.

Although not officially part of the Belgian Suite, the Carnarvon Room is allocated to a visiting Head of State as a dining room. This comfortable room, with its golden flocked wallpaper and yellow silk curtains and chairs, was named after the Marquess of Carnarvon, the nobleman who is thought to have drawn King George III's attention to the then Buckingham House. It is interesting to note that the present Earl of Carnarvon has also been of great service to the monarch. He has been Her Majesty's Racing Manager for more than twenty years.

Before a Head of State is expected The Queen will attach her own personal equerry to the visiting suite, to look after any problems that might arise. He accompanies the visitor at all times, smoothing the way and helping to make the Head of State and his or her entourage as comfortable as possible.

Obviously a number of things may be strange to visitors from different countries staying at Buckingham Palace for the first time. If they have particular dietary requirements – some like to bring their own cooks for religious reasons – the Equerry in Waiting is there to make sure they have everything they need. Most Heads of State are very appreciative of this help and occasionally valuable gifts are presented to the equerry at the end of the visit. Tipping is actually forbidden within the Royal Household, but nobody wants to offend a distinguished visitor, and if a present of gold cufflinks or a diamond tie pin is offered, a blind eye is turned to the rule.

Some Middle Eastern potentates arrive with enormous entour-

The Amir of Bahrain is given a royal chauffeur as Prince Philip drives a 'coach and four' through the grounds of Windsor Castle. The other passenger is the man who was in charge of the royal mews at the time, the then Crown Equerry, Lt. Col. Sir John Miller.

ages, and one or two have been known to employ the extra precaution of having a servant sleep across their doorway all night. Whatever the particular foible, the likes and dislikes, The Queen takes it all in her stride and behaves as if these customs were perfectly normal in her house. Nothing puts her out – apart from unpunctuality – and her attention to every aspect of the programme always guarantees a successful visit. She may be the most experienced monarch in the world but she is also 'mistress of the house' (Buckingham Palace is the largest house in the country with more than 600 rooms) and as such it is her responsibility to arrange the immense programme of entertainment.

A king would not need to involve himself in the day-to-day running of any of his palaces; that would be left to his queen. When the monarch happens to be a woman, she has to assume the additional responsibility of a hostess and give personal thought, care and attention to the comfort and well-being of her guests. The Queen has never shirked this duty. She considers it as important as any of her other functions as Head of State. True, she is served by the most experienced and capable of servants, who, if left to their own devices, would in all probability carry out their duties in an exemplary manner. But servants, no matter how dedicated, need to be supervised, and The Queen realises how important it is for her to be seen by those who work for her, and for them to know that she is taking an active interest in what they are doing.

So when the Head Chef presents his suggested menu for a State Banquet or a Lunch party, he knows that it is not simply a question of Her Majesty's 'rubber-stamping' his selection. She will go to endless lengths to ensure that her guests are offered the very best to eat and drink, that this particular menu will appeal to their particular tastes, and will suit the time of year. Even though her own tastes are simple in the extreme – she dislikes elaborate dishes with fancy sauces – she is knowledgeable about food, both English and foreign, and will often make suggestions of her own. The Master of the Household says it is essentially a team effort, 'but no one is in any doubt who is the captain of the team'.

One of the most delightful traditions continued by The Queen is the invitation to 'Dine and Sleep' at Windsor Castle. It was Queen Victoria who first introduced this novel way of meeting people, but in those days the guest lists were restricted to the leaders of society, all from similar backgrounds. Today, there is a much more catholic selection with film producers dining alongside eminent surgeons, and archbishops sharing a joke with authors and scientists.

The idea of these Dine and Sleep nights is for The Queen and the Duke of Edinburgh to meet, in a comparatively informal manner, men and women who have achieved success in a variety of fields. Usually six couples and up to four single persons will be asked for a night on three separate dates during the time The Queen is in residence at Easter. Also present will be the usual house guests, so the party numbers around twenty.

The guest list at Windsor Castle for Thursday, 9 April 1987 is a perfect example of the variety of interests represented: The Ambassador of Kuwait and Madame Al-Rayes; the High Commissioner for Canada and Mrs McMurty; The Chairman of the National Westminster Bank and Lady Boardman; the Leader of the House of Commons and Mrs Biffen; the Bishop of Guildford and Mrs Adie; The President of the University of Manchester Institute of

His Holiness Pope John Paul II paid a courtesy call on the Queen during his first visit to the United Kingdom in May 1982. They spoke privately for an hour before Her Majesty accompanied the Pope to the grand entrance at the conclusion of the visit.

Science and Technology and Lady Mason; Professor John Ashworth, Vice-Chancellor, University of Salford; The Chairman of W.H. Smith (the booksellers) and Mrs Hornby; The Surveyor of The Queen's Works of Art and Lady de Bellaigue; The Commanding Officer, 1st Battalion Scots Guards, and Mrs Kiszely; and Mr Hugh Robertson, The Life Guards.

The Queen likes to include young officers from the regiments which are on duty at Windsor, but it can be something of an ordeal for first-timers. There is a story told of one young Guards officer being invited to sit near The Queen on one of these occasions. He was wearing the usual mess dress, which these days includes a soft, white shirt instead of the boiled, hard-fronted variety which were de rigueur at all evening meals until comparatively recently. Her Majesty, no doubt with a twinkle in her eye, asked innocently if it was no longer the custom for her officers to wear the traditional 'boiled' shirts at dinner. The subaltern, obviously speaking without thinking, replied: 'Oh no, Ma'am, only on special occasions.' He spent the remainder of the meal fervently praying for the ground to open up and swallow him.

The invitation is sent by the Master of the Household at least four weeks in advance, so that in the unlikely event of a refusal, a reserve couple can be asked. Spouses are always included and the invitation specifies that 'dinner jackets will be worn'. Guests are asked to arrive between six thirty and seven in the evening and are greeted by members of the Household.

After being shown to their rooms, they are helped to unpack by a valet or housemaid, and then assemble in the Green Drawing Room for a drink. This is when they meet their hostess for the first time. While they are waiting for Her Majesty to appear they are able to admire the magnificent collection of blue Sèvres porcelain obtained by King George IV which is displayed in glass-fronted cabinets.

The Queen and the Duke of Edinburgh, together with any other members of the Royal Family who happen to be staying at Windsor, mingle easily with their guests, displaying a remarkable knowledge of what each individual has achieved. Of course the guest list was worked out many months in advance and a full briefing on every person has been given to The Queen long before the night in question.

After half an hour or so, everybody disperses to their bedrooms to change and they reassemble in the Green Drawing Room for a glass of sherry before dinner. The meal begins at eight-thirty and The Queen leads the way into the dining room accompanied by the senior male guest. The others follow in no particular order of precedence.

The dining room is in what is regarded as the coldest corner of the castle, the north-east, where the Private Apartments meet the State Apartments. But the white and gold panelled walls give out a warmth of their own and the painting of an equestrian scene of Queen Victoria which adorns them provides an instant topic of conversation. The Queen has personally arranged the seating plan in such a way that all the guests are within talking distance of a member of the Royal Family or the Household. In spite of the grandeur of the setting, there is a cosy informality about the occasion and a lot of animated talk around the table. It is all rather different from the days of Queen Victoria, who would allow only those of royal birth to sit next to her, and who spoke only to fellow royalty during dinner.

In pre-war days there would have been music throughout the meal, provided by a small string orchestra from the regiment of the Household Division currently on duty in the Castle. But The Queen decided to discontinue this practice. She thought the music a distraction from the conversation.

Once the meal has ended The Queen takes her guests on a tour of some of the treasures stored at Windsor. She pays particular attention to the interests of each and always has something to show them. For example, a war historian might be shown the actual bullet which killed Admiral Nelson at Trafalgar. An explorer would be able to see a relic of Captain Scott's journey to the South Pole, while someone interested in old books would see some marvellous examples of early printing. All are priceless treasures about which The Queen shows considerable knowledge which she is happy to share.

After a nightcap in the drawing room, at about midnight The Queen and the Duke of Edinburgh retire; and protocol dictates that nobody leaves the room until they have done so. Guests may then remain drinking as late as they wish, but most retire shortly after their royal hosts. They will have thanked Her Majesty for her hospitality and said goodbye, because that is the last they will see of her – for this visit anyway.

Breakfast, which has been ordered the night before, is served in the guests' suites, and once the Visitors' Book has been signed, guests leave at whatever time suits them – so long as it is before lunch.

The Dine and Sleep tradition not only gives The Queen and her husband an opportunity of meeting many distinguished men and women for more than just a quick word, but also allows people from different walks of life to see the sovereign and her consort in the privacy of their own home.

Much more frequent than Dine and Sleep invitations are those to join Her Majesty for luncheon at Buckingham Palace. These take place every month in the 1844 Room, so named because in that year it was used by Emperor Nicholas I of Russia during a State Visit to Queen Victoria. The colour scheme is white and gold and the room has a cosy and warm atmosphere, mainly due to the beautiful Axminster carpet made in honour of the room's first royal occupant. This is also the room in which The Queen receives all foreign ambassadors who come to present their credentials, and where meetings of the Privy Council are held. The 1844 Room contains one of the most unusual of the 300 clocks in the palace. It is a 'Negress Head' clock in which one of the eyes displays the hours of the day; the other shows the minutes. The eyelids open and close and the pedestal contains a working music box. Nobody claims the 'Negress Head' clock to be a beautiful work of art but it is certainly different and provides guests with a ready talking-point.

Again the guest lists show how wide are the interests and occupations of the men and women invited to The Queen's table. For example, on Wednesday, 28 October 1987, the Duke of Edinburgh, who normally attends these lunches, was abroad and therefore Princess Margaret was invited to replace him. Accompanying Her Royal Highness was her Private Secretary, Lord Napier and Ettrick, and Mrs Robert de Pass, who is an Extra Lady-in-Waiting to The Queen, also attended. The guests were: Dr Pauline Cutting, the surgeon who had recently returned from a refugee camp in Beirut; Dr Douglas Acres, Chairman of the Magistrates Association; the Reverend Michael Bourdeaux, General Director, Keston College, Kent; George Cole, the actor best known for his comedy roles in television series such as 'Minder'; Sir Ronald Dearing, former Chairman of the Post Office; Dr Eric Duckworth, Managing Director of the Fulmer Research Institute; Mr Anthony Loehnis, Executive Director of The Bank of England; and Mr Peter West, one of Britain's most successful broadcasters and sports journalists. Truly a mixture of talents, each person with something special to contribute and providing opportunities for The Queen to learn something new.

They had been asked to arrive at Buckingham Palace shortly before 1.00 pm, where they were met by a member of the Household who knew exactly who each one was. They were taken to the 1844 Room and offered drinks and cigarettes. When all the guests had arrived, the door opened and half a dozen corgis charged into the room followed by their mistress, Her Majesty The Queen. (This must be a standard ploy to break the ice with newcomers to the palace. When Jocelyn Barrow was lecturing at London University she was invited to lunch by The Queen and said the same thing happened to her: 'We were standing around a little nervously when all of a sudden the doors burst open and half a dozen dogs exploded into the room, running around, barking and charging between furniture and people, all over the place. When The Queen followed them she had a handful of biscuits which she gave them, and I was also offered a couple of biscuits to feed the corgis. Immediately the atmosphere became relaxed and everyone settled down to enjoy themselves.')

Each of the guests was presented individually and then those members of the Household who were not staying to lunch left the room and The Queen led the way to the table.

It was a simple but perfect three-course meal consisting of: scrambled eggs in pastry, garnished with asparagus; roast beef, new potatoes and green beans; ice-cream and fruit. White wine and red were served, but The Queen confined herself to a single glass of white wine throughout the meal. The conversation ranged from the theatre to the problems of the refugees in Beirut. Princess Margaret talked animatedly with George Cole about his television programmes and with Peter West about his long and varied broadcasting career. The Queen was fascinated by Dr Cutting's description of life in war-torn Beirut and was able to compare the doctor's views with those of her own daughter, the Princess Royal, who had also recently returned from visiting Save the Children Fund projects in the area.

Lunch lasted for just over an hour and a quarter and was followed by coffee, and liqueurs for those who wanted them. These were served to everyone standing, which enabled The Queen and Princess Margaret to circulate amongst those guests with whom they had had no chance for a real talk before or during lunch.

At 2.45 pm The Queen left to continue her afternoon engage-

E II R

*The Master of the Household
has received Her Majesty's command to invite*

The Reverend Canon William Down

*to a Luncheon to be given at Buckingham Palace
by The Queen*

on Tuesday, 4th November 1986 at 12.50 for 1pm.

*The reply should be addressed to
The Master of the Household, Buckingham Palace*

Dress: Lounge Suit

---

ments, and the guests, most of whom had not previously met one another, chatted for a few minutes longer before they too departed. The Queen had been able to add to her store of knowledge and experience and her guests had gained a unique insight into another aspect of royalty.

Much rarer than the invitations to luncheon or even to Dine and Sleep is being asked to spend the weekend at Sandringham. The house is the private property of The Queen and one she regards, as did her father and grandfather before her, with great affection. It was first bought by Prince Albert for the Prince of Wales, later King Edward VII, for the not inconsiderable sum, in those days, of £220,000. The house was rebuilt in 1870 and at that time had 365 rooms – one for every day of the year. However in the 1970s The Queen decided that Sandringham was far too large for her requirements and had 91 rooms demolished, so today a mere 274 are left. Much of the furniture and decorations and, certainly, the atmosphere of the house reflect the Edwardian tastes and style of its original royal occupant, and The Queen is perfectly happy that it should remain so. Guests who are invited are not always personal

An invitation to one of the Queen's informal lunches she holds every two months. The invitation is sent only after a preliminary telephone call from the Master of the Household to make sure there isn't a refusal.

friends but as the house is in the middle of the Norfolk countryside, those asked to stay can be expected to be *au fait* with a typical English countryhouse weekend.

If it is your first visit and you are not well known to the Royal Family a member of the Household will telephone the week before and discreetly ask what size shoes you wear. You will then find in your room a pair of green Hunter Wellington boots your size – an indication of the sort of weekend it is going to be.

An estate car meets your train unless you come by road, and at Sandringham House itself an equerry greets you and shows you to your room. You will be invited to 'come downstairs and meet The Queen' while your suitcase is unpacked, your nightclothes laid out on the bed and the remainder of your wardrobe pressed and carefully put away. The coathangers have all been branded with the royal cypher EIIR.

The weekend will probably be in January or early February, and you will be expected to shoot with the rest of the houseparty; if you have not brought your own guns, a pair will be supplied. The entire weekend will seem to pass in a haze of continuous gunfire, punctuated by picnic lunches, afternoon teas and formal dinners. A royal weekend is one where nobody gets a moment to themselves and the most important prerequisite for any guest is an inexhaustible supply of energy.

The rooms for guests at Sandringham are spacious and comfortable but the elegant little fireplaces have all been blocked up years ago and now the heating is provided by an electric fire which, if you leave it on all day, will warm the room nicely by the time you get back from shooting, ready to change for dinner. All the beds are large doubles, and every room contains a desk complete with writing-paper and envelopes, pens, pencils, letter opener, scissors, a ball of string, calendar and an ashtray. In fact everything you could possibly need if you decided to keep a daily journal – and then seal it against possible prying eyes. The room has a fitted carpet, paintings on the walls and a fully stocked library. In addition The Queen will have chosen several books herself which are placed on the small table beside the bed. All you need is twenty-five hours in the day.

Evening entertainment at Sandringham is very much self generated. The Royal Family enjoys party games such as charades, and no one is excused. The former Lord Chamberlain, Lord Maclean, and his wife were invited to spend a weekend just once during his thirteen years as head of The Queen's Household, and he found it very strange to see The Queen and her family letting their hair down in no uncertain fashion. Sandringham is one of the places where members of the Household take all their meals with the Royal Family and join in all the other family activities. Which is partly why most of the senior courtiers come from similar backgrounds. It is important for them to 'know the form'.

Back in London the never ending round of entertaining and being entertained continues; even when The Queen goes to the theatre she provides her own refreshments. If she has accepted an invitation to the Royal Opera House at Covent Garden she takes all her own food and drink and her own servants. The Palace Steward will telephone the head waiter at the Opera House to let him know how many will be in the royal party and to ask him to provide tables and chairs, in a private room near the Royal Box. Usually the palace staff will bring their own tablecloths and napkins, but occasionally the Opera House is able to provide them. Hot soup is brought in a container, but the main course is always something cold – salmon is a favourite. Footmen from Buckingham Palace serve the food – one to every four guests.

It is a bit like a picnic, albeit a rather grand picnic, and although some might think it is an unnecessary extravagance on the part of The Queen, it is in fact exactly the opposite. Her Majesty pays for all her private entertaining, and even though her visits to the theatre are rarely for personal enjoyment only – she nearly always goes on behalf of a charity – by providing her own food and servants she is able to control the expense and at the same time prevent her hosts being put to the trouble and inconvenience of having to pay for her supper. In any case, if the theatre were to provide a meal for The Queen and her party, there is little doubt that they would mount, with the best possible intentions, a far more lavish affair than Her Majesty does herself.

Similarly when The Queen goes to the races the catering is

provided by her own staff from the Royal Household. On Wednesday, 15 June 1988 Her Majesty invited the Princess Royal and Prince and Princess Michael of Kent to join her in the Royal Box at Ascot to see some of the finest racehorses in the world. Millions watched on television and saw The Queen and her guests cheering on the winners from the balcony in front of the Royal Box. What they didn't see was the private dining room immediately behind which was laid out for tea.

The Royal Suite, which contains a sitting room, viewing room and cloakrooms, is carpeted and glassed in on its balcony with reinforced, electric windows. There is a small lift at the rear of the suite but most of the Royal Family, including Queen Elizabeth the Queen Mother, prefer to use the stairs. Tea is served at a number of tables, with those guests who are invited to join Her Majesty being told discreetly by an Equerry or Lady-in-Waiting. The rest can sit where they choose.

The room was decorated with baskets of flowers, and hours before the royal party arrived, a small team from Windsor Castle turned up to prepare for tea. A van containing tables and chairs, tablecloths, china, crystal and cutlery pulled in just behind the grandstand, and footmen from the castle began unloading and setting the tables. Each place was laid as carefully as for an official dinner party, with Minton china (plain white with a gold band and the royal cypher), solid silver centrepieces, flowers for the tables and gilt chairs for The Queen and her guests. A television set was installed just in case the weather became too bad (and also because the Duke of Edinburgh, when he attends the races, prefers to watch cricket or some other sport once he has done his duty and made a brief appearance). The tiny sandwiches and fruit cakes were brought in airtight containers, and the staff spent several hours polishing the glasses and making sure everything was as perfect as they know the sovereign expects. Once The Queen and the rest of the party had finished their tea, and those who wanted it had had a glass of champagne, the servants cleared everything away and carefully repacked the china, glassware and cutlery before returning to Windsor to resume their normal duties.

The same procedure was followed every day during the Royal

Ascot meeting when The Queen was joined in the Royal Box by up to twenty guests each afternoon.

ROYAL WEDDINGS

Not only did The Queen act as hostess when her only daughter Princess Anne was married to Captain Mark Phillips in 1973, she also took on the responsibility of providing the wedding breakfast for two of her sons, firstly in 1981 when the Prince of Wales married Lady Diana Spencer and again in 1986 on the occasion of the wedding of the Duke and Duchess of York. There is no requirement for The Queen to give the wedding breakfasts for all her children, but it is a thoughtful and generous gesture; she realises only too well the difficulties that could arise if the families of her sons' brides had to host these events.

The three wedding breakfasts were almost identical in format: comparatively simple meals compared with the sumptuous royal feasts of Victorian and Edwardian times, when it was customary to have a fifteen-course meal lasting up to five hours. Princess Anne had four courses: scrambled eggs, lobster, shrimps and tomato in mayonnaise to begin with, followed by a main course of partridge with fresh mushrooms, peas, cauliflower and new potatoes; then came a salad; and the dessert was Bombe Glacée Royale – peppermint ice-cream filled with grated chocolate. (Dessert is often an ice-cream dish at royal meals.)

The Band of the Grenadier Guards under their Director of Music, Major P. W. Parkes, played selections by Novello, Strauss, Elgar, Purcell and Mozart, before ending with the 'Radetsky March', the regimental march of 1st The Queen's Dragoon Guards – Mark Phillips' regiment.

For the wedding breakfast of the Prince and Princess of Wales on Wednesday, 29 July 1981, the menu was slightly more sophisticated. They began with quenelles of brill in a lobster sauce, with which they drank Brauneberger Juffer Spätlese 1976. The main course consisted of chicken breasts sautéd, stuffed with lamb mousse, covered in brioche crumbs and served with a creamy mint-flavoured sauce, the whole being garnished with samphire – a Norfolk seaweed delicacy long enjoyed by the Royal Family when they are in residence at Sandringham. On the menu the dish was called Suprême de Volaille Princesse de Galles in honour, of course, of the new bride.

The vegetables accompanying the main course were broad beans, sweetcorn and new potatoes. To go with the chicken the Yeoman of the Wine Cellar had come up with one of his finest clarets, Château Latour 1959. The usual salad to refresh the palate was served next and they ended with fresh strawberries with Cornish clotted cream delivered from a farm in the Duchy of Cornwall. A splendid champagne, Krug 1969, was served for the toasts and the port was Taylor 1955. Prince Andrew and Prince Edward were delighted and relieved to find that at a royal wedding the best man, or 'supporter' as he is called, is not required to make a speech.

The wedding cake was a present from the Royal Navy. It stood five feet (1.5 m) high with five tiers surmounted by a bouquet of fresh flowers. It had come from the Royal Navy Cookery School at HMS *Pembroke* at Chatham, and because it was so delicate in spite of its weight – two hundredweight (102 kg) – they made a second cake in case the first was damaged in transit. The officer responsible was Lieutenant Fred Motley, assisted by cooks Dave Avery, David Scott and Ken Fraser. But as Lieutenant Motley said at the time, 'I guess everyone at HMS *Pembroke* had a hand in it – at least we all had a stir.'

The guest list at royal wedding breakfasts is usually restricted to around 120; so of the 2,500 people invited to the wedding service in St Paul's Cathedral all but a very few had to make their own arrangements for lunch.

These wedding breakfasts were held in the Ball Supper Room, one of the State Apartments at the palace. It is situated next to the State Ballroom on the first floor and seats 120 guests in comfort. In the case of the Prince and Princess of Wales they were arranged at twelve tables of ten and, in addition to the Royal Family, included the immediate Spencer family (with both the Countess Spencer, the bride's step-mother, and the Hon. Mrs Shand-Kydd, the Princess of Wales' mother). Also present were various members of foreign royal families who were staying either at Buckingham Palace or Windsor

Castle, among them several relatives of the Duke of Edinburgh, plus the bridesmaids and pages. It was a delightfully informal occasion, The Queen and Queen Elizabeth the Queen Mother chatting with all the guests almost like any family wedding.

Entertainment was provided from the next room by the Band of the Welsh Guards, of which regiment Prince Charles is Colonel-in-Chief. Under their Director of Music, Major D. N. Taylor, they played selections from *Bless the Bride*, *My Fair Lady* and *South Pacific*, together with the song 'The Princess of Wales' as a tribute to the bride and ending appropriately with another tribute, 'The Belle of the Ball' by LeRoy Anderson.

The wedding breakfast of the Duke and Duchess of York followed a similar pattern: 120 guests in the Ball Supper Room, all seated at tables for ten. It was another moment calling for diplomacy in the seating arrangements, as both the bride's mother, Mrs Susan Barrantes, and her step-mother were present.

After the formal photographs had been taken the guests sat down to diced lobster, egg and tomato in a Marie Rose sauce, decorated with prawns and washed down with Piesporter Goldtröpfchen Auslese 1976. Then came roast best end of lamb, garnished with tomatoes filled with mint-flavoured hollandaise sauce, accompanied by ring mould of spinach soufflé with mushrooms in the centre, broad beans with butter and new potatoes; to go with this there was Château Langoa Barton 1976. An asparagus salad prepared them for the strawberries and whipped cream in the form of the cross of St George on a base of strawberry fool. By this time they were all ready for the Bollinger 1966 and the port, a Graham of the same vintage.

It is noticeable that none of the dishes in this menu was named for the bride. Her husband had been created Duke of York only two hours before the ceremony, so the chefs and the Master of the Household, who had arranged the menu, could not know in advance that the newest member of the Royal Family would be the Duchess of York.

Even though by some standards these meals would be considered modest, they were all a far cry from the wedding breakfast of The Queen herself when, as Princess Elizabeth, she married Lieutenant

The menu for the wedding breakfast of Princess Elizabeth and the Duke of Edinburgh in 1947. A far cry from the sumptuous feasts of Edwardian and Victorian times. Food rationing was still in force in Britain and all the ingredients for this meal came from the Royal Estates.

BUCKINGHAM PALACE
THURSDAY, 20TH NOVEMBER, 1947
WEDDING BREAKFAST

Filet de Sole Mountbatten

Perdreau en Casserole
Haricots Verts   Pommes Noisette
Salade Royale

Bombe Glacée Princesse Elizabeth
Friandises

Déssert

Café

Philip Mountbatten on Thursday, 20 November 1947. This was of course still a time of austerity in Britain. The Second World War had ended barely two years earlier and food rationing was still very much in evidence. So, the wedding breakfast reflected The King's intention to show his people that, even for his daughter's wedding, he was not prepared to step beyond the limits imposed by the regulations of the day.

The meal began with Filet of Sole Mountbatten – named in honour of the bridegroom. This was followed by a casserole of partridge, the birds having come from the Sandringham estate; and the green beans, potatoes and salad were all grown in the royal gardens. It finished with Bombe Glacée Princesse Elizabeth and coffee. It was the sort of meal one could buy in almost any decent restaurant at the time and was well within the restrictions imposed by rationing.

It was also a royal function at which no delicate balancing of guests was required, unlike the weddings of the Prince of Wales and the Duke of York, when the parents of both brides had been divorced. In 1957 the Lord Chamberlain issued the following directive:

Guilty parties in divorces cannot be invited to functions held by The Queen within her royal palaces. (The royal yacht *Britannia* would come within this category.)
Innocent parties in divorces can be invited.
Persons in public office are received on account of the office.

There has been no official relaxation of these rules but The Queen, who is certainly a realist in such matters, has wisely decided to ignore the conventions of the fifties. If she didn't, the guest list at almost every royal function would be severely curtailed.

Her Majesty is very conscious that getting to know her people, and allowing them to meet her as informally as the occasion will allow, is a vital element in establishing that special feel and relationship between a monarch and her subjects. She has inherited from her mother the very special gift of sensitivity to the feelings, thoughts and reactions of both the individual and people in the mass. This talent is fine-tuned and exercised during the many different entertainments which she hosts, and the happy spin-off is that her guests depart from the royal home, not only having enjoyed themselves greatly, but with an enhanced knowledge and admiration of The Queen, as a person, and in the role she plays in the national life.

This is equally true for the peoples of the Commonwealth, whilst at the level of Heads of State, be it a Commonwealth or foreign country, the goodwill which has been generated by a happy social occasion can set the tone for successful relationships and oil the 'hard-grinding' wheels of twentieth-century politics. There can be little doubt that The Queen's great care and interest in every facet of her role as hostess aims not only to give real pleasure to her guests but also to promote the many benefits which, from time immemorial, have flowed from these happy gatherings.

3

Court Entertainments

Apart from the State Banquets which are held at Buckingham Palace and Windsor Castle in honour of a visiting Head of State, the most sumptuous entertainment provided by The Queen is the annual evening reception for the Diplomatic Corps. It takes place in November on an evening when all the magnificent State Apartments are brought into use and is an occasion to which every diplomat in London exerts all his influence to get himself invited. All the ambassadors and high commissioners receive invitations but because there simply is not enough room for all their suites to accompany them the guest list is worked out by the Marshal of the Diplomatic Corps (who answers directly to the Lord Chamberlain) in strict order of precedence. All sorts of cajoling and pleading take place in the weeks leading up to the reception, but to no avail. Precedence in the Diplomatic Corps goes according to seniority in years of service, so if, for example, the Belgian representative has been in London for longer than the United States Ambassador he is placed higher on this particular list. The size of the legation and the wealth and power of the country have no bearing at all.

In the early part of this century the diplomatic reception was one of four Courts held in the State Ballroom at Buckingham Palace. The Marshal of the Diplomatic Corps would present the wife of the doyen of the Corps to the sovereign and his consort; she would curtsey before the thrones, and the Court was then said to be officially opened. Then followed two hours of presentations, all in

The Lord Steward

is commanded by Their Majesties to invite

The Right Hon. Sir Alexander Hardinge
and the Hon. Lady Hardinge

to a State Banquet at Buckingham Palace, in honour of

The King of Roumania,

on Tuesday the 15th November, 1938, at 8·10 o'clock.

It is requested that the reply to this invitation may be
addressed to the Master of the Household at Buckingham Palace.

Full Dress.

1938 was the last year of full Court ceremonial before the outbreak of the Second World War brought Royal entertaining to a halt for six years. Sir Alexander Hardinge, as Private Secretary to King Edward VIII, had been closely involved with the abdication crisis two years earlier.

strict order of precedence, starting with the Archbishop of Canterbury, the Lord High Chancellor and the Prime Minister, then the ambassadors, each resplendent in the prescribed Court Dress of black velvet breeches buckled below the knee, black silk stockings and patent leather pumps. The rules governing the wearing of Court Dress occasionally caused a certain amount of embarrassment and disunity. The older established traditionalists from the European countries were used to the ritual surrounding royalty and at ease in the formal uniforms with decorations, sashes and even black silk stockings. One or two American diplomats, however, felt that to put on what they regarded as an outdated and unnecessary garb would be seen as 'bending the knee' back home, and bluntly refused to wear knee breeches at Court. In 1929, Ambassador Charles Dawes took up his post in London and immediately announced that he would not wear knee breeches and silk stockings 'at Court or anywhere else'. King George V was acutely upset, particularly as, owing to his own illness, the Court at which Mr Dawes was to be presented was to be presided over by The Queen alone, and the decision of the new Ambassador might be seen as a public insult to Her Majesty. The row grew to immense proportions, involving the Foreign Office, the Lord Chamberlain and even the Prince of Wales, who was a personal friend of Charles Dawes. But the American was adamant: he would not be budged from his original decision. It was even suggested that as a compromise he could leave the embassy wearing trousers over his knee breeches and change at the palace, thereby avoiding a public display in Court Dress. But it was all to no avail. When the time came for him to be presented to Queen Mary he advanced towards the throne – wearing full evening dress, but no knee breeches. When the evening was over Her Majesty was heard to mutter: 'What a pity that such a distinguished man should be so difficult.' His immediate successor, Robert Bingham, restored Anglo-American relations when he appeared at the 1935 Jubilee Banquet in full Court Dress, but his successor Senator Joseph Kennedy refused to have anything to do with knee breeches, saying: 'If I were to wear knee breeches I'd offend folks in America.' Post-war American ambassadors found no difficulty in conforming to the custom of wearing Court Dress as and when required, but today the practice is to don full evening dress: white tie, tails and decorations for the evening reception, and morning suits at other times.

It is not only Americans who have objected to conventional Court Dress. When the Labour party first came into power in the nineteen twenties there was a considerable difference of opinion within the new government about whether or not to wear it. The Prime Minister Ramsay MacDonald didn't mind at all – he rather enjoyed the glitter and pomp of dress uniforms and wearing swords and spurs, but many of his colleagues felt it was ridiculous to expect them to appear in clothes they could not afford and that were quite alien to their class.

As far as the cost was concerned, The King's Private Secretary, Lord Stamfordham, tried to make things easier. He made enquiries at Moss Bros Ltd of Covent Garden (who today hire morning suits and evening wear for most royal functions) and discovered that they could undercut the then current price of a full Levee Dress, which was £73. 25s. 6d, to £30 complete; this included cocked hat and sword. But this did not overcome the objections of the dissenters. The cost was only part of it. Men who had only recently been working with their hands felt that for them to be seen parading in cocked hats with swords strapped to their sides would be a betrayal of their origins. The issue went to cabinet level, and in true political style a compromise was reached. They would wear knee breeches but with evening dress coats. The King took the matter very seriously and felt that unless some form of uniformity were adopted the whole Court would be left open to ridicule.

Even so at the first reception attended by the new Labour ministers, several were in full Court Dress while others wore a combination of knee breeches, dinner jackets and tail coats. The headgear ranged from cocked hat with plumes to silk opera hats – but happily no bowlers or The King would have had a heart attack. By the time of the first post-war Labour government in 1945 the regulations regarding Court Dress had been dropped and now very few people wear it apart from the male members of the Royal Family and the Household. Evening dress, even black tie and dinner jacket, are now acceptable at all State functions and since 1978 lounge suits have been permitted. The Roumanian State Visit took place in that year and it was agreed in advance that Roumanian men could wear lounge suits at State Banquets and receptions.

Today the Diplomatic Reception is attended by some 1,200 guests, most of whom attend a private dinner party before the function, which begins promptly at nine thirty. Members of the Royal Household who occupy Grace and Favour apartments in St James's Palace usually host dinners for twenty or thirty diplomatic guests, who can then simply walk the few yards to Buckingham Palace. The Lord Chamberlain's dinner party is the most prestigious, with the Prime Minister, the Archbishop of Canterbury and the senior diplomats and their spouses all arriving at seven o'clock in the spacious corner apartment overlooking Marlborough House. Once the meal is over the Lord Chamberlain accompanies his guests, if it's a fine evening, on the short walk across Stable Yard, through Milkmaids Passage skirting the edge of Green Park and across the road to Buckingham Palace, where he leaves them temporarily as he will be on duty for the rest of the evening.

The guests enter the palace by the Grand Entrance and proceed up the Grand Staircase to the Green Drawing Room and the Picture Gallery where drinks are served. It is a scene of unsurpassed splendour. Every nationality, colour and creed are represented; diamonds sparkle, tiaras glint in the light from the crystal chandeliers; diplomats are weighed down with medals, crosses, stars and sashes.

The ladies and gentlemen of the Household are in attendance making sure that everyone has everything they need. No one is left alone; no glass is left empty. The Master of the Household has arranged the evening's entertainment with his usual care and attention, the footmen and pages are standing by in full State livery, the band of the Household division is playing in the Gallery of the State Ballroom. Even Queen Victoria would have been proud of the spectacle. Once all the guests have arrived they assemble to await the appearance of The Queen and the Royal Family.

The royal party enters from the White Drawing Room and walks slowly down the two ranks of waiting diplomats and their spouses. As they number well over a thousand it would be impossible for each to be presented individually as in the past, so as The Queen and other members of her family walk past, the gentlemen bow from the neck and ladies curtsey. Once Her Majesty has passed through all the State Rooms and been seen by all her guests, they congregate in the Ballroom where later there will be dancing to a band provided by whichever regiment is on duty. A buffet supper has been laid out and champagne is served throughout the remainder of the evening.

The longest serving member of the Diplomatic Corps is presented to The Queen, and certain other guests, who include the Prime Minister, the Lord Chancellor and the Archbishop of Canterbury, are guided to the royal presence by the Lord Chamberlain and his staff. Shortly after midnight the band plays the national anthem, The Queen and the Duke of Edinburgh leave the reception and the most sparkling evening of the year is over. For a few brief hours Buckingham Palace has regained some of its former glory, the grandeur and magnificence of bygone days, and the Lord Chamberlain, the Master of the Household and the Palace Steward have shown that when it comes to entertaining on a truly royal scale, they have few equals.

A much more exclusive function is the one held at Windsor Castle every year to commemorate the Duke of Wellington's victory over Napoleon in 1815. It takes place on or around 18 June – the date of the battle – in the Waterloo Chamber and was originally conceived by King George IV who commissioned Sir Thomas Lawrence to paint a series of portraits of all the monarchs, statesmen and soldiers who had played a part in the historic victory. An immense painting of the Duke dominates the room from its position above the doorway. Fifty-two people sit down for the Waterloo Banquet at a table decorated with flowers of blue and yellow, the colours of the first duke. His descendant, the present holder of the title, is guest of honour and before the dinner is required to present the sovereign with a silk tricolour flag, the annual rent for his country estate at Stratfield Saye in Hampshire which was given in perpetuity to the great duke by a grateful nation. Visitors to Windsor can see the flag displayed in the Queen's Guard Chamber.

A few days before the Waterloo Banquet, another pleasant Court entertainment takes place at Windsor. It is the annual luncheon which precedes the Garter Service in St George's Chapel. New knights are installed in a private ceremony at noon and this is followed by a delightful meal at which The Queen and her family are joined by the Knights of the Garter and their wives. Sir Cennydd Traherne, a Knight since 1970, described it as one of the most enjoyable of all royal functions because of the informality. The Knights have shed their ceremonial robes after the instalment, and their wives, who take no part in the formal part of the proceedings, are able to mix with their husbands' colleagues and also with the Royal Family. The Queen and the Duke of Edinburgh are always present. So too are Queen Elizabeth the Queen Mother, the Prince and Princess of Wales and the Duke of Kent, who has been a Royal Knight since 1985. Foreign royalty also attends on occasion. King Olaf of Norway, the Grand Duke of Luxembourg, the King of the Belgians and the King of Sweden are all Extra Knights who are welcome guests at Windsor; when they all turn up for the Garter Luncheon it is quite a party.

Court entertainment in Scotland is restricted to the one week in the year when The Queen takes up residence at the Palace of Holyroodhouse. There is always a garden party at which kilts of every tartan are to be seen. An added attraction is the presence of two of the most colourful of The Queen's ceremonial bodyguards: the High Constables of Holyroodhouse, who patrol the grounds wearing distinctive blue uniforms and cockaded silk bonnets (approved by King George V in 1914), and The Queen's personal bodyguard in Scotland, the Royal Company of Archers, each clad in Sherwood green with a feathered bonnet and clutching a long-bow (which he has paid for personally). However, the service for the Most Ancient and Most Noble Order of the Thistle – the sovereign's personal Order of Chivalry in Scotland – does not take place every year. Her Majesty gives at least one formal dinner party in the palace and if it is to be a State Banquet, it is held in the Long Gallery which can accommodate 100 guests.

One particular aspect of dining at Holyroodhouse is special. The silver used was a Silver Jubilee present in 1935 to King George V and Queen Mary from Sir Alexander Grant (then Chairman of McVities) and his fellow Scottish Royal Warrant Holders. It was a magnificent gift consisting of a full banquet service for 108, including all cutlery and serving dishes. It was designed by the principal architect for Scotland at the time in the style of the late seventeenth century. When the complete service is being used, more than 2,000 pieces of solid silver are on view.

Apart from these regular formal entertainments in Scotland and England, The Queen also acts as hostess at a variety of functions for special groups. If leaders of the Commonwealth are meeting in London Her Majesty always invites them and their spouses to a cocktail party at Buckingham Palace; participants in the Duke of Edinburgh's Award Scheme are given a reception and in the early years of her reign The Queen gave a garden party for delegates from the American Bar Association conference, when they were served with hamburgers to make them feel at home.

GARDEN PARTIES

One centuries-old social tradition was carried on by The Queen for only the first six years of her reign. She then realised how outdated it was and decided to end it. It was the tradition of Presentation Parties, the custom by which young unmarried girls were presented at Court during their 'Season', after which they were considered of an age to wed.

The Presentation was a formal occasion at which each debutante –
a word invented during the reign of Queen Victoria – dressed in a
long white evening gown and with a headdress of three ostrich
feathers formed into the crest of the Prince of Wales, was invited
to make an individual curtsey to her sovereign. Once that all-
important curtsey had been made and observed, the young lady was
said to have 'come out' and was then eligible for the marriage stakes.
Hence 'debutante' – one who had made her debut at Court. Mothers
vied with each other to make sure their daughter had the best guest
lists of the Season at her dinner parties and ball. Fathers patiently
put up with the frantic merry-go-round and paid the bills, which
even in the early nineteen fifties could run to several thousand
pounds.

The Royal Household took the Presentation Parties as seriously
as the would-be guests and each year the regulations governing
the ceremony were published with due formality by the Lord
Chamberlain. This is the list for the final year:

The Lord Chamberlain announces that The Queen, with the
Duke of Edinburgh, will hold afternoon parties for the pres-

In the 1920s debutantes – and their mothers – took the business of 'being presented' very seriously indeed. A number of ladies made a good living by coaching young ladies in the correct way to curtsey before they were allowed into the royal presence.

entation of ladies at Buckingham Palace next year. Ladies whose applications include the names of debutantes will be summoned to make their presentations at one of the parties to be held on March 21 and 22. Ladies whose applications do not include the name of a debutante will be summoned to attend one of the Garden Parties in July. The regulations are as follows:

Ladies, who have already been presented in their present name and style, wishing to make presentations, should forward the names as soon as possible to The Lord Chamberlain, St James's Palace, London SW1.

Any lady who has attended, or been presented at a Presentation Party in 1956 or 1957, is not eligible to attend in 1958, except for the purpose of presenting an unmarried daughter.

No applications can be accepted from ladies wishing to be

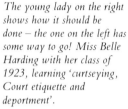

The young lady on the right shows how it should be done – the one on the left has some way to go! Miss Belle Harding with her class of 1923, learning 'curtseying, Court etiquette and deportment'.

presented; their names must be forwarded by the ladies who wish to present them.

Unmarried ladies are ineligible to make presentations even though they themselves have been presented.

No applications can be accepted for attendance only.

A lady eligible to make a presentation who wishes to present her daughters and/or daughters-in-law may, in addition, present one other lady. Otherwise ladies are limited to one presentation only.

On the occasion of their own presentation, ladies may only present their daughters and/or daughters-in-law.

Invitations will be extended to the husbands of ladies making presentations or being presented, only if their names are submitted in the original application. It is emphasised that the

After weeks of training, the moment of truth. A young lady arrives at Buckingham Palace in 1927 to be presented to King George V and Queen Mary. She is accompanied by her sponsor who would also have had to have been previously presented at Court.

attendance of gentlemen at these presentation parties will not count as presentation at Court.

Ladies domiciled in the Commonwealth countries and colonies wishing to be presented, must make application to the High Commissioner, or Secretary of State, concerned, for presentation by his wife.

Ladies of foreign nationality, either by birth or by marriage, can only be presented through the diplomatic representative of the country concerned, except when they are in possession of British passports.

Far from being put off by the strict rules governing the Presentation Parties, mothers flocked to have their daughters' names included in the invitation lists. Each party, at which only about 200 girls could be presented, was oversubscribed fifty times at least. If the Lord Chamberlain had charged a thousand pounds a time he would still have been besieged with applications from socially ambitious parents, and not only from the British upper classes. Wealthy American fathers were prepared to go to almost any lengths to get their daughters presented at Court, and the wife of the United States' Ambassador was deluged with requests.

The position became ridiculous; so much so that it soon became apparent that the Presentation Parties would take up far too much of The Queen's time if all requests were granted. So after consultations with the Lord Chamberlain Her Majesty decided to bring to an end a practice that had lasted for more than two and a half centuries. On 14 November 1957, the following world-shattering announcement was issued from St James's Palace:

> The Lord Chamberlain gives notice that there will be no Presentation Parties after 1958. The Queen proposes to hold additional Garden Parties in order that larger numbers may be invited to Buckingham Palace.

There was panic in fashionable houses throughout the land as mothers rushed to make sure their daughters' names were included in the final invitation lists. Extra Presentation Parties were held at

Buckingham Palace to accommodate the final numbers and the last Presentation Party of all at which The Queen was present was held in the Throne Room of the Palace of Holyroodhouse in Edinburgh on 3 July 1958. The distinction of being the last debutante to curtsey formally before Her Majesty fell to Miss Fiona Macrae, daughter of Mr and Mrs Kenneth Macrae of Edinburgh. She was not aware at the time that she would one day occupy a unique place in the history of British society because two other Presentation Parties at Buckingham Palace were planned for later that same summer. However, nature intervened and The Queen had to withdraw from the ceremonial occasions through illness and her place was taken by Queen Elizabeth the Queen Mother. The custom by which the cream of society was honoured by the sovereign had given way to the more democratic system of the Garden Party.

It is usual for between 8,000 and 9,000 guests to turn up at Buckingham Palace on the day of a Garden Party. Most arrive by car – with a special pass to allow them to park in The Mall and on

''Twas ever thus' – the scene on The Mall on 21 July 1936 as taxis and private cars jam the approach to Buckingham Palace shortly before an afternoon party given by King Edward VIII – when they all came out at 6 o'clock it was even worse!

Constitution Hill – and the traffic jams when all 9,000 emerge at the end of the afternoon are truly horrendous, causing taxi drivers and regular business commuters to curse long and loud.

The first indication that one has been invited to a Garden Party is a large white envelope dropping through the letterbox. There is no stamp; simply a legend containing the royal cypher in the lower left-hand corner. And the envelope, which is addressed to the lady of the house, has always been handwritten. Inside the envelope is a stiff white paste-board, which says:

> The Lord Chamberlain is commanded by Her Majesty
> to invite (the names follow)
> to a Garden Party at Buckingham Palace on
> (the appropriate date) from 4 to 6 pm

There is also a small numbered blue card which has to be surrendered to a Footman when you enter the palace. This is how they can tell who has turned up because no r.s.v.p. is required. In addition there will be a car-sticker to allow your driver to park in one of the approach roads to the palace and a map showing the three entrances to be used on the day, which even points out the nearest underground railway station.

The guest lists for Garden Parties are the responsibility of the Lord Chamberlain's Office, where the names of every person who has ever been invited is retained in a card index system. These cards also record the number of times each person has attended and whether their children have accompanied them: unmarried daughters aged eighteen and over are allowed to join their parents at a Garden Party – a throwback to the days of Presentation Parties. However, sons are not included in the invitation. While married women are accompanied by their husbands, unmarried ladies who are invited must come alone; no companions are permitted. In Queen Victoria's time Garden Parties were held so that Her Majesty could meet more of the upper classes. In Queen Elizabeth II's time the guest lists range from archbishops, diplomats and senior politicians, who come every year, to the council worker who has been invited as a reward for long service to the community.

It wasn't only British girls who yearned to be presented at Court. These two young ladies are from Canada and they travelled 6,000 miles for this one royal occasion. It was a garden party at Buckingham Palace in July 1956. The dresses are organdie – the invitations obtained through the Canadian High Commission.

When the guest lists were extended to include people from all walks of life and every social category, The Queen was anxious to ensure that nobody would be put to the expense of hiring a morning suit if this was going to be a hardship, nor did she want any of her guests to be embarrassed, so she insisted that the invitation should state that lounge suits would be acceptable. Nevertheless, they are the exception; the majority of male guests are still attired in formal morning dress complete with top hat and silk gloves. Ladies always

Windsor Castle was the setting for a splendid garden party in July 1912. King George V and Queen Mary welcomed the cream of Society – some of whom are here seen walking to the Henry VIII gate at the castle.

wear hats, and trouser suits are definitely frowned upon. The majority of the guests opt for the Grand Entrance because this gives them the opportunity, albeit a brief one, of going inside Buckingham Palace itself rather than directly into the gardens. For many of them it may well be the only occasion they will be able to do so.

The queues start forming shortly after lunch and at 3.15 pm guests are permitted to enter. After crossing the forecourt and passing through the arch into the inner Quadrangle one enters the Grand Entrance to the Marble Hall. Once you have delivered up any cameras to the courteous but firm attendants, who politely inform you that photography of any sort is strictly forbidden, you ascend the shallow staircase with its rich crimson carpet to the Bow Room. This is where first-time guests like to linger a while to see a tiny fraction of the treasures in the palace. In recesses in the four corners is assembled the Mecklenburg-Strelitz table service of Chelsea porcelain which was commissioned by King George III and Queen Charlotte and completed in 1763. The Bow Room itself was redecorated in 1902, and the gold and white ceiling, supported by columns of grey Carrara marble, is enriched by the deep crimson colours of the carpets and velvet curtains.

After the Bow Room guests pass through the glass doors on to the Terrace at the rear of the palace and descend the stone steps to the most exclusive lawns in the world. The gardens are spread over 40 acres (16ha) and there are magnificent displays of lilies, delphiniums, rhododendrons, azaleas, camellias and several varieties of rose, including Queen Elizabeth, Silver Lining and Peace. There is also a splendid lake at the west end of the gardens containing a flock of pink flamingoes who have been in residence since 1959. As the coolest part of the gardens the lake is particularly attractive on very hot afternoons.

The tea tents are arranged along the southern wall and experienced Garden Party goers usually aim for their refreshments as soon as they arrive. They know it will be at least three-quarters of an hour before The Queen makes an appearance and that newcomers will

High Society dressed to kill. Guests arriving at Buckingham Palace for an afternoon party in July 1926. This photograph was taken just a few months after our present Queen was born.

wait until after that before trying to get served. Then there is a dreadful crush as several thousand people try to attract the attention of the hard-pressed waitresses.

The catering at Garden Parties is left in the experienced and capable hands of J. Lyons and Co. (of Corner House fame). They provide 27,000 cakes, 36,000 sandwiches, 10,000 cups of Indian tea and 10,000 glasses of iced coffee (by far the favourite beverage) for each of the three parties. But they do not look after the refreshments for the Royal Tea Tent. Everything eaten and drunk by The Queen and the Royal Family is the responsibility of the palace kitchens.

Garden Parties are expensive to mount. Each one costs more than £30,000 and this The Queen pays for personally. In addition to the tea and buns, she has to provide first-aid and ambulance facilities, bandstands, the hire of the marquees and temporary toilets. The cloakrooms in the gardens at Buckingham Palace must be among the most luxurious anywhere; each one being completely carpeted.

The Garden Party proper starts at exactly 4 o'clock when the royal party step through an open glass door on to the Terrace. The Queen is always accompanied by the Duke of Edinburgh and several other members of the Royal Family. They chat to each other as they stroll towards the top of the steps where they pause as one of the two military bands on duty plays the national anthem. Any latecomers among the guests who have not managed to get into the gardens by this time are kept in the Bow Room until the anthem is finished.

Immediately in front of The Queen at the foot of the steps, a group of people is waiting to be presented. They are tenants from the Royal Duchies of Lancaster and Cornwall and official guests such as incoming High Sheriffs, Lords Lieutenant and High Court judges. Meanwhile the rest of the assembled guests have formed themselves into a number of 'lanes' down which the royal party will walk – each one taking a separate lane. It is easy to see which lane The Queen will use because a detachment of the Yeomen of the Guard have formed up to line the route, which is always the most densely packed.

Meanwhile a small group of rather distinguished looking gentlemen, all very tall, with the unmistakable air of former officers in the three Armed Services and each wearing a yellow carnation in his buttonhole, has marshalled the guests and gone through the preliminary task of sorting out those who are to be 'presented'. These are members of the Household in Waiting and all have years of experience in dealing with Court protocol. They know exactly the type of person The Queen wants to meet – and it has nothing at all to do with rank. Her Majesty is totally unimpressed by the social standing of any of her subjects. We are all equal in her eyes. So the choice depends on whether the guest in question has something outstanding about him. If he or she is wearing an unusual uniform or perhaps a particular decoration, it could mean that they have something interesting to tell The Queen. The usher will have a short chat to find out one or two personal details and also to point out what happens when the guests meet Her Majesty. Gentlemen are asked to bow from the neck and ladies to curtsey and both are advised not to shake hands unless The Queen offers her hand first. As Her Majesty walks slowly through the lanes acknowledging the polite applause of her guests, one of the Gentlemen Ushers will perhaps murmur in her ear that: 'The gentleman you are about to

meet, Ma'am, has been a refuse collector at Windsor for forty years and never had a day off sick.' This is, of course, why he was invited. When The Queen reaches him she will offer her hand and remark to his astonishment that she is truly delighted to meet him, particularly as they both come from Windsor, and she also congratulates him on his remarkable work record. Even more astonishing is the fact that she makes him believe that she really means it!

After a few minutes Her Majesty smiles and moves on to the next couple. If someone gets a little nervous or tends to talk for too long through over-enthusiasm, royalty has the knack of being able to bring the conversation to a close and moving on without giving offence, and almost without the offender being aware of what is happening.

At garden parties in the grounds of the Palace of Holyroodhouse in Edinburgh the atmosphere is somehow much more informal. Peter Heatly, Chairman of the Commonwealth Games Federation, tells a story of the party held in 1986 to which the competitors at the Commonwealth Games were invited. The afternoon was wet and dismal and the guests huddled under the tents for protection. The lanes down which The Queen walked were very narrow and just as she reached a certain point one of the Scottish team stepped out in front of her. Her Majesty was surprised – it had never happened before. The athlete (who shall remain nameless) spoke in a broad Glaswegian accent. He asked The Queen if he could ask her a personal question. She replied, guardedly, that he might; whereupon he said, 'How old was your last corgi dog when it died?' The Queen thought for a moment and replied, 'Fifteen years and she just collapsed one day and that was it.' Her guest then said, 'Just the same as mine, Your Majesty – no signs, just keeled over and died.' The Queen smiled and walked on. They had established a common link – two dog lovers with a shared experience.

Meanwhile, at Buckingham Palace, the other members of the Royal Family will have been 'working' their lanes in the general direction of the Royal Tea Tent, where the diplomatic guests, who received special passes, are already gathered. The area immediately in front of the Royal Tea Tent is clear of people except for lines of folding chairs arranged in a large semi-circle. A number of ladies who are obviously old hands at this Garden Party game has laid claim to these chairs, so that they can watch, from a respectful distance, the royal party take its tea. The distance covered by The Queen from the foot of the Terrace to the Royal Tea Tent is no more than 300 yards (274m), but it will have taken Her Majesty about an hour and twenty five minutes to walk it. Inside the Royal Tea Tent there is more small talk to be made with diplomats of every race, creed and colour and then, at ten minutes to six, The Queen smilingly leaves the Tea Tent and leads her family party slowly (they never hurry) back across the lawns to the palace. The invitation was from 4 to 6 pm and now the guests, some of them reluctantly, start to make their way home. If they are lucky they will be away from the palace within the hour, if not, it could take much longer. But they have enjoyed their brief moment of glory, rubbing shoulders – almost – with royalty. The bandsmen pack away their instruments, the employees from J. Lyons salvage what is left of the food and collect the tea cups, plates and cutlery. In the old days, guests used to take the spoons home as souvenirs because they had the royal cypher on them. These days they are plain stainless steel so nobody bothers. Another Garden Party is over, and The Queen has completed another duty she has made to seem a pleasure.

INVESTITURES

Some fifteen times a year The Queen acts as host to nearly 500 people who come to Buckingham Palace for a couple of hours but are offered neither food nor drink – and they don't mind a bit! The occasions are the Investitures, when Her Majesty presents decorations to those men and women who have been mentioned in either the New Year or the Birthday Honours List. Investitures always take place on a Tuesday morning at 11, when honours are received by about 150 people, the number that can best be processed in exactly one hour. It is all over on the stroke of twelve.

Those who are to be honoured by The Queen receive two invitations: one of fawn cardboard on which the words 'This cannot be replaced' is underlined, the other a slightly larger, white paste-board which one is asked to show to the usher at the entrance to the Ballroom where the Investiture is to take place. The cards also inform guests that entry is from 10 o'clock and that 'dark suits' should be worn. The invitations, issued in The Queen's name, are signed by the Earl of Airlie, the Lord Chamberlain.

On the day of the Investiture a long procession of motor cars approaches Buckingham Palace, usually on the dot of ten. Although they will have an hour to wait, most of the recipients and their guests want to make the most of every minute they can spend inside Buckingham Palace, so turn up as early as politeness allows.

The drivers of their cars have been issued with special large passes bearing the letter X. These allow them into the forecourt of the palace – a more than useful perk in central London at any time of the day. The cars, and visitors on foot, enter the forecourt by the South Front Gate (the one on the left as you look at the palace from The Mall). They are directed to a policeman standing near the central arch who then points them towards the inner Quadrangle. This is the square you cannot see from the outside and for most of those arriving it affords their first glimpse of the hidden side of Buckingham Palace. Nearly everyone has brought a camera and photographs are being taken all over the place by proud relatives. No one takes too much notice of the squads of police with dogs, and mirrors on long handles which they push under the vehicles in case any has explosives attached. It is a sign of the times we live in that booby-trapped cars may be used by terrorists in many parts of the world.

Once all the photographs have been taken the family groups move towards the Grand Entrance, where they surrender the smaller, fawn cards to a waiting doorman clad in scarlet livery. They walk up a few, shallow steps, then turn to the left to proceed up the Grand Staircase.

The ladies' cloakrooms are on the right; gentlemen on the left. Coats are handed to a footman who gives a plastic token in return. Guests are politely but firmly reminded that *all* cameras must be left behind – no photography of any kind is allowed inside the palace.

The cloakrooms themselves are very modern and up to date, in fact rather like those you would find in any top class hotel. They are in complete contrast to the lavatories elsewhere in the palace, which are Victorian in the extreme – ornate, imposing, and very comfortable.

At the foot of the Grand Staircase signs direct recipients of honours to the right and guests straight on. In a separate room those involved in the ritual of the Investiture are told what they should do during the ceremony. A small hook may be attached to their clothes, so that The Queen can hang their medals easily without having to fuss with a pin on heavy material. Meanwhile their guests are free to meander towards the State Ballroom at their own pace. A number of dismounted Troopers of the Household Cavalry are standing guard at intervals on the Grand Staircase, drawn swords resting on their right shoulders, cuirasses (body armour) gleaming and thigh boots polished until you really can see your face in them. The Life Guards are resplendent in their scarlet tunics with white plumes flowing from their burnished helmets; the Blues and Royals are equally striking in their dark blue uniforms and sporting distinctive red plumes. In the East Gallery, at the top of the Grand Staircase, most of the guests linger to admire the magnificent portraits of past members of the Royal Family. There are two truly impressive paintings of Queen Victoria, one showing her wedding to Prince Albert, the other, on the opposite wall, a charming family group.

A slightly jarring, but nonetheless essential, note is introduced by a white placard indicating where the First Aid Room is located.

Any royal occasion can be nerve-wracking for those taking part, and a sympathetic nurse is on duty to help with aspirins, smelling salts – even a friendly cup of tea.

At the entrance to the State Ballroom stands the imposing figure of the Chief Usher. He is usually a former officer from one of the services. On this occasion he comes from the Brigade of Guards and is dressed in a black frock tunic (without the sword) and spurs. He is accompanied by four other senior officers, two from the Royal Navy and two from the Royal Air Force. Each has a copy of the morning's programme showing the number and identity of recipients, which band is playing and who will be in the royal party. The Ushers are friendly, charming, with exquisite manners and throughout the morning give no sign of irritability or any other indication that they have been through this same procedure many times.

Inside the Ballroom 200 gilt chairs have been set out in rows immediately in front of the dais on which stand the two thrones

One unusual item of furniture which is carried on board 'Britannia' is the kneeling stool used when the Queen bestows a knighthood. Surely there can be no more romantic setting for such a ceremony?

under a silk canopy. Only fifty of these chairs are occupied by guests, the remainder being left empty for the recipients once they have been given their awards. The rest of the guests are seated on three banquettes permanently situated around the walls. They are tiered so that everyone is able to see what is happening without standing up. Near the front is a special section which, at The Queen's request, is reserved for children.

As the guests enter the Ballroom the band of the Welsh Guards, seated in the Minstrels' Gallery, is playing selections from *Oklahoma* and other well known musicals. About fifteen minutes before the Investiture is due to begin, one of the Ushers stands at the lectern and welcomes everyone to Buckingham Palace. He then proceeds to give a short briefing on what is going to happen. In a moment a detachment of the Yeomen of the Guard, the oldest military bodyguard in the world, will march into the room and shortly afterwards the royal party will arrive. We are asked to stand up when Her Majesty enters the room but not to applaud, either then or later, 'no matter how enthusiastic you are about the person receiving the honour'. In fact, there is only one record of applause in the entire history of investitures and that was on 15 November 1977. The Queen was slightly late in arriving in the State Ballroom, an unusual occurrence in itself. When she took her place on the dais she apologized and explained that she had just heard that she had become a grandmother for the first time (with the birth of Princess Anne's son, Peter). There was a gasp from the assembled guests and then, encouraged by the then Lord Chamberlain, Lord Maclean, everyone broke into a round of spontaneous applause. The Queen was delighted.

We are reminded that no photography of any kind is permitted inside the palace and informed that 'conversation during the Investiture is allowed, but please keep it to a pleasant murmur'.

A buzz of excitement passes through the assembled guests as the band breaks into 'The Men of Harlech', the regimental march of the Welsh Guards. This signals the entrance of a detachment of five members of the Yeomen of the Guard, in their elaborate scarlet Tudor uniforms and carrying pikes, the original weapons used to protect Henry VII, their first sovereign, in the fifteenth century.

The first recruits to the Yeomen of the Guard came from Wales, which is why 'Men of Harlech' is played for them.

As the Yeomen take up their positions behind the thrones, The Queen enters from the top right-hand door. She is wearing a purple woollen dress and a triple strand of pearls. She is accompanied by the Earl of Airlie, the Lord Chamberlain, two Gurkha orderly officers (by tradition Her Majesty always has two Gurkhas in attendance at the palace), and bringing up the rear is Lieutenant-Colonel George West, the Comptroller of the Lord Chamberlain's Office, with several members of his staff.

Her Majesty stands in the centre of the dais while the national anthem is played, then bids us all good morning and invites us to be seated.

The Lord Chamberlain moves to the lectern, switches on the microphone and announces the name of the first person to receive an award this morning. The recipient moves to a spot immediately in front of The Queen, gives a neck bow (King George V said that only headwaiters bow from the waist) and takes three paces towards Her Majesty. She takes the insignia with its ribbon from the velvet cushion on which it has been placed by the Comptroller, puts it around his neck, shakes his hand and exchanges a few words. He then walks backwards for three paces, turns smartly to his right and walks out of the room. In an ante-room he is given a small leather case in which to keep his award and is then guided back into the Ballroom at the top entrance to take his seat at the front of the centre aisle. Meanwhile, the rest of the recipients are being herded in groups of twenty around to the side entrance nearest the Lord Chamberlain. As he calls out the name of the next person to meet The Queen, the one behind moves to a position about ten feet (3m) away. It's a conveyor belt, albeit the most genteel conveyor belt, and with 150 people of varying ages and degrees of agility to get through, there's no time for idle chatter. The Queen speaks to every single one of the recipients and the entire process for each takes no more than forty seconds. The band continues to play throughout the ceremony as the empty seats in the centre of the room fill up.

On the dais the little tableau is enacted time and time again. The Secretary to the Lord Chamberlain's Office has a list of all the names;

one of his colleagues places the medal on the velvet cushion, and Colonel West offers it to Her Majesty. Every man and woman receives the right award; there is never a mistake.

At precisely twelve o'clock the Lord Chamberlain signals us all to stand once more; the national anthem is played and The Queen leads her Household out of the Ballroom. The recipients join their families and friends to show their latest treasured possession; they linger as long as they can in the State Apartments, and then, after collecting coats and cameras, leave the palace reluctantly. It has been a memorable morning for them all, and The Queen has made it appear an equally unique occasion for her. That is the secret of her success. She never loses her enthusiasm for the job and turns the most mundane task into a joyful event for all concerned. As the guests leave for private celebratory lunches in nearby restaurants and hotels, perhaps returning their hired morning clothes to Moss Bros Ltd, the Household gathers in the Equerries' Withdrawing

Another occasion when the Queen brought the full majesty of the monarchy to her people. An investiture in Fiji meant that this recipient, although confined to a wheelchair, could still meet Her Majesty in person and enjoy a day to remember!

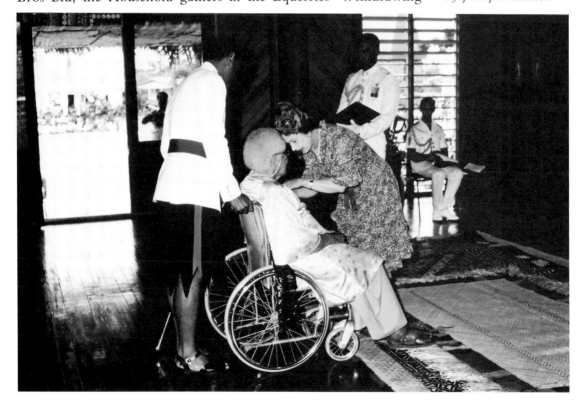

Room for a much needed drink and Her Majesty goes back to her first-floor office to continue the never ending work of monarchy. On another Tuesday she will go through exactly the same routine, and still make it seem to be the first time for her as well.

Occasionally there is an Investiture with a difference. This was the case on Tuesday 8 March 1988, when twenty-seven men and women who had acted with great courage during the Zeebrugge ferry disaster a year earlier were honoured by The Queen. Among the recipients were eleven Belgians; it was an unprecedented gesture to foreign nationals in peacetime, and during the ceremony Her Majesty spoke to each of them in French.

She also gave a private audience to the widow of Mr Michael Skippen, one of the heroes of the disaster who had died while helping others to escape. Mrs Skippen received her husband's George Medal at a private Investiture in the Blue Drawing Room of the palace shortly before the main ceremony. It was another example of The Queen's thoughtfulness; she realised that if she bestowed the medal in public at such a highly emotional moment, it might have been a little too much for the young widow.

Mrs Skippen said afterwards that The Queen had been sympathetic and understanding, and that it was both the saddest and proudest day of her life.

THE ROYAL CHRISTMAS

The Queen gives the impression that she really enjoys being a hostess, even on those stiff, formal occasions when she can have little if anything in common with the guests who have been invited because of the position they hold. Differences of language, culture, creed and religion make no difference to her attitude; she treats everyone alike: Arab and American, communist and capitalist.

However, the one time in the year when Her Majesty can really be said to enjoy her role as hostess is at Christmas. Windsor Castle is the romantic setting for one of the largest family gatherings each year when more than forty of The Queen's nearest relations join her and the Duke of Edinburgh for the festive season. Until 1964 the Royal Family always spent Christmas at Sandringham, but with the growing number of Kents and Gloucesters the party is now so large it has to take place at Windsor. As it happens, Windsor is the biggest castle in the world, so there is plenty of room for all; the youngest members in particular love the miles of corridors and secret passages where they can ride their bicycles, use their skateboards and play any number of fascinating games.

Christmas actually begins for The Queen and some members of the family a few days before they all assemble at Windsor. The occasion is The Queen's Staff Party, which is held in alternate years at Buckingham Palace and Windsor Castle. The invitations are sent by the Master of the Household on behalf of Her Majesty, and as all the recipients are allowed to bring a partner they receive invitations only every other year – there simply isn't the space to accommodate everybody at one time. The party is held on the Tuesday or Thursday evening of the week before The Queen leaves for Windsor for her own Christmas celebrations, and at Buckingham Palace it is held in the State Ballroom with all the other State Apartments opened up so that spouses and sweethearts can have the opportunity of seeing the splendour that is usually reserved for those attending State Banquets.

As everyone in the royal service is invited – grooms, secretaries, housemaids, kitchen porters and chefs – the catering is done by J. Lyons Ltd (who also look after Garden Parties) so that they can all have the night off. The invitation specifies 'Black Tie' and all the male guests wear immaculate dinner jackets, having swopped their usual attire of livery or kitchen whites. The ladies are in long evening dresses and when The Queen and the other immediate members of the Royal Family arrive there is little to distinguish the gathering from any other royal occasion. The Prince of Wales often attends and likes to break the ice by dancing with the youngest housemaid, to the music of Joe Loss and his Orchestra. Until recently The Queen made a point of dancing with some of her footmen, but these days she prefers to mingle with as many guests as she can, and the conversation between servant and mistress is as informal as such an occasion will allow.

The week prior to Christmas is a busy one for everybody connected with the Household. Princess Margaret, who employs only nine or ten staff herself, still gives a special Christmas cocktail party for nearly a hundred or so guests, all of whom work in one of the Royal Households. It is a very popular party and an invitation to Kensington Palace is regarded as a special prize among royal servants.

Queen Elizabeth the Queen Mother also likes to show her appreciation to her staff by giving them a thank-you party at Christmas. Clarence House takes on a special glow of its own and the hostess makes a point of personally greeting every one of the two hundred guests who join her. The best crystal and china are used. The guests can drink anything they want – from real ale to vintage champagne – and the sophisticated palates of the 'below stairs' staff match anything the most exalted formal guest list can produce.

Once the staff parties are over The Queen settles down to her own preparations. She likes to take a personal interest in everything to do with Christmas, and in the days before the holiday begins she and the duke will sign hundreds of cards which they send to other members of the family, personal friends and senior and long-serving members of the Royal Household. The usual Christmas card is a photograph of The Queen and the Duke of Edinburgh.

A great deal of thought is given to the choosing of presents which The Queen also likes to do herself. Because of security problems she no longer visits Harrods or Fortnum & Mason, as she used to, and today one of her Ladies-in-Waiting will arrange for samples of suitable presents to be sent to Buckingham Palace for her approval. In recent years a couple of the more distinguished mail-order catalogues have found their way into the Royal Apartments so that The Queen can browse through them at her leisure – though there is precious little of that. Her Majesty is very selective about what she buys and how much she pays.

Her Christmas present list is a long one with every member of staff at all the royal residences receiving a gift, which they have been able to choose themselves from a list which is circulated by the Master of the Household some weeks earlier. The further up the ladder they progress, the better the present they receive. Everyone is handed his or her present personally by The Queen in the Bow Room at the palace.

As far as the family is concerned The Queen's gifts are likely to be on the practical side: perhaps something to do with horses for the Princess Royal and the Prince of Wales. The Duke of York will probably find a useful addition to his photographic equipment. The Princess of Wales might well receive a set of records (nearly always pop or ballet music) while the Duchess of York is always glad to receive clothing, preferably something she can wear while skiing. The Duke of Edinburgh is the easiest of all to buy for because he is the most avid reader in the family and the latest books – on practically any subject – are all gratefully received.

When the younger members of the family want to know what to buy each other they employ the 'jungle telegraph' of the servants. They prime their own servants to find out from the valets, housekeepers and policemen attached to the others just what is needed in that particular household that Christmas. Prince Charles once produced a door-mat for Princess Anne with the word Welcome written on it. When she asked how he knew that that was exactly what she wanted, he just tapped the side of his nose mysteriously.

The decorations in the Private Apartments at Windsor are supervised by The Queen, who likes to make the finishing touches herself, especially to the Christmas tree. Christmas trees were first introduced into England by Prince Albert, husband of Queen Victoria, in the middle of the nineteenth century, and since then they have played an important part in royal Christmases. A giant tree is erected in the Crimson Drawing Room at the Castle, while smaller trees are put up in The Queen's Sitting Room, the nursery and each of the staff dining rooms. Trees from the royal estates at Sandringham are also given to Westminster Abbey, St Paul's Cathedral and St Giles' Cathedral in Edinburgh, as well as some of the smaller parish churches near the various royal homes.

In the days leading up to Christmas the family starts to congregate. All the members have been given instructions that they are to arrive no later than lunchtime on Christmas Eve, and no one ever breaks The Queen's rules on punctuality at Christmas – not even the Queen Mother, who is notorious for being late. Queen Elizabeth usually drives from London with Princess Margaret, while Viscount Linley and his sister Lady Sarah Armstrong-Jones turn up independently after attending numerous private parties. The Prince and Princess of Wales, with two of the youngest members of the family, Prince William and Prince Harry, are early arrivals, with the Princess Royal and Captain Mark Phillips the last to arrive. They have the longest distance to travel, having come from their home in Gloucestershire. They travel in two vehicles: the Princess driving Captain Phillips and their two children Peter and Zara, with an estate car carrying all their luggage and the presents, just behind.

The Yorks, with Princess Beatrice, Prince Edward, the Duke and Duchess of Kent, the Duke and Duchess of Gloucester, Princess Alexandra and Prince and Princess Michael of Kent with their families complete the royal party. The Queen loves to be surrounded at Christmas by cousins, nieces, nephews and grandchildren; it is just as well that she has a large number of rooms to accommodate them all.

The Private Apartments at Windsor are all located in the south-east corner, overlooking Home Park. Right in the corner is The Queen's Tower where Her Majesty, the Duke of Edinburgh and Prince Edward have their living quarters. There is also a nursery wing in The Queen's Tower where the Prince and Princess of Wales and their two children are housed. The nursery is quite large with four rooms plus its own kitchen and two bathrooms, but these days, unlike in Victorian times, it is used only as a day nursery, where the youngest children have their meals and play throughout the day with their nannies. At night they all return to their parents' quarters where they have their own bedrooms alongside.

Next door to The Queen's Tower is the Augusta Tower where the Princess Royal and her family usually stay at Christmas, and moving farther down the south-east wall is the York Tower which provides the quarters for the Duke and Duchess of Gloucester, and right at the end of the same wall is King Edward III's Tower, where Prince and Princess Michael of Kent are lodged.

Although there is plenty of room for everyone, the arrangement is not ideal from a domestic point of view because the servants are housed in three different towers which are some distance from the living quarters of the Royal Family, so there is a lot of walking to be done.

The Royal Family traditionally exchanges its presents at tea-time on Christmas Eve, not on Christmas morning, so during the early afternoon of 24 December they all visit the Crimson Drawing Room, trying hard to be as secretive as they can, and lay out their presents on long trestle tables which have been set up with each section marked off with tape, and large place names arranged in front. Only the presents for the young children are placed around the Christmas tree.

At four o'clock precisely the Duke of Edinburgh marshals every-one in the drawing room and under his supervision the gifts are distributed. There is one golden rule: all presents must be opened immediately in the presence of the rest of the family. The Duke of York and Prince Edward are known to enjoy slipping embarrassing little gifts in alongside their main presents and the duke insists that everyone shares the joke.

Midnight mass is held at St George's Chapel in the Lower Ward of the castle, and this is open to members of the public who have to apply for tickets beforehand. Most of the congregation are local people who belong to the Friends of St George's, the voluntary organization which provides guides to the chapel throughout the year and prepares the magnificent floral arrangements for Sunday services. Not all members of the Royal Family attend the midnight service, but the Duchess of Kent likes to go and join in the carol singing and Princess Margaret is another regular.

The Queen always goes to early morning communion on Christ-mas Day in her Private Chapel, which is situated in the Brunswick Tower. It is not open to the general public, but members of staff who wish to attend are welcome and they use any pews except the front one which is reserved for The Queen's private worship.

The entire family, with the exception of the youngest children, then walk down the hill to St George's Chapel for the main morning service at eleven o'clock. This is conducted by the Dean of Windsor, the Very Revd Michael Mann, a close friend of the Duke of Edinburgh, who likes to chat after the service with Captain Mark Phillips if he can. They have a lot in common as both were officers in 1st The Queen's Dragoon Guards for many years.

After church and before lunch, some of the family walk in the grounds before they all gather for the main meal of the day, Christmas lunch at 1.15. In fact there are five Christmas lunches served at Windsor. The first is at 11.30 when the junior staff sit down. At noon the senior staff have their lunch, and at 12.45 the youngest children are taken to the nursery dining room for their meal. The head chef won't have his own lunch until The Queen and her family have finished theirs, so it is sometimes around 4pm by the time he eats his turkey and plum pudding.

The royal luncheon is presided over by the Duke of Edinburgh and is the most relaxed and informal of occasions. It is also the only time of the year when The Queen sees her head chef officially as he comes to carve the turkey. At all other times she orders her meals via the Royal Menu Book in which every meal ever eaten in the royal residences is recorded. The servants who wait on the Royal Family will have already started to celebrate Christmas, and if they have enjoyed a glass or two beforehand The Queen diplomatically ignores the fact that they are perhaps not quite as formal as usual.

The State Dining Room is beautifully decorated with flowers from the royal greenhouses and this is the one occasion when chocolates, sweets and sugared almonds, a royal favourite, are placed on the table. Boxes of crackers have been ordered and the resulting bangs add to the general merriment. It's a traditional Christmas lunch with roast turkey and all the trimmings. The one exception to the usual family menu is that there is always a fancy fish course to start: lobster or crab dressed in an exotic sauce.

If there is a senior member of the Household on duty at the Castle, he or she will be invited to join the family celebrations, but most of the equerries and Ladies-in-Waiting are given leave to spend the holiday with their own families.

Lunch always ends by 2.45pm so that all the family can gather to watch The Queen's Christmas broadcast on television at three o'clock. Then the party divides for the rest of the afternoon. Queen Elizabeth the Queen Mother likes to take a short nap; the Princess Royal and her husband join some of the others for a brisk walk, and Princess Margaret watches television. They all assemble once again at 4.30 for tea which consists of tiny sandwiches, scones and a massive iced cake baked some weeks earlier in the royal kitchens. The Queen really likes tea-time and she personally pours for every-one present.

After tea most of the adults rest for a couple of hours and then they all join The Queen once more for yet another splendid meal. Christmas dinner is served at 8.15 and is a 'black-tie' affair, the gentlemen in dinner jackets and the ladies in long evening dresses. But this is still quite some way from the formality of the days when The Queen's grandfather King George V was on the Throne. He insisted on formal evening wear every night, even when he and Queen Mary dined alone. Roast lamb is the traditional dish served on Christmas night, with the other courses kept fairly simple after the huge lunch that has been consumed.

Once dinner is finished the family plays party games such as charades for a while, but generally Christmas night is a quiet time and as everyone has had a tiring day they usually try to relax in the evening. When The Queen retires around midnight the younger members of the family stay up playing music, or occasionally slip downstairs to the staff disco which goes on until the early hours.

Everybody gets up early on Boxing Day and breakfast is a noisy, good-humoured meal as each person prepares for the day's sport, which at Windsor means shooting. Prince Philip organizes the party into Land Rovers just after 9am, with all the men taking part and the Duchess of York and the Princess Royal joining in also. The gundogs have been brought from Sandringham where they are kennelled, and the estate workers, all volunteers, are glad to earn an extra day's pay by acting as beaters.

The royal chefs have prepared a picnic lunch which has been laid out in advance in the Village Hall in Windsor Great Park, and footmen from the Household are on hand to serve the hot soup and cold roast beef. It is a pleasant meal with ample food for everyone but a far cry from the elaborate picnics prepared for King Edward VII when he went shooting – or even for King George V, who also liked plenty of good, plain food after a day in the field.

The shooting party returns to the castle in time for tea and in the evening everyone gathers in the Garter Throne Room to watch one of the latest films. The Throne Room has been equipped as a modern cinema with cinemascope and stereophonic sound, with the projection booth discreetly hidden behind the Throne itself. Comfortable armchairs are provided, and all the family, including the children, settle down in what must be one of the strangest, and certainly the grandest, cinemas in the world. The films chosen are of the type that can be enjoyed by all the family and if there is a new James Bond you can be sure that it will be high on the list. Action films with plenty of electronic gadgetry are particular favourites. When the film show has ended the youngest children are packed off to bed, while the adults move to the Oak Room for sandwiches and drinks.

The day after Boxing Day is another shooting day and shortly after that the members of the family start to return to their own homes to prepare for New Year. The Queen, the Duke of Edinburgh and sometimes the Princess Royal and her family leave for the drive to Sandringham where Her Majesty spends the next six weeks. Because Sandringham was where the Royal Family used to spend their Christmas holidays, The Queen goes through the whole rigmarole once again – even down to the Christmas lunch with turkey and all the trimmings. This is so that the staff at Sandringham will not feel left out of the celebrations. Various other members of the Royal Family will join The Queen and the duke at some time during January or early February. At Sandringham Her Majesty breaks with one long-held Christmas superstition: she allows the decorations to remain way past twelfth night; in fact they are not taken down until the last day of January.★

★ Because of extensive repair work being undertaken at Windsor Castle at the time of writing, the royal Christmas has been temporarily moved back to Sandringham.

4

Bon Appétit

Catering at Buckingham Palace and all the other royal residences is today far less elaborate than it was in the days of The Queen's grandfather, King George V, and even less so than in the days of her great-grandfather, Edward VII. By the standards of Edwardian days the present Royal Family would be considered meagre eaters, and indeed, their appetites are extremely modest. The Queen and the Duke of Edinburgh restrict their private meals to never more than three courses, and very often two. At breakfast, neither eats porridge or any heavy cereal to start with. They both like cooked breakfasts of scrambled eggs, accompanied by sausages or bacon, but just as frequently will simply have fruit juice, toast and tea or coffee.

Although The Queen can, if she so wishes, call on the services of liveried footmen at any hour of the day or night, she prefers to serve herself at breakfast from the hotplates which line the sideboard in her private dining room. Similarly she insists on making her own tea, pouring the hot water into the teapot from a kettle which has been mounted on a swivel stand designed by Prince Philip in order to do away with the need for lifting a kettle full of boiling water. His Royal Highness never drinks tea himself, preferring coffee at all times – he drinks it black with no sugar. The Queen likes tea with breakfast, with milk but no sugar. If there are no guests for lunch, The Queen either eats alone or with the duke. It's always a simple meal with no starter, and a main course which is invariably something light such as fish or lamb, with fresh vegetables and salad, and very few potatoes. Dessert is often a selection of fresh fruit, and while the Duke of Edinburgh likes a glass of beer with his lunch, The Queen rarely has anything other than mineral water or orange squash.

Dinners at the palace today contrast considerably with those of previous reigns. When King George V was in London, even on those evenings when he and Queen Mary dined privately, he never sat down to dinner without changing into a frock coat and donning the Order of the Garter, and his wife always wore a tiara at dinner, even when she dined alone. Today The Queen and the Duke of Edinburgh do not change into evening dress. Her Majesty wears a short daytime dress and the duke a comfortable lounge suit. But both Queen Elizabeth the Queen Mother, at her home in Clarence House, and Princess Margaret, in Kensington Palace, always dress for dinner, whether with guests or alone.

At Buckingham Palace dinner usually follows the pattern of lunch; once again there is no soup or fish course, simply a main course of perhaps lamb once more (said to be The Queen's favourite meat), poultry or, very occasionally, steak. (Red meat is eaten less frequently at royal meals these days.) There is always a side salad, and both Her Majesty and His Royal Highness prefer a savoury dish to a dessert, so perhaps a quiche lorraine or kidneys rolled in bacon will be served followed by fruit. The Queen rarely eats cheese and so the chef does not bother to include it on the list of suggestions he sends up from the kitchen and from which she makes her daily selection. Wine is served at dinner, The Queen drinking only the lightest of white wines and, more often than not, sticking to her usual Malvern water throughout the meal.

THE PRINCE AND PRINCESS OF WALES

The system of picking a number of dishes from a list suggested by the chef is one which is followed by all the ladies in the Royal Family. At the beginning of each week the Princess of Wales chooses from such a list all the meals she requires over the next five days.

Friday lunch is the last meal of the week to be eaten at any of the London royal residences; they all retire to their country homes shortly after lunch on Friday, returning just before lunch the following Monday.

Since their marriage in 1981 Prince Charles's tastes have altered considerably under his wife's influence, not only in the way he dresses, but also in what he eats. When he was single he loved all the things he should not have had: stodgy puddings, heaps of potatoes and gooey desserts. These days he is practically a vegetarian, and red meat is never served at apartment Nos 8 and 9 Kensington Palace, the home of the Prince and Princess of Wales and their two children Prince William and Prince Henry.

Fish is included on the menu and chicken, but the main course is frequently something like macaroni cheese, eggs Florentine or just plain spaghetti. Salad is served every day and potatoes baked in their jackets are favourites of the royal couple. Neither the prince nor the princess cares a great deal about desserts but sorbets are often to be found on the Waleses' menus. They particularly like the champagne sorbets made to the following recipe:

Ingredients: 1lb 6oz (600g) sugar, 2 quarts (2.2l) water, juice of two lemons, juice of 1 orange, 8 whipped egg whites.
Flavouring: 1 bottle of Champagne.
Method: Boil sugar and water to a syrup. When cool, whip in the egg whites, fruit juice and flavouring. Freeze.

Serves 25.

Prince Charles claims that he is the one who started the move to vegetarianism in his family but those who have known the princess for some time say that she has always been keen on dishes without meat. All their vegetables are grown in the garden at Highgrove, their home in Gloucestershire, and they are always served boiled or steamed. Nothing fried is ever allowed to leave their kitchens, in spite of the fact that the children love hamburgers and a visit to a McDonald's is a real treat. The chef at Highgrove helps Prince Charles to choose vegetables from his garden, and His Royal

Highness also likes to experiment with soups made from wild plants such as nettles.

The Prince and Princess of Wales entertain frequently at home and their dinner parties are elegant, formal and impeccably presented. They tend to keep their guest lists apart; one for family and close friends and the other for people they have both met, or want to meet, from the worlds of show business, the arts, business and politics. A Kensington Palace dinner party is rarely just for fun. There is always something or someone that the prince or princess wants to learn about, and the comparatively informal atmosphere of the dinner table is a good place both for sparkling conversation and animated talk and for picking up useful snippets of information.

The Duke and Duchess of York are regular guests at these dinner parties, while the duchess often calls in for lunch during the week. The Princess of Wales hates to eat alone. Princess Margaret is another family guest on the 'A' list, but the Princess Royal, who spends as little time as possible in London, is a much rarer visitor. Prince Edward comes whenever he is invited, usually with his latest girl friend. The other royal residents of Kensington Palace, however, the Gloucesters and Prince and Princess Michael of Kent, are not often asked to join their cousins for a meal.

Outsiders who have dined with the Prince and Princess of Wales include Bob Geldof, the fund-raising pop singer who is much admired by them both; Viscount Tonypandy, who as George Thomas, Speaker of the House of Commons, was asked to read the lesson at their wedding in 1981; and the Prime Minister Mrs Margaret Thatcher and her husband Denis. The dancer Wayne Sleep, with whom the princess once danced on stage, has been invited on several occasions, and Aled Jones, the brilliant young Welsh treble, was delighted to be asked to dine at Kensington Palace, even if he did have to 'sing for his supper' afterwards. Placido Domingo is another world-famous artist who has entertained the prince and princess and their other guests after dinner, along with Dame Kiri Te Kanawa, the New Zealand soprano who was specially chosen by the prince to sing at his wedding service in St Paul's Cathedral.

The entrance to Kensington Palace is alongside the towering

Kensington Garden Hotel and is guarded by officers of the Royal Protection Squad, who thoroughly check everyone before letting them through the barrier and up the drive. Once inside the palace though it's a different world – of history, romance and discreet but superb comfort. Dinner guests are welcomed by the Waleses' butler, Harold Brown, a shy and retiring man, not at all the 'superior' head servant one might expect the heir to the Throne to employ.

The entrance hall to apartments 8 and 9 is spacious, light and elegant and dominated by a large green and grey carpet patterned with the Prince of Wales feathers. On the ground floor are the separate cloakrooms for ladies and gentlemen, the latter decorated with Prince Charles's unique collection of original newspaper cartoons. Next door, in what is known as the 'Throne Room', is his even rarer collection of vintage lavatory seats – all in splendid mahogany.

The drawing room is on the first floor and is approached via a magnificent, broad Georgian staircase which was damaged by German bombs during the Second World War, but is now restored to its original grandeur. It is lined with valuable paintings, but one stands out. It is the picture of the Princess of Wales in her wedding dress, painted by John Ward, and commissioned by the prince when he learned that his wife was expecting their second child, Prince Henry.

It is unusual for the couple to invite more than ten guests for dinner even though they have on occasion had up to thirty-six. The men all wear dinner jackets, the ladies long evening dresses as they meet their hosts in the drawing room for pre-dinner drinks. The room is warm and inviting with yellow walls and comfortable chairs and sofas upholstered in the lightest shade of peach. The tone of the evening is set by the liveried footmen handing round the drinks. It is always the very best vintage champagne; neither the prince nor the princess will drink spirits and they will only offer it to their guests if there is a special request – Princess Margaret likes a glass of whisky. It is unusual for anyone to smoke in the drawing room before dinner; Prince Charles is passionately anti-smoking and most guests know this and refrain – even if privately they long for a cigarette.

Dinner is served at eight thirty and both the prince and the princess have taken endless pains with the seating plan. Everybody has a place card, and the dining table is such that the royal couple can chat with everyone throughout the meal. The food is superbly cooked and beautifully served, but the fare is comparatively simple. They do not stray a great deal from their normal diet and most dinner parties consist of soup (it might be one of Prince Charles's specials from the garden at Highgrove) followed by a fish course – eaten with ordinary knives and forks in common with the rest of the Royal Family. (At a private house, King George V was once offered a Dover sole at a table laid with fish knives and forks. He asked what they were for and when told it was the custom in middle-class houses to eat fish with special knives and forks, remarked 'How extraordinary.') At Kensington Palace a salad is often served either with the main course or afterwards, and pudding is either a light ice dish or a fresh fruit salad. The wines drunk with the meal will invariably be light and white, probably German, whatever the food. Prince Charles never drinks red wine, and only takes white wine at dinner parties to be sociable. He would prefer to keep to mineral water. Port and liqueurs are offered at the end of the meal, but cigars are not available.

Dinner parties normally end at around eleven and Prince Charles bids his guests farewell upstairs. If a member of the Royal Family is present, however, he will accompany him or her to the door, and if it is Princess Margaret, will walk her home. She lives nearby and he does not have to venture outside. A passage connects their apartments inside the palace.

Princess Margaret

Apartment number 1a is the most dramatic of all the apartments in Kensington Palace, which is quite fitting, as its occupant is far and away the member of the Royal Family with the most interest in the theatre.

Her Royal Highness loves to entertain. An evening spent alone is an evening wasted so far as she is concerned. Artists, film stars, musicians, stars of the opera and ballet, all come to Princess Margaret's table – and depart having had a marvellous time.

When Princess Margaret was first married, she and her husband Lord Snowdon were housed in apartment No 10 – described by reporters as 'the Dolls' House' because it was so small. In fact it has ten rooms and Prince and Princess Michael of Kent now occupy it during the week. Princess Margaret persuaded her sister The Queen to allow her to move to her present apartment from No 10 because, as she put it, 'It was too small for the amount of entertaining we do.' Apartment 1a has twenty rooms. Of course, she has now been divorced, but the entertaining continues. Every morning her secretary will telephone the princess's friends to find a companion for lunch. If no one is available a Lady-in-Waiting usually eats with the princess in the dining room on the ground floor, where the oval-shaped table can seat up to fourteen. Lunch is normally restricted to two, while ten or twelve are the numbers favoured by Princess Margaret for dinner parties – but she is not averse to adding a couple of names at the last minute, much to the annoyance of her long-suffering chef, who has yet to be unable to come up with the extra food. Actually 'long-suffering' is an unkind description to apply to the chef or any of her servants. Princess Margaret has the longest serving household in the Royal Family, and her staff are among the most loyal and happiest to be found.

The princess's guests are given drinks in the drawing room, the largest room in the apartment, which leads directly off the spacious hall, paved with black and white Welsh flagstones, obtained from a North Wales quarry by Lord Snowdon when he was helping to design the apartment's interior. The style of the drawing room is a cross between palace and country house. Decorated in the princess's favourite colour scheme of blue, the room contains a superb Spanish carpet in blue and gold which was a wedding present from the City of London. It was designed by Carl Toms, the theatrical designer who was introduced to the princess by Lord Snowdon, and who also helped design the interior of Caernarvon Castle for the Investiture of the Prince of Wales in 1969. Blue and gold are also the colours of the deep armchairs and comfortable sofas in the drawing room, while the centrepiece is the elegant baby grand piano with its lacquered lid; this was another wedding present, from her former parents-in-law, the Earl and Countess of Rosse.

The princess is an accomplished pianist, with a melodious singing voice – and a wicked line in mimicry. Noël Coward once said that if she had not been of royal birth, she could certainly have graced the concert platform, and at most of her dinner parties she will entertain her guests with songs from some of the West End musicals. Her tastes are fairly predictable: middle of the road standards – and no pop!

Princess Margaret's dining room is on the ground floor and the colour scheme is beige with lots of blue glassware on shelves and tables. She drinks wine with all her meals, including lunch, and, unlike her nephew the Prince of Wales, enjoys red as much as white, so both are served as appropriate. Her Royal Highness also drinks the Malvern mineral water which is favoured by The Queen. Her meals are planned on a weekly basis; the menu card, which has been printed by the Master of the Household's department at Buckingham Palace (which carries out the same service for the Prince and Princess of Wales), being presented for her approval. The princess ticks the items she wants and indicates when she will be out.

Lunches are fairly easy and light. As the princess doesn't usually rise very early in the morning, she isn't ready for a large meal at 1.15pm when lunch is normally served. Poultry in the form of boiled chicken appears regularly on the menu, served with mange tout and duchesse potatoes, and the princess does not seem to tire of it. She has no starter at lunch but enjoys fruit or an ice afterwards.

Like her mother and sister, Princess Margaret is a firm believer in the ceremony of afternoon tea. In the summer it is served in the one-acre (0.4ha) garden, the largest of any of the royal apartments, and takes place at 4.30pm promptly. The table is set with delicate bone china and crisp tablecloths and the bite-sized sandwiches have their crusts cut off. She has been known to ask for unusual items on occasion, such as biscuits with marmalade, but normally her tea-time tastes are more conventional.

Her dinner parties attract a sparkling array of guests and as she herself is very much a night person, the evenings tend to go on well after midnight. The occasions are always formal, black tie for the men and evening dresses for the ladies. The princess grew up in an age when people of her class always dressed for dinner and she still enjoys making the simplest event into an 'occasion'.

Champagne is served as an aperitif, but if anyone wants whisky, brandy, gin or any known cocktail it is immediately available. Princess Margaret's proud boast is that she has never been caught out when a guest has asked for a drink. If any bar in the world serves it – so does she! Officially dinner is served at 8.30pm but she doesn't object if it is nine o'clock before they sit down – so long as the food hasn't been spoiled. The first course is usually smoked salmon (from the royal estates on Deeside) or her own favourite, asparagus. The main course will often be either Scotch beef, cooked rare, or Welsh lamb with fresh vegetables. A salad is served between the main course and dessert, which is always cold – strawberries in season or perhaps an exotic ice dish made into an artistic design by her chef.

Princess Margaret enjoys French champagne and German wines but her taste in food is strictly patriotic. Almost all the food served at her table is British. The finest port and liqueurs are offered and there is an ash tray and cigarette lighter alongside every place. Her Royal Highness likes to smoke and the atmosphere in the dining room and afterwards in the drawing room is always thick with cigarette and cigar smoke.

These evenings invariably end with the princess sitting at the piano, enjoying a glass of whisky and leading her guests in a robust sing-song until the early hours. It's a good job the walls at Kensington Palace are two feet (60cm) thick.

PRINCE AND PRINCESS MICHAEL OF KENT

With only ten rooms No 10 Kensington Palace is the smallest in the royal complex, but it is built on three floors and, mainly through the influence of Princess Michael, has been transformed into an elegant town house of which any society hostess would be proud.

The top floor has been made into a nursery and the princess designed a roof garden which leads off the children's bedroom. The master bedroom is on the floor below with 'his and hers' dressing-rooms and bathrooms adjoining. There is a spacious study which spans the width of the house, and the two main reception rooms, the drawing room and dining room, together with cloakrooms and kitchen, are on the ground floor. The servants' quarters and Household offices are in the basement.

The drawing room is the princess's delight. Decorated in blue moiré, its walls are adorned with works of art and the furniture is modern, comfortable and very stylish. The princess herself designed the low, glass-topped coffee table with special drawers for part of the Fabergé collection Prince Michael inherited from his mother.

The princess, who is married to The Queen's cousin, the younger son of the late Duke of Kent, is an accomplished interior decorator who has stamped her own personality on every aspect of the apartment. Her tastes are even reflected in the design of the kitchen, where she insisted that the grain on the wood finishes for working surfaces, washing machine and dishwasher should all run the same way. It is attention to tiny details such as these that has made her one of the most successful royal hostesses and her dinner parties are banquets in miniature.

Many of the priceless treasures in her home, such as the silver cutlery, candelabra, and Fabergé *objets d'art*, belonged to her husband's mother the late Princess Marina, and were brought out of storage after many years languishing in an attic at Hampton Court Palace. Princess Michael is regarded as an authority on antiques and she was delighted to find so many valuable pieces lying there, long forgotten and unused.

Many items of furniture which were once the property of the late Duchess of Kent are still stored at Hampton Court, and both Princess Michael and the present Duke of Kent, her brother-in-law, visit the palace to choose suitable pieces from time to time. The man charged with looking after all the stored items is the Chief Steward of Hampton Court Palace, Lord Maclean (the former Lord Chamberlain), and he needs all his diplomatic skills at times when both members of the family decide they would like the same article.

As a hostess Princess Michael is charming, gregarious and generous to a fault. Her table is always elegantly set with masses of cut flowers which she arranges herself and she takes endless pains over the seating plan, making sure that everyone is placed near someone compatible. She likes to think of herself as a good social mixer and since her husband is involved in a number of business enterprises in the City, their guest lists nearly always include a sprinkling of international tycoons.

As they do not employ a permanent large staff (there is no butler – the duke's valet acts in this capacity when necessary), they use the services of a group of domestic servants from Buckingham Palace when they give a dinner party. The servants are well experienced in this type of work and are always pleased to earn extra money by this 'moonlighting'.

Prince Michael is a little like Prince Philip where food is concerned: both will eat anything that is placed in front of them; but Princess Michael is more discerning. She enjoys finding new dishes for her menus and her starters range from unusual soups to Stilton fritters or the lightest of soufflés, while her Australian background comes to the fore when the main courses are decided. She still enjoys a good steak or Beef Wellington and her idea of making a party go with a swing is to ensure that her guests' glasses are never empty. Prince Michael acts as the barman – under his wife's instructions – while she flirts outrageously with any attractive men. And there usually are plenty. The Kents like the company of 'beautiful' people, also successful television stars, international financiers, leading politicians (Mrs Thatcher has been to dinner more than once) and occasionally, very occasionally, other members of the Royal Family.

The main attraction of a dinner at Prince and Princess Michael's home is the couple themselves. She is a brilliant if at times overpowering conversationalist, and guests love to watch the way she appears to order her husband around (in fact he allows her to do the ordering; they are excellent partners) while ensuring that his name is prominently mentioned if there is any prospect of business coming their way. Her personal magnetism is so powerful that she can switch it on and off at will, and it is equally appealing to men and women. In fact some men find her intimidating, her physical presence and flashing wit often causing them to feel inadequate. If this happens and she becomes aware of it, and she usually does, she can tone down her performance a shade and use her undoubted feminine charms to make them feel important once more. Women either love or hate her, but a surprising number of women who have said they could not stand the sight of her before actually meeting her in person have changed their opinion as soon as they are in her company. She is a complex person with that magic ingredient known as charisma and as a hostess has few equals.

THE DUKE AND DUCHESS OF GLOUCESTER

The Gloucesters are the royals everybody likes, but few people know. And that's the way they want it to remain. Two families of Gloucesters live together in Kensington Palace: Princess Alice, Duchess of Gloucester, the widow of Prince Henry (a brother of King George VI), and her son and his wife the present Duke and Duchess. They all live in apartment 4, next door to Princess Margaret. They rarely receive any publicity, yet are on the Civil List and perform a large number of royal duties. The duke is a qualified architect and he met his wife, who is Danish by birth, while they were both students at Cambridge.

They have three children who all live at home and any entertaining they do is quiet, unobtrusive and homely. The house they occupy is large, comfortable and splendidly Georgian. As you enter it for the first time the main impression is of colour and flowers. The duchess arranges them herself and, with her Danish tastes, the rooms have been decorated and furnished to make them seem even more spacious than they are.

The Gloucesters' appetites for food and drink are Spartan to say the least. The duke says he still enjoys nothing more than the nursery food he grew up with, so cottage pie and boiled fish are often on the menu. He does not drink any alcohol, even when they give a dinner party, nor does he care for tea or coffee. Plain water and fruit juice are the only drinks he takes regularly, with the odd glass of milk at breakfast with his grapefruit and toast.

He does have one consuming passion in food and that is chocolate in all its many forms. He will eat it in puddings, cakes, ice-cream or simply on its own. Rarely a day goes by without the Duke of Gloucester having some chocolate. The duchess likes to start the day with a substantial breakfast of cereal and eggs. She also likes a cooked lunch and a hot meal in the evening. Unlike her husband, she does enjoy good wine with her meals and has assumed the role of connoisseur in their household. When they have a dinner party Her Royal Highness chooses the wine.

They have a large staff to look after them, second in size only to that employed by the Prince and Princess of Wales. There is a butler, under-butler/valet, two chauffeurs (provided by the Royal Corps of Transport, one of the regiments of which Princess Alice is Colonel-in-Chief) plus a cook, nanny and maid.

Dinner parties are usually fairly small, intimate gatherings of close friends or business acquaintances from the architects' practice the duke has established. Not for them the glitterati of the society pages or luminaries of the stage and television screen. They like their privacy and keep their public and private lives entirely separate. But when they entertain there is no doubt in any guest's mind that he or she is in the presence of royalty. Everything is perfect; quiet efficiency is the watchword and a recent guest said after attending his first dinner party at apartment 4 that it was the most enjoyable evening he could remember.

QUEEN ELIZABETH THE QUEEN MOTHER

Clarence House, the London home of Queen Elizabeth the Queen Mother, is easily the most relaxed and comfortable of all the royal homes. An invitation to lunch or dinner is a passport to an age of perfect manners, an atmosphere of country house gentility – and the largest gin and tonics served in London. Most octogenarians tend to slow down a little as they reach the autumn years of their lives; Queen Elizabeth (nobody who knows her ever calls her the Queen Mother and *never* the Queen Mum) seems to thrive on activity and her engagement book is as full today as it has been for many years past. As old as the century, she is still going strong and shows no sign of reducing either her public duties or her entertaining.

Her Majesty takes a delight in inviting old friends to join her in the elegant and gracious dining room of the home she has occupied since she was widowed in 1952. Most of her friends come from the same generation as herself, if not the self same vintage. Her Household has all been with her for years; the 'junior' member is Major John Griffin, her Press Secretary, who joined her staff as a 'temporary' Equerry more than twenty years ago, while her Private Secretary Sir Martin Gilliat has been in her service for more than thirty years.

Inside Clarence House the atmosphere resembles that of one of the more exclusive and old established London clubs. Visitors are welcomed by Sir Alastair Aird the Comptroller in his room just to the left of the rear hallway, where, if it is the right time of day, they will be offered one of the legendary gin and tonics. Small measures are unknown at Clarence House and a tumbler three-quarters full of gin with just a dash of tonic is guaranteed to make eyes water if the recipient is not used to it.

If Her Majesty is spending the day at home she will often lunch with the senior members of her Household or perhaps she will give a lunch to a long serving member of The Queen's Household who has just retired. She did this for Lord Maclean before he retired from the office of Lord Chamberlain in 1984, and also paid him the compliment of asking him who else he would like invited on that very special day. Senior politicians of every persuasion come within the ambit of the royal invitation list; the former Speaker of the House of Commons George Thomas (now Viscount Tonypandy) is a frequent guest. If only his old 'Mam' from the Rhondda Valley of South Wales could have lived to see him in these surroundings, he says, how proud she would have been. James Callaghan, the former Labour Prime Minister (now Lord Callaghan of Cardiff), is another regular at Clarence House in spite of the fact that his background is far removed from that of his hostess. Lord Callaghan is also one of the few ex-prime ministers who is still on The Queen's private guest list and he and Lady Callaghan have been asked to stay at Balmoral during the long summer break.

Other leading political figures who rank as friends of Queen Elizabeth are Lord Hailsham and another ex-prime minister Lord

Home of the Hirsel. There is also a strong sprinkling of personalities from the world of the arts, including Sir Hugh Casson, who advises her on paintings and drawings. The late Sir Frederick Ashton, who shared a love of the ballet with Her Majesty, was another popular guest.

The Provost of Eton, Lord Charteris of Amisfield, loves joining Queen Elizabeth for a meal, particularly if it's one of her *al fresco* lunches. In the early summer Her Majesty likes to have meals out of doors in the splendid garden at Clarence House. The table is laid with spotless linen, Minton china, silver cutlery and sparkling crystal beneath a plane tree, alongside the wall which divides the garden from the outside world. The liveried footmen carry the dishes from the kitchen into the garden where Her Majesty enjoys holding court in the sunshine – and listening to the talk that drifts over the wall as tourists pass by.

When her guests arrive they are invited to assemble in the garden for a pre-lunch drink and the sudden flurry as a couple of corgis hurtle out of the French windows heralds the arrival of the lady of the house. She joins her guests, perhaps with a gin and Dubonnet, and as they are nearly always old friends, the conversation is easy, relaxed and comfortable. Horses figure strongly in Queen Elizabeth's life; her house is the only royal residence fitted with a 'blower' – the direct information service from race courses with the latest news of runners and riders – so guests are very understanding if they know that Her Majesty has a horse running or a particular interest in that day's racing.

Queen Elizabeth always takes her drink standing up, in fact her many years of royal training have enabled her to remain on her feet for hours on end without showing the slightest hint of tiredness. She says she prefers to stand than sit and at receptions has been known to remain standing for two hours or more – sometimes to the dismay of her more elderly fellow guests.

Lunch will probably start with a little asparagus, one of Queen Elizabeth's favourites, though she tends to keep it as a 'little treat' – not to be enjoyed too often. Then lobster might be on the menu, another of her weaknesses, and dessert could well be strawberries and cream which Her Majesty enjoys even out of season. Wine will be served with each course and mineral water is also put on the table before each place. After lunch a glass of champagne is sometimes offered if it is a special occasion. For her guests every opportunity to dine with Queen Elizabeth is a special occasion – her very presence makes it so.

THE DUKE AND DUCHESS OF KENT

York House, which is part of St James's Palace, is the London home of the Duke and Duchess of Kent. It is a delightful and impressive house which was once home to the late Duke of Windsor when he was Prince of Wales. It has recently undergone a massive improvement programme which took nearly two years to complete and which means that the house, while retaining its historic characteristics, now also possesses all the comforts of a modern home. The kitchen is a designer's dream and as the duchess herself likes to cook whenever she can the chef has to guard his province. But the Kents are an easy family to work for. The duke is involved in many outside organisations and consequently spends most of the day away from home, and the duchess, whose work for the Samaritans and many other charities is well known, also eats very few meals at York House.

The royal couple breakfast together; it is usually something light such as muesli, grapefruit and coffee with the occasional foray into cooked dishes, perhaps at weekends. Lunch is equally simple. Soup, cheese and fruit with the main course left out.

Dinner is the only formal meal of the day and is usually eaten at 8.30pm. If any of the children are at home they will join their parents but, with their eldest son recently married, the younger boy, Lord Nicholas Windsor, at university and Lady Helen Windsor working at her own career in the art world, they are likely to be in some distant part of the world. Then it will be just the duke and duchess and perhaps their Private Secretary.

The duchess never drinks alcohol, even with meals, taking only mineral water and fruit juices. Nor is the duke a big drinker. He likes a whisky and soda before dinner and a glass of wine with his food. Their guests often come from the world of music. The duchess is a member of the Bach Choir and a lover of most kinds of music, whilst the duke is an acknowledged expert on opera and enjoys the company of some of the world's leading singers.

THE PRINCESS ROYAL AND CAPTAIN MARK PHILLIPS

Gatcombe Park in the heart of rolling Gloucestershire countryside is the home of the Princess Royal and her husband Captain Mark Phillips. Their entertaining has to be fitted into busy diaries. The princess heads the royal league table in the number of public engagements she undertakes so an early evening at home is something to be cherished, and Mark Phillips has an equally full calendar, with a thousand-acre (405ha) farm to manage, many outside business commitments which take him to Australia, New Zealand and the United States for long periods every year, plus his riding in international competitions. A private dinner party, therefore, has to be arranged with great care and usually a long time in advance.

Gatcombe is a charming house which is not nearly as big as it looks from the outside. The dining room leads directly to the right from the stone-flagged hallway. It is an oblong room which doubles as a meeting place for Mark's business colleagues – the table is often covered in papers, contracts and all the other paraphernalia without which it appears no company can function these days. However, when the Princess Royal and her husband entertain, the room takes on a glamour and sheen which compare favourably with those of any of the royal residences. The table is polished to a high gloss with centrepieces of solid silver candelabra and beautiful arrangements of fresh flowers grown in the superb conservatory which is one of the outstanding features of the house. They can seat ten people comfortably and when the guests arrive they are admitted by the butler who doubles as Captain Phillips's valet. Throughout the day he is likely to be found dressed casually in open-necked shirt and corduroy trousers, but for a formal occasion he dons the traditional white tie and tails.

The hall at Gatcombe is littered with Wellington boots, children's toys and copies of *Country Life* and *Field*. There is a bowl of water waiting for any of the Phillipses' dogs who needs a drink and the whole scene is one of slightly disorganised chaos in a typical English country house.

The drawing room leads off the hall immediately opposite the dining room and as soon as you enter it you are in another world. It is immaculate, comfortable and furnished in exquisite taste. The colours are light and airy pastel shades, the tables laden with photographs of other members of the Royal Family, near and distant, and if you arrive in wintertime, a huge log fire will be blazing to welcome you. Neither the princess nor her husband drinks but a trolley containing whisky, brandy, gin, vodka and sherry stands ready to quench the thirst of new arrivals.

Because both the princess and Captain Phillips are so involved in equestrian matters it follows that many of their friends have the same interests and the conversation at dinner parties often revolves around the latest happenings in the 'horsey set' – but not exclusively. Former racing driver Jackie Stewart is an old friend with little or no knowledge of horses but a regular guest at Gatcombe. (His wife Helen is godmother to the princess's daughter Zara.) Other friends come from the acting profession and the world of films, television and business.

The Princess Royal freely admits that she is no gourmet. She eats to live rather than the other way around. But as she says, 'I am getting better'. David Dixon, who is a fellow member of the British Olympic Committee, says he and his colleagues are always amused when the princess turns up for one of their working lunches and she is discreetly handed a packet of Ryvita by her Lady-in-Waiting. At home, the food she offers will be fairly conventional, fish and meat, lamb or beef, and no exotic sauces – Her Royal Highness likes her food plain. There will probably be avocado pears at some stage of the evening – they are her one passion. She loves them at any time of day, in any country in the world. When she is on one of her major overseas tours, her staff go to endless lengths to find avocados. As one of her secretaries said, 'It's her great weakness.' The princess also enjoys cheese, unlike most of the other members of her family, who rarely eat it, with the exception of Queen Elizabeth the Queen Mother. Two non-starters at the Princess Royal's table are celery and pea soup.

Mark Phillips eats anything that is placed in front of him. He says there is nothing that he does not like: 'After my years at school [he was at Marlborough] and in the army, I am not fussy about food so long as there's plenty of it.'

The Phillipses' dislike of alcohol extends even to wine with meals. The princess sticks to mineral water or Coca-Cola while Mark drinks only fruit juice. But that doesn't prevent their providing excellent wines for their guests and encouraging them to experiment with little known or newer labels. Hospitality at Gatcombe means enjoying yourself. Anything you want is available – all you have to do is ask.

PRINCE PHILIP DUKE OF EDINBURGH

One of the most pleasant dinners of the year is the one given by Prince Philip on the evening before the annual Birthday Parade (Trooping the Colour). In 1988 it took place on Friday, 10 June, which also happened to be His Royal Highness's 67th birthday. It is a most exclusive gathering with just nine people sitting down, and they are all, with one exception, the most senior officers in the Household Division. The exception is the Temporary Equerry attached to Prince Philip (on this occasion Captain James Fraser).

Before dinner a brief conference was held in Prince Philip's Library at which they discussed the coming Sovereign's Birthday Parade and any problems which might arise. It didn't take long and shortly afterwards His Royal Highness led his guests to the Chinese Dining Room, one of the most exotic of all the State Rooms in Buckingham Palace. It is located at the north-east corner of the East Front of the palace and much of the decoration and furniture comes from the Prince Regent's Banqueting and Music Rooms in the Brighton Pavilion. The room is gloriously decorative and evokes memories of Britain's most lavish royal patron of the arts.

The Duke of Edinburgh is Senior Colonel of the Household

The Chinese Dining Room on the first floor in the north east corner of Buckingham Palace. Most of the furniture and exotic decorations were brought from George IV's banqueting and music rooms at Brighton Pavilion. Today the room is occasionally used by the Duke of Edinburgh for informal luncheon parties.

Division and his guests on that glorious June evening were: Major General Sir George Burns, Coldstream Guards; HRH The Prince of Wales, Colonel Welsh Guards; Major General Lord Michael Fitzalan-Howard, The Life Guards; General Sir Desmond Fitzpatrick, Colonel Blues & Royals; HRH The Grand Duke of Luxembourg, Colonel Irish Guards; Major General Christopher Airy, Major General Commanding the Household Division; Lieutenant Colonel D. V. Erskine Crum, Brigade Major Household Division; and Captain James Fraser, Temporary Equerry.

Having disposed of the business side they settled down to a relaxed and enjoyable meal. It consisted of:

Gratin de Crabe
Caneton au Miel
Fresh Peas
Mashed Potatoes
Salade
Profiteroles au Chocolat

Prince Philip is a generous and congenial host. He was among friends and their only worry was the following morning, when they all had to parade on horseback in full ceremonial dress uniform for more than two hours. A tight bearskin can be a bit of a headache at the best of times; with a hangover in addition and temperatures in the upper seventies, it needs all the self-discipline at a trained soldier's command to remain cool, calm and, apparently, good humoured. That the Trooping the Colour ceremony that year was considered one of the finest ever is itself a tribute to the stamina and self-control of Prince Philip and his guests of the previous evening.

THE ROYAL KITCHENS

The lower ground floor at Buckingham Palace is a world of its own. For it is here that the kitchens are located and the non-stop activity of providing up to 600 meals every day goes on throughout the year.

Even when The Queen is on *Britannia* or at Balmoral (when some of the cooks from the palace will be looking after her) meals for a reduced number are served by the royal kitchens in London throughout the period.

Apart from any of the immediate Royal Family who may be at home, about 200 lunches are served daily in other parts of the palace, while for those domestic staff who are accommodated (the married ones live out), breakfast and dinner are also available. Different sections of the Household need to eat at different times, and there are several dining rooms for the many people to be fed.

The menus are chosen each week by the Master of the Household, and when the number for a particular meal is known (at least twenty-four hours' notice is the target), a computer will inform the head of catering how much beef to order for the beef olives, the quantity of potatoes and runner beans, and the amount of apples and raisins for the Dutch apple tart. The computer is even pro-grammed to give the perfect cooking time, thus avoiding any over-cooking when, of course, the quantity is reduced.

The kitchens are enormous and are run on military lines with the Head Chef in total command. The staff is arranged in 'Brigades' of eight to twenty, depending on the function they are catering for. When a State Banquet is being prepared, they work in Brigades of ten – Head Chef, Sous Chef, Chef de Partie, Vegetable Chef, Fish Chef, Sauce Chef, Apprentice Chefs and Scullery Hands.

Not all the staff at Buckingham Palace work full-time. In the past an advertisement for the extra help used to be placed in the London *Evening Standard* but nowadays most of the part-timers have helped out a number of times before and the Master of the Household's department now knows how to contact them when they are required. The chefs all wear full whites on duty while the rest of the staff wear overalls.

Until as recently as twenty years ago there were two separate kitchens at Buckingham Palace: one for the Royal Family and one for the Household. This was to minimise the possibility of any royal food drifting on to a non-royal table. Of course it also meant a huge duplication of effort and manpower and, despite considerable opposition from some of his colleagues, the then Master of the Household, Sir Geoffrey Hardy-Roberts, amalgamated the kitchens into a single unit. In recent years a major modernisation programme has seen the installation of gas convection ovens (converted to North Sea gas as soon as it became available) to replace the old coal-fired stoves, and dish-washing machines for the everyday crockery (but not that used at State Banquets, which is still washed by hand). Microwave ovens were tried as an experiment for a time but they failed to meet the specific needs of the Household and were dispensed with.

In spite of the modernisation, the kitchens still have a few relics of the past including the giant cast iron frames on which whole oxen were roasted on spits. (The kitchens in the Crown Equerry's house in the Royal Mews contain cooking ranges that are so large they cannot be taken out – even though they have not been used for generations.)

At Buckingham Palace the kitchens are located far from the dining rooms, a deliberate plan in the building of most great houses to prevent smells from the kitchen from permeating the rest of the house. It also meant that much of the food was cold by the time it reached the dining room, so Sir Peter Ashmore, when he was Master of the Household, introduced heat-insulated trolleys to carry the food up to the first floor.

The kitchens themselves used to be divided up into various rooms, each a 'mini-kingdom' of its own, and some of them still remain. The glass rooms contain The Queen's vast collection of crystal and here all the sinks are wood (no stainless steel), to reduce the danger of glasses being chipped. All the glasses are washed by hand. One of the most unusual rooms is the Copper Room in which hundreds of saucepans, other pans and copper moulds used for jellies, mousses and other dishes in unusual shapes, are arranged in long lines. The moulds date back to the reign of George III (1760–1820) and there are pieces of copper with the initials VR, POW (Prince of Wales), ER, GR and even LC, for the Lord Chamberlain, from the days when members of the Royal Household would order their own individual dishes. The copper is kept in its original condition by cleaning with a special solution of vinegar, lemon and salt and the total collection is estimated to be worth several hundred thousand pounds. A former Master of the Household wanted to sell the lot but was told that the cyphers and initials would have to be removed first. Of course this would also have greatly reduced the value of the utensils so the idea was dropped.

The floors of the kitchens are made of genuine quarry tiles and the shelves in the pantries are pure marble.

Two areas are kept locked at all times. They are the wine cellar, which has a permanent store of a hundred dozen bottles of Krug champagne alone, and the Kitchen Vault, room number 465, where part of the silver and gold plate is kept. There is a story, perhaps apocryphal, that some years ago there was only one key to both the cellar and the Vault and it was carried by a servant with a liking for the bottle. One evening, he and the key went missing, only to be found hours later in his 'Grace and Favour' apartment, blind drunk and surrounded by the Royal Plate. Since then security has been tightened and there is no possibility of such an incident happening these days. Also the bulk of the Gold Plate is now stored in the most secure room of the palace – the old air raid shelter. Next door to the wine cellar, the Yeoman of the Wine Cellar has his own sitting room which also doubles as his office, with the Livery Porters' Dressing Room alongside. Perhaps appropriately, the locksmith's workshop is also nearby. A number of ladies are employed in the kitchens just to make coffee. They have their own work room and bedrooms on the first floor of the Kitchen Wing, next door to the Servants' Hall, while the staff coffee room is one of the most popular meeting places below stairs.

The Pastry Cook also has his own sitting room, alongside the Pastry Kitchen. The vegetable store is another large room. For a formal function one person is responsible for the preparation of each separate vegetable as all the sprouts or pieces of carrot have to be of identical size. There used to be separate rooms for roasting and even for boiling but a single large kitchen is now used for both. Although fresh bread is no longer baked on the premises, the croissants for breakfast are, as is The Queen's special chocolate cake, with the chocolate delivered from Harrods.

Even though in the entire palace only one open fireplace is still in use a firewood store and a log room remain, and the kitchens are littered with pantries and larders, plus offices for the ordering clerks and typists who maintain the tightest control over the vast stocks of food and drink.

When the modernisation programme was introduced at Buckingham Palace and the amalgamation of the two separate kitchens reduced the warren of mini-kitchens to two larger rooms, one for pastry, the other for all other food, the same system was established at Windsor Castle, where the kitchen staff work in a room with one of the finest oak hammer beamed roofs in existence. At Holyroodhouse the kitchens are smaller than at the other two palaces but have a charming, domestic atmosphere as they are situated on the ground floor of the inner Quadrangle, which means that the staff are able to see members of the Royal Family and their guests as they go in and out. They were modernised fifteen years ago, when the improvements included an entrance made through one wall of the Long Gallery so that food can now be served to the guests at a State Banquet from either side.

The kitchens at Buckingham Palace are run with the smooth efficiency that characterises the rest of the Royal Household. Each person knows his or her own job perfectly and keeps to his particular area of the domain. There isn't much overlapping in the royal kitchens – the only person who dares to interfere, on rare occasions, is the Head Chef. In the hierarchy of royal catering, his word is law and for him there is only one standard – perfection. Buckingham Palace is probably the last house in Europe where the old qualities of service remain. In many ways it is like going back to another century, when the aristocracy maintained huge households to look after their families and friends. Cost was never a consideration and servants were expected to stay for life. Buckingham Palace is unique in that, physically at least, it has changed very little in the last hundred years; and, in the kitchens, it is still possible to recapture some of the glamour of a bygone age.

5

The Royal Household

Because the present monarch happens to be a woman she also has to assume the responsibilities of a housewife with all its attendant problems, though in her case they are magnified many times over. The size and scale of the five royal residences of Buckingham Palace, Windsor Castle, the Palace of Holyroodhouse, Sandringham and Balmoral only increase the domestic difficulties which might be experienced by other women throughout the world.

It is perhaps antiquated in the latter part of the twentieth century to talk about the 'servant problem', but in The Queen's household, the problem is very real and it is not always easy to recruit enough of the right sort of people at the wages offered. Until the outbreak of the Second World War, there was a plentiful supply of servants only too willing and anxious to work for the Royal Household. In fact, the domestic side of the Household was virtually a 'closed shop', the only way in by personal recommendation from someone who already worked there, probably a relation. Generations of the same families worked at the same jobs in the palace kitchens, the pantries and the Servants' Hall, and outsiders were not welcome.

The wages were never high. At the beginning of this century a kitchen apprentice earned £15 a year, out of which he was expected to provide his own 'working whites' – and he needed six sets. The man at the top of the tree, the Royal Chef, was paid £10 a week, a very handsome wage on which he could afford to keep servants of his own. One thing has remained constant. All single men and women, then and now, are offered accommodation at Buckingham Palace. Each one gets his or her own room on the top floor. They are furnished simply but comfortably and are rent free with all heating and light included. Meals are provided free also. Married couples are usually offered apartments or houses in and around the Palace, and when a loyal servant retires after perhaps many years' service, he or she is sometimes allowed to stay in their quarters or, more usually, offered alternative pensioners' quarters.

So, while the salaries paid today are still not among the highest in the catering industry, and realistically everyone, from The Queen down, knows that they could earn more outside, there are several advantages. Security for life is there if you want it, and if you don't, there is never much of a problem in getting a well paid job once you have a reference from the palace. At the same time there is virtually a 'standing order' at several leading domestic employment agencies, not only for staff at Buckingham Palace, but for nearly all the homes of other members of the Royal Family also.

Before we examine the jobs of the full-time employees in the Royal Household, it might be as well to look briefly at two categories of royal servant who operate on a part-time basis.

LADIES-IN-WAITING

The Queen has fourteen Ladies-in-Waiting which might seem an exorbitant number, but they are never all on duty at the same time. Besides each of them has to shoulder the usual responsibilities of a home and family, notwithstanding periodic assignments to royal duties. At the top of the list is the Mistress of the Robes, the Duchess of Grafton; the Mistress of the Robes is always a Duchess. As the senior Lady-in-Waiting she organises the working roster for the other Ladies and is always in attendance at the coronation and other State occasions such as the State Opening of Parliament, when, as her title indicates, she is responsible for supervising the Robing of Her Majesty.

Then there are two Ladies of the Bedchamber, the Countess of Airlie (whose husband is the Lord Chamberlain), and Lady Farnham.

Their duties are irregular in that one of them will usually accompany The Queen on all overseas tours, but in the United Kingdom they attend Her Majesty only on the more important public occasions. There are also two Extra Ladies of the Bedchamber, the Countess of Cromer and the Marchioness of Abergavenny.

The bulk of the work is carried out by the Women of the Bedchamber. There are four: The Hon. Mary Morrison, Lady Susan Hussey, Mrs John Dugdale and Lady Elton. Each is on duty full time for two weeks, during which period they stay at the palace and deal with Her Majesty's private correspondence, of which there is a considerable amount. Letters from old people or children are usually answered on The Queen's behalf by one of her Ladies-in-Waiting, and they also do any personal shopping Her Majesty might need.

Strange as it might seem, it is easier for Ladies-in-Waiting to serve a Queen Regnant than a Queen Consort. Our present Queen has a Private Secretary and various Government departments to assist her in answering official correspondence, so the Ladies-in-Waiting have nothing to do with that side of her work. With a Queen Consort, there is very little administrative back-up, and the Ladies-in-Waiting assume the responsibility for the bulk of their mistress's correspondence.

The ladies have a comfortable sitting room on the second floor of the south-east corner of the palace where a lady clerk looks after the administrative details. At Buckingham Palace they eat in the Household Dining Room (it is immediately adjacent to the Bow Room on the ground floor), while at Windsor and all other royal homes they take their meals with the Royal Family.

Five Extra Women of the Bedchamber can be called upon in the event of an emergency. They are Mrs John Woodroffe, Lady Rose Baring, Lady Abel Smith, Mrs Robert de Pass and Mrs Michael Wall, who was given the honour when she retired as Assistant Press Secretary to The Queen after more than a quarter of a century's service.

Ladies-in-Waiting are not paid a salary for their duties but are reimbursed for any out of pocket expenses they may incur. They come from similar backgrounds and each has the ability to mix with people of all nationalities and walks of life. The Queen regards them more as personal friends and companions than as staff – and none has ever spoken publicly about her job.

THE EQUERRY IN WAITING

The Equerry in Waiting is a serving officer, selected in rotation from one of the three armed services, who is seconded from his unit to the Royal Household for a period of three years. He is in immediate attendance on Her Majesty and accompanies her on all engagements. His responsibilities include making all travel arrangements for The Queen and he introduces guests into the royal presence when they arrive for an audience. The Equerry in Waiting needs to be gregarious, good-humoured and a man of infinite patience.

THE MASTER OF THE HOUSEHOLD

The Queen does not maintain large permanent staffs at all her residences. Most of the domestic staff are based at Buckingham Palace and travel with her wherever she goes: to Windsor at weekends; Sandringham for New Year; Balmoral and Holyroodhouse in the summer and even on board the Royal Yacht *Britannia* when required. Throughout the remainder of the year the other royal homes are maintained by a skeleton staff.

The nearly 200 domestic servants all come under the jurisdiction of the Master of the Household. This office is one of the more recent appointments and came about through the reforming zeal of Prince Albert, who was exasperated by the utter confusion he found in the Royal Household during Queen Victoria's reign. Until 1844, the rooms at Buckingham Palace (except kitchens, sculleries and pantries) came under the Lord Chamberlain's Office. The Lord Steward controlled the kitchens and the Office of Woods and Forests looked after the outside of the building. So one department provided the wood and coal for the fires, but another department had to light those fires. If the fires were in the kitchens, yet a third department took over. And this process was repeated for most of the household requirements.

Prince Albert brought his orderly mind to bear on the problem and the result was the appointment of a Master of the Household with responsibility for all domestic arrangements in all the royal residences (including the Royal Yacht when a member of the Royal Family is on board).

The Master of the Household is one of the most senior of The Queen's servants and even though he has been described variously as the top hotel manager in the world or the most exalted major domo, his is a job that requires the utmost skill, tact and diplomacy and the ability to deal equally with Heads of State, foreign royalty and junior footmen. It is no accident that before taking up their appointments the present Master of the Household and his immediate predecessor were both senior career officers in the Royal Navy.

This distinguished office is currently held by Rear Admiral Sir Paul Greening, who was formerly Flag Officer Royal Yachts, in effect Captain of *Britannia*. So he has a wealth of experience in dealing with members of the Royal Family and their guests, both at home and abroad. He is assisted by a Deputy, Lieutenant-Colonel B. A. Stewart-Wilson, and most of the day-to-day administrative details are left in the capable hands of the Chief Clerk, Mr A. Hancock, who has been made a Member of the Royal Victorian Order (the sovereign's personal Order of Chivalry) for his long years of loyal service.

Only fourteen people work in the offices of the Master of the Household's department, which is ludicrously small when one considers the overall task. Three hundred meals are served every day in Buckingham Palace alone and it can be up to six hundred if all the staff are in for every meal. In addition there are the functions, eighty every year from State Banquets to Garden Parties. The Master of the Household is also responsible for the palace post office and is the point of liaison with the police who guard the Royal Family and all the royal homes, and with the Department of the Environment who look after the structure of the three royal palaces, in London, Windsor and Edinburgh.

With nearly 200 men and women to supervise (which includes

the skeleton staff at royal homes outside London and teams of craftsmen, cabinet makers, gilders, polishers, upholsterers etc.), there is naturally a number of problems to deal with, some of which would tax the patience of Job. When members of the Royal Household are travelling by air to an overseas destination, perhaps to join up with *Britannia*, the Master of the Household advises on the allocation of seats on the aircraft. He has to be particularly careful to get the precedence right. It wouldn't do for a junior footman to be seated next to a royal chef, or in a better position than a Page of the Presence. Protocol and precedence don't end with the Royal Family!

Of all the domestic staff employed at Buckingham Palace, less than a dozen or so come into regular contact with The Queen. The majority look after the people who work for her. Members of the Royal Household are waited on by footmen and the chauffeurs in the Royal Mews spend much of their time driving other employees of The Queen about their business. Until recently two men were employed to wind and maintain the 300 clocks, but these have recently been removed from the Master of the Household's department and now come under the jurisdiction of the Surveyor of The Queen's Works of Art.

There is a fairly rigid pecking order in the Household. At the top are the *Members*, consisting of Private Secretaries, Controllers and Assistants. Then come the *Officials* who look after the administrative details and clerical work. Finally there are *Staff*: junior office workers, domestic staff and craftsmen.

Members all address each other by Christian name, regardless of rank or position. Officials are called Mr, Mrs or Miss and never address Members by their first name. Staff call everybody above them Sir or Madam but the rest of the Household usually address them by their first name. It's all rather subtle, but seems to work to everyone's satisfaction.

If you are ever invited to have lunch with The Queen, you will first of all receive a telephone call from the Master of the Household, followed by an invitation. He also issues all invitations to State Banquets and Official Lunches or Dinners – perhaps for a visiting Head of State not on an official State Visit. Invitations to Garden Parties and royal weddings come from the Lord Chamberlain.

A number of domestic servants within the Master of the Household's department bear job titles whose names go back several centuries, even though the work they do has been brought up to date.

PALACE STEWARD

This is the head servant in the Royal Household. He is a man of great importance and vast experience in all matters concerning the domestic requirements of The Queen and her family. At present the position is held by Cyril Dickman who has been in royal service for more than forty years. Known to everyone in the palace, even The Queen, as Cyril, he can be seen closest to Her Majesty at all State Banquets. From his position immediately behind her chair he controls all the serving arrangements and his eyes miss nothing. If the Master of the Household is the Commanding Officer, the Palace Steward is the Sergeant Major.

Mr Dickman is responsible for the work of all the male servants in the Royal Household, namely the Page of the Chambers, the Pages of the Presence, the Pages of the Backstairs, the Sergeant Footman and all the other Footmen, and the Yeomen of the Gold and Silver Pantry, of the China and Glass Pantry and of the Royal Cellars, together with their respective Under-Butlers and Assistants. The Palace Steward is in charge of the Stewards' Dining Room and also looks after the training of all male domestic servants in the palace.

When the Prince and Princess of Wales were married, the Palace Steward was responsible for the serving arrangements at their wedding breakfast. He also performed the same task for the Duke and Duchess of York.

A pre-wedding dance for the Prince of Wales and Lady Diana Spencer was held in Buckingham Palace. Cyril Dickman looked after the arrangements for supper and refreshments and then, at four o'clock in the morning, after the last revellers had departed, made sure that the Ballroom was cleared and preparations made for a supper party for sixteen that evening. It was no easy task, as a fountain had been installed in the Ballroom for the festivities and this had to be dismantled and taken away.

The Palace Steward is an authority on the serving of food and wine and is kept fully informed by his colleagues, the Yeomen of the Cellars, the Glass and China Pantry and the Plate Pantry; so that he knows exactly which piece of china, gold plate or cutlery has been used on every occasion. When the tables are being set for a State Banquet, his day starts shortly after dawn and rarely ends before the early hours of the following morning. Even though each place is measured with a ruler by the Yeoman of the Glass and China Pantry, Cyril Dickman can tell immediately if a glass, knife or fork is a millimetre out of line.

It is impossible to overestimate the importance of the Palace Steward in the domestic arrangements in the royal homes. Without his expertise, the Master of the Household would find life 'below stairs' difficult indeed. Most of the recent Masters have recognised this fact and, apart from exercising an overall supervisory role, have left their Palace Steward to get on with the job. It's a system that appears to operate rather well.

PAGE OF THE CHAMBERS

Contrary to the impression which might be given by the title, the various Pages within the Royal Household in no way resemble the pageboys who were employed in hotels some years ago. In addition to acting as Deputy Palace Steward, the Page of the Chambers also has particular responsibilities of his own, for all The Queen's official engagements within Buckingham Palace come into his area of responsibility. When a foreign ambassador presents his Letters of Credence to The Queen on his appointment, the Page of the Chambers makes the arrangements within the palace. At the fifteen or so Investitures every year, the 150 men and women presented with honours by The Queen are each allowed to bring a small number of guests to witness the ceremony, so a number of footmen, cloakroom attendants and so on have to be on duty. The Page of the Chambers makes the necessary arrangements and looks after the serving arrangements at Cocktail Parties and other receptions.

PAGES OF THE PRESENCE

These are senior servants in the Royal Household who work very closely with the Royal Family and with the suites of visiting Heads of State who stay at Buckingham Palace, Windsor Castle or Balmoral. They also look after the Grand Entrance to the palace and are the servants who come into most contact with the outside world when they are on duty at the Privy Purse Door, the entrance used by most visitors who come to see a member of the Household. It is the one on the extreme right of the palace as you look at it from the front and is also the door to which the government boxes containing State and other official papers are delivered several times every day. One daily task of Pages of the Presence is to see that members of the Royal Household have fresh stationery on their desks every morning. And a Page of the Presence oversees the serving arrangements at Household meals. All of them are experienced servants who have come up from the junior ranks of the domestic staff, and have been chosen for their discretion, tact and supreme ability. One long-serving Page who recently retired was asked what he considered the most important assets for someone in his position. He replied, 'Good feet, hollow legs and a strong sense of humour.'

PAGES OF THE BACKSTAIRS

Two Pages of the Backstairs serve as The Queen's Pages: both of them very senior male servants who have been in royal service for many years. They take it in turn to wait in attendance on Her Majesty, so one is always on duty. If a Member of the Household needs to see The Queen he telephones the Page to find out if she is free. This is a position very close to the sovereign and her Pages are required to be models of discretion.

Two other Pages of the Backstairs perform a similar function for the Duke of Edinburgh.

TRAVELLING YEOMAN AND SERGEANT FOOTMAN

With his deputy, the Sergeant Footman, the Travelling Yeoman is directly in charge of all the footmen in the palace. This means that he acts as a sort of foreman or supervisor, carrying out the instructions of the Palace Steward on a day-to-day basis. When the Court moves from Buckingham Palace to Windsor or any of the other royal residences, he makes sure that the right number of footmen are allocated to move with the Court.

As his title implies, he is also responsible for certain travel arrangements. In fact, he is indispensable for his duties include supervising the transport of the luggage of The Queen and other members of the Royal Household. When one realises that more than five tons of luggage may be taken on a foreign tour, the size of the task can be imagined.

During a long overseas tour – perhaps to Australia and New Zealand – he will make the detailed plans for moving baggage from the palace to London's Heathrow Airport. Then from the airport of arrival to (say) *Britannia* and a week later to an hotel in Melbourne. It may then go by air to another hotel in Adelaide and by air again to Auckland, New Zealand to rejoin *Britannia* for the latter half of the tour.

The Travelling Yeoman moves with The Queen whenever she travels – to any of her other homes or even on board *Britannia*, the Royal Train or aircraft of The Queen's Flight. His proud boast is that so far he has never yet lost a single one of Her Majesty's bags!

FOOTMEN

As the name implies, these men (in spite of the sex discrimination act there are no footwomen in royal service) have general duties around the palace. They act as messengers for The Queen, for her page or any other members of the Household when required and also escort visitors from the Privy Purse Door. They are used as valets to visiting male guests and to members of the Household.

One rather pleasant aspect to working at Buckingham Palace is that if you need to stay the night for any reason, a charming room is placed at your disposal and a footman unpacks your suitcase, lays out your nightwear and presses your suit if required.

Footmen are also seen on State occasions when they ride, in full State Livery, on the carriages in the royal processions, and also on the back of the smaller carriages which are sent to carry new ambassadors to the palace to present their Letters of Credence.

It is not very difficult to get a job as a footman at Buckingham Palace. The requirements are intelligence and a capacity for hard work. There are usually several vacancies and, because full training is given on the job, no experience is required. You apply by writing to the Master of the Household.

YEOMAN OF THE GOLD AND SILVER PANTRY

The Queen's priceless collection of gold and silver plate, with its cups, candelabra and other ornaments, is the finest in the world. Its value runs into millions of pounds and much of it is irreplaceable, so the holder of this position has a very responsible job. His duties include keeping an inventory of every article and making sure each piece is in perfect condition. When there is a State Banquet he has to provide the required displays of gold plate as well as the items used for the meal itself. Then when the function is over, he must make sure that everything is returned to its proper place. After one State Banquet at Buckingham Palace, a solid gold fork was found to be missing. The kitchen staff stayed behind all night before they finally found the missing piece of cutlery – in a refuse bag which was about to be thrown out.

YEOMAN OF THE GLASS AND CHINA PANTRY

With more than eighty functions a year at Buckingham Palace alone, apart from those at other royal residences, this man has a massive task. He provides glass and china for all State Banquets –

800 glasses simply for the meal itself – and keeps an inventory of the china used at the 300 meals served at Buckingham Palace every day. He also has to look after the very valuable dessert and fruit sets used by the Royal Family and make sure that the delicate porcelain is kept in conditions which will allow it to breathe.

YEOMAN OF THE ROYAL CELLARS

The cellars at Buckingham Palace and Windsor Castle are vast and compare with those of the finest hotels in the world. Vintage wines are stored in perfect conditions, the very best pure malt whiskies (favoured by the senior members of the Household), beers and soft drinks are all available in large quantities. Even though The Queen herself and the Duke of Edinburgh are abstemious to a degree unknown in previous monarchs, their hospitality is legendary and every kind of drink is kept for their guests.

At one time it was decided to make members of the Household pay for the drinks they consumed. But the cost of collecting the money was more than the amount collected so the practice was dropped. These days if you arrive in the palace at the appropriate time in the early evening you will probably be invited to join one of the Private Secretaries, or whoever you are visiting, in a glass or two of the finest Scotch whisky money can buy.

CHIEF HOUSEKEEPER

This is a fairly recent addition to the Master of the Household's department. The position of Chief Housekeeper was created in January 1970 to oversee the housemaids at all the royal residences. Previously, Buckingham Palace had its own Housekeeper, but there was no one with a coordinating function over the housekeepers at all the other royal homes. The present occupant of the post is Miss Heather Colebrook.

The Chief Housekeeper has overall responsibility for all house-keeping matters at Buckingham Palace, Windsor Castle, the Palace of Holyroodhouse, Balmoral Castle and Sandringham House, but there are also permanent housekeepers at Windsor, Balmoral and Sandringham and a deputy at Buckingham Palace. She looks after the Royal Family and Household requirements for linen, daily cleaning and the provision of materials and cleaning machines. At the beginning of each year she sends a list of major items needed to the Master of the Household – carpet sweepers, washing machines and so on – and he then has to obtain the approval of the Keeper of the Privy Purse.

Housekeeping in the royal residences is in no way a matter of simply replacing anything worn with a new item. These households are arguably more cost conscious than any other in the world, and the amount of darning, mending and making do that goes on would perhaps surprise many people in the outside world.

There are twenty-four housemaids employed at Buckingham Palace as well as a number of daily women who come in to help with the cleaning of the 600 rooms. The housemaids do not, as a rule, come into contact with their royal employer; in fact they have been known to go to quite extraordinary lengths to avoid being seen by The Queen or the Duke of Edinburgh if they happen to be working in one of the corridors when one of them passes – dashing into tiny cupboards or even hiding behind the curtains until the Royals pass. This is not because The Queen herself has issued orders that the domestic servants are to be neither seen nor heard, but because their immediate superiors feel it is better that way. The ladies are also well segregated from the male members of staff; they live in one corner of the Palace while the men occupy another. Most of their duties involve dusting, polishing and cleaning, but the housemaids also serve breakfast to any ladies staying at the Palace. Footmen are not permitted to enter a bedroom if it is occupied by a lady.

There is one golden rule which affects all the housemaids. They must be single and remain so if they wish to continue in royal service. Many of them marry other members of the staff, but exceptions to the rule are never made. The wife of the Palace Steward, Cyril Dickman, used to be a housemaid. She had to give up her job once she got married. She, and all the others who have

married, are still welcome at the Palace as guests, when The Queen
gives a dance or reception for her staff and their families, but not as
working members of staff.

FLAGMAN

This man is a serving soldier from the Household Division who has
been recommended by his Commanding Officer and selected by the
Master of the Household. Apart from running up the Royal Standard when The Queen is in residence (and taking it down when she
is not) he also despatches flags to other places when they are needed
for a royal visit. He then sees that they are returned safely afterwards.
His other duties include acting as the principal operator in a team
of three which scrutinises by fluoroscope every single item of mail
that arrives at Buckingham Palace. This is to make sure no letter
bombs or explosive parcels are delivered.

Many other people are of course employed at Buckingham Palace
and the other royal homes. There are cabinet makers, daily cleaners,
gilders, carpet planners, upholsterers as well as all those working in
the Royal Mews maintaining the State Livery and carriages – scores
of royal servants carrying out an astonishing number of different
tasks to maintain the splendour of the monarchy.

The engineers, electricians and plumbers of the special Depot of
the Department of the Environment which is based inside Buckingham Palace (and at Windsor Castle and the Palace of Holyroodhouse) are responsible for the upkeep of the building itself and
the machinery.

The royal Staff belong to the Civil Service Union and their pay
is negotiated on an analogous scale. So when, each year, an increase
is announced in the Civil List (the allowance paid to The Queen by
Parliament) the bulk of that increase is taken up by pay rises awarded
within the Civil Service. The Union, recognising the unique position
of its members in the Royal Household, normally excuses royal employees from taking part in industrial action. In its 200-odd years as
a royal residence, there has not been a strike at Buckingham Palace.

The Queen has compared life in the palace to living in a small village. Certainly there are similarities. There is a Royal Household Social Club, with all the usual outings, parties and other activities. There is a Royal Household Football Club which doesn't play in any local league but whose team is seen frequently in charity matches and whose opponents' secretaries love getting letters with the Buckingham Palace letterhead.

Inside the palace is a post office which is used by all members of staff, regardless of rank. There is also a swimming pool which only the senior members of the Household are able to enjoy – and that at times when none of the Royal Family is present. The unwritten rule is that if you are already swimming when a member of the Royal Family arrives, you get out unless invited to remain. If you turn up and find one of the royals in the water, you do not go in.

The most frequent and regular user of the swimming pool is the Princess of Wales, who likes to swim several lengths every morning. The Household has come to know her time and leave her to enjoy her swim in peace.

A 'perk' for domestic servants is that they are allowed to invite friends and relatives into their rooms for a drink in the evenings or on a day off. For reasons of security they have to notify the Master of the Household beforehand, and no guests are allowed to remain overnight. It is indeed a pleasant privilege to be able to ask a friend to join you for a drink inside Buckingham Palace.

The work of the domestic staff in the Royal Household does not usually receive a great deal of publicity – and that is the way they prefer to keep it. But it is vital to the wellbeing of The Queen and her family, and its continuous and efficient operation contributes enormously to the smooth running of the royal palaces and castles.

THE PRIVATE SECRETARY

Sir William Heseltine, a fifty-six year old Australian, is The Queen's closest and most influential aide. Although not primarily concerned with The Queen's entertaining, he plays a vital role in the monarch's daily life. He is in daily contact with Her Majesty and arranges

ABOVE: *The Queen and her guest, King Fahd of Saudi Arabia, are quietly amused at the Duke of Edinburgh's attempts to guide Queen Elizabeth The Queen Mother towards the royal group prior to a State Banquet at Buckingham Palace in 1987.*

RIGHT: *The Queen, who prides herself on her knowledge of Scottish regiments and their music, has obviously found something worth pointing out to this drummer lining the steps at a State function.*

BELOW: *The Archbishop of Canterbury, Dr Robert Runcie, escorts Queen Elizabeth The Queen Mother into the banquet given for King Olaf of Norway at Windsor in April 1988. The Duke of Edinburgh, the Prince of Wales and the Duke of York are all wearing the 'Windsor Coat' of blue with scarlet collar and cuffs.*

RIGHT: *The Blue Drawing Room is said by many visitors to be the most beautiful of all the State apartments. Guests at State Banquets and official receptions move from the Music Room, through the B[lue] Drawing Room into the State Dining Room en route [to] the State Ballroom.*

LEFT: *President Reagan was given a full State Banq[uet] at Windsor Castle (April 1982), although officially h[is] was not a State visit. The Palace Steward, Cyril Dickman, stands immediately behind the President's chair.*

BELOW: *The view The Queen sees from her place a[t the] head of the horse-shoe shaped table in the State Ballro[om] at Buckingham Palace. The organ at the far end was brought from the Royal Pavilion in Brighton, and the Regimental String Orchestra plays in the minstrels' gallery.*

ABOVE: *Part of the Duke of Manchester service of Sèvres porcelain purchased by the Prince Regent in 1802. It was a present from Louis XVI to the Duchess of Manchester, whose husband had signed the treaty bringing the war of American Independence to an end in 1783.*

LEFT: *A comport with pierced bowl, part of a Minton service made for Queen Victoria. Turquoise is its main colour and, as with many of the finest pieces in the Royal Collection, it contains the royal monogram 'VR'.*

BELOW: *The Yeoman of the Glass and China Pantry is responsible for the priceless collection of crystal and porcelain at Buckingham Palace. This group of pieces by Tournai is brought out only on the most special occasions such as the wedding breakfast of the Duke and Duchess of York.*

THE ROYAL WEDDING BREAKFAST

·THURSDAY·27TH·APRIL·1882·

Potages.
À LA BRUNOISE   À LA CRÈME DE RIZ.

Entrées.
LES COTELETTES D'AGNEAU, PANÉES ET SAUTÉES.
LES FILETS DE POULETS BIGARRÉS AUX TRUFFES.
LES ESCALOPES DE RIS DE VEAU À LA CHICORÉE.
LES FILETS DE CANETONS AUX POIS.

Relevés.
LA PIÈCE DE BOEUF BRAISÉE, SAUCE RAIFORT.
LES POULARDES À LA JARDINIÈRE.

Entrées Froides.
LA SALADE DE HOMARDS.
LES OEUFS DE PLUVIERS.

Rôt.
LES POULETS GRAS AU CRESSON.

Entremêts.
LES POIS SAUTÉS AU BEURRE.
LES ARTICHAUTS À LA LYONNAISE.
LE GATEAU DE GÉNOISE AU CHOCOLAT.
LA CRÈME À LA D'ORLÉANS
LA GELÉE GARNIE D'ORANGES
LA MERINGUE SUISSE À LA CHANTILLY

Relevés
LE PUDDING À LA DIPLOMATE.
LES SOUFFLÉS À LA CANELLE.

Royal wedding breakfasts in the last century were sumptuous feasts compared with the modest meals of today. When Queen Victoria's eighth child, Prince Leopold, married Princess Helena of Waldeck-Pyrmont in the Chapel Royal at Windsor Castle, every guest at the wedding breakfast belonged to a European royal family and the meal lasted four hours, to be followed by an equally elaborate banquet that evening.

ABOVE: *The State Dining Room at Buckingham Palace is used for formal lunches and dinners which are not State Banquets.*

RIGHT: *Occasionally other members of the Royal Family stand in for The Queen at official functions. Here the Prince of Wales carries out an investiture on behalf of his mother; in the Ballroom at Buckingham Palace 150 men and women receive their awards in a ceremony which lasts exactly one hour.*

ABOVE: *The days when the Royal Train could truly be described as 'a palace on wheels'. This is the elaborate drawing room on Queen Victoria's train in which she frequently travelled from Windsor to Ballater in Scotland en route to Balmoral.*

LEFT: *There was very nearly a clash of colours when The Queen welcomed Queen Beatrix of the Netherlands at the start of her State visit in November 1982. Her Majesty always meets the Royal Train at Victoria station accompanied by Prince Philip and members of the Government. In the background are the Prime Minister, Margaret Thatcher, the Foreign Secretary, Sir Geoffrey Howe, and the Home Secretary, Douglas Hurd.*

ABOVE: *Once a year the Court moves to Scotland for a week. The Queen takes up residence in the Palace of Holyroodhouse in Edinburgh where a full programme of social events and Court entertainment is arranged. In this photograph The Queen is joined by Princess Margaret and the Princess Royal, all wearing tartan sashes.*

LEFT: *'Don't worry, you look perfect': the bridesmaids of the Princess of Wales get ready for the official photographs in the Picture Gallery at Buckingham Palace in July 1981. The mother of the groom looks on reassuringly.*

BELOW: *The Queen is at her happiest when she is able to relax among friends and household on board the Royal Yacht Britannia. Here the men are wearing 'Red Sea Rig' – short sleeves and open-necked shirts.*

her complete programme of events. His office sees every piece of correspondence that is addressed to her and, as Keeper of the Royal Diary, no one, not even the Lord Chamberlain, who is Head of the Royal Household, gets to see The Queen without the Private Secretary's knowledge.

He accompanies her on all overseas visits where his considerable diplomatic skills are very much in evidence and is Her Majesty's link with Government. There are two other Private Secretaries. The Deputy, Robert Fellowes, a former discount broker who gave up a large income in the City to enter royal service, is married to the former Lady Jane Spencer, the eldest sister of the Princess of Wales. The other Private Secretary is the Assistant, Kenneth Scott, who was formerly British Ambassador to Yugoslavia. Another of the Private Secretary's responsibilities is to produce the Court Circular which lists the engagements of the Royal Family every day. Until recently this task was carried out by the Master of the Household, but it was decided that it would be more logical for the Private Secretary to circulate the information.

The Press Secretary, Robin Janvrin, works to the Private Secretary. There are now two Assistant Press Secretaries to cope with the avalanche of queries that descend on Buckingham Palace twenty-four hours of every day, plus a Deputy Press Secretary, John Haslam, a former BBC producer who looks after the press requirements of the Princess Royal and the Duke of Edinburgh. The two newest recruits are Dickie Arbitter, another former radio man, and Geoffrey Crawford. He is an Australian on temporary attachment to the palace for three years.

Keeper of the Privy Purse and Treasurer to The Queen

Major Shane Blewitt is the man who signs the cheques that pay for The Queen's entertaining. He has a dual responsibility: he looks after Her Majesty's private financial affairs, the Royal Estates, the Stud and her racing expenses. And he is also responsible for all Civil List finances, the allowance that is paid to The Queen and certain other members of the Royal Family to cover their official expenses for public duties. Major Blewitt also has one other centuries-old responsibility. He looks after the administrative details of the annual Maundy Service when The Queen gives a bag of coins to the elderly poor.

THE CROWN EQUERRY

Efficiency is taken for granted in every aspect of the sovereign's life. Parties always start on time, guests are never left alone. If The Queen is going out to an engagement everything runs like clockwork and according to a predetermined plan. She never appears to hurry yet always arrives in exactly the right place at the appointed moment. The reason is the most extraordinary attention to the tiniest detail, especially when she is travelling.

The man responsible for ensuring that Her Majesty is never late is the Crown Equerry, Lieutenant-Colonel Seymour Gilbert-Denham of the Life Guards. He not only provides cars for the Royal Family for every occasion (there are five State Rolls Royces in the Royal Mews) but he looks after the State Coaches used for State occasions such as the Opening of Parliament, and provides smaller, horse drawn carriages to transport new ambassadors from their homes, when they come to present their Credentials to The Queen. He also plays an important role when a garden party is planned because the royal lawn-mowers and hedge trimmers come under his umbrella. Altogether he has a staff of twelve chauffeurs, forty-odd grooms and coachmen and more than ninety maintenance men and women, including the seamstresses who sew the exquisite uniforms worn by the coachmen, and the upholsterers who look after the padding in the coaches and carriages.

THE LORD CHAMBERLAIN'S OFFICE

The Lord Chamberlain, the Earl of Airlie, is Head of the Royal Household and responsible for all ceremonial surrounding the mon-

archy. So when a royal wedding is planned it is the Lord Chamberlain who takes over a massive operation and heads the team which produces the final result. If attention to detail is taken for granted in the Royal Household, it is a prerequisite for those who work in this department.

The actual day-to-day running of the office is left in the capable hands of the Comptroller, at present Lieutenant-Colonel George West, who looks after all incoming State Visits, part of the State Opening of Parliament, under the direction of the Earl Marshal (Lieutenant-Colonel West is the figure you see on television carrying the Imperial State Crown on a velvet cushion up the steps of the House of Lords), and the awards of Royal Warrants to those tradespeople who have served the Royal Family with distinction for the required period of time (see chapter on Royal Suppliers).

In terms of The Queen's entertaining, perhaps the most important of the sub-departments within the Lord Chamberlain's Office is the Garden Party Office. This is staffed by a number of ladies who in early summer write out in longhand some 31,000 invitations to the

The State opening of Parliament, when the Comptroller of the Lord Chamberlain's office and his assistant are responsible for bringing the royal regalia to the Palace of Westminster. Here the former Comptroller, Lt. Col. Sir John Johnston (right) is joined by the present Comptroller, Lt. Col. George West.

annual garden parties. These ladies are still known as 'Temporary Lady Clerks', even though some of the 'Temps' have been doing the same job for more than twenty years. You cannot apply to attend a Garden Party. You are invited either on the recommendation of a senior member of the Household or through your local authority, Lord Lieutenant or other public body, who every year are asked to submit names of people they feel deserve an invitation because of their public work. Every name is filed and indexed at the palace; including the information on whether you turned up or not. One of these ladies' most important tasks is to find the correct title, decoration or professional qualification of every guest. The Lord Chamberlain's Office prides itself on never making a mistake when writing to a guest of The Queen – whether it be Earl, Duke or just plain Mr and Mrs.

THE ROYAL COLLECTION

Until 1988 two departments were responsible for The Queen's art works: The Surveyor of The Queen's Pictures and The Surveyor of The Queen's Works of Art. However, it was decided to amalgamate these two offices under the title of The Royal Collection and the present Director is Sir Geoffrey de Bellaigue, formerly Surveyor of The Queen's Works of Art. He works from an attractive office in St James's Palace and has the awesome responsibility of looking after more than 5,000 pictures in The Royal Collection, plus all the other priceless works of art from Fabergé eggs to Chippendale furniture.

Guests at royal homes are shown tiny parts of the Collection which have been suggested by Sir Geoffrey, and there is also a delightful custom in the Royal Household whereby its members are allowed to borrow certain paintings to decorate their offices and, in some cases, their homes. The pictures are usually changed around every six months or so, so nobody gets too attached to any one work, and the idea is yet another example of The Queen's thoughtfulness to her staff in allowing them to share the exquisite and, in some cases, priceless paintings in her collection.

THE HONOURABLE CORPS OF GENTLEMEN AT ARMS AND THE YEOMEN OF THE GUARD

The Honourable Corps is in attendance at all State Occasions and is composed of former officers in the Army and Royal Marines. It provides the Gentlemen Ushers at Investitures and Garden Parties and does much to ease the progress of The Queen and her family at crowded functions.

No formal ceremonial occasion would be complete without the presence of The Queen's Bodyguard of Yeomen of the Guard. It is the oldest military bodyguard in the world, having been founded

The Princess Royal was once asked what happens if it rains at a garden party. 'We get wet', was the crisp reply. Guests at Buckingham Palace on 21st July 1987 made sure umbrellas were the order of the day – but no protection for the Yeomen of the Guard.

in 1485, after the Battle of Bosworth. Its members are drawn from senior non-commissioned officers of the army, marines and Royal Air Force – personnel from the navy are not permitted to join because in the old days when press gangs were used to 'recruit' sailors, their loyalty to the Crown could not be taken for granted. In royal circles old customs die hard!

The Yeomen have their headquarters in St James's Palace and a detachment is always close to The Queen at State Banquets, royal Garden Parties and all formal receptions. These days the pikes they carry are intended to be purely symbolic, although anyone who tried to get too close to The Queen would find the Yeomen did not hesitate to use them in the manner for which they were designed five hundred years ago.

This then is the Royal Household. Its people come from many different backgrounds today; from business, the professions and the armed forces. They are intelligent, cultivated and articulate men and women who work as a team, united in their loyalty to The Queen.

In their efforts to oil the machinery of monarchy they use the latest technology and methods, yet at the same time they preserve the traditions of the past – a royal history which has lasted a thousand years.

It was Disraeli who once remarked, 'Everyone likes flattery; when you come to royalty you lay it on with a trowel.' In Victorian times that may well have been the custom among courtiers. Today the relationship between the sovereign and her Household is a much more practical, working arrangement. Both she and they are professional in their approach to their jobs.

6

Royal Travel

———

Wherever and whenever The Queen travels, by land, sea or air, the Court and all that implies goes with her. If she is journeying by rail, not for her or her Household the inconvenience of queuing up at the buffet for a coffee or an 'all-day breakfast'. The Royal Train is equipped with the most modern kitchen facilities and when The Queen dines, even at 100mph, it is off the best china and cutlery, with spotless linen and in an elegant salon.

In the air Her Majesty is equally well served. Whether it is in an aircraft of The Queen's Flight, to which the latest additions are two BAe 146 medium haul jets, or using a commercial service, the standard of catering is never allowed to fall below the levels expected in any royal residence. But of all the methods of transport used by The Queen and her family, there is one which easily outshines all the others in glamour, comfort and service: the Royal Yacht.

British monarchs have always loved the sea, and every one has had the use of a royal yacht since King Charles II was given his first yacht by the Dutch East India Company in 1660. Queen Victoria had a number of yachts apart from the *Victoria and Albert*, built in 1843, which was used extensively to carry her to parts of the British Isles that would have been otherwise inaccessible. In fact she had six steam yachts built during her reign and several of them were used regularly to convey her ministers to and from the mainland when Her Majesty was in residence at Osborne, her home on the Isle of Wight.

Menu:

Tortue Claire.

Whitebait.

Darnes de Saumon à l'Écossaise.

Cailles à la Valenciennes.

Côtelettes d'Agneau à la Masséna.

Jambon d'York au Champagne.

Poulardes Rôties flanquées d'Ortolans.

Salade.

Petits pois à la Française.

Moscovites de Framboises à la Montreuil.

Biscuits à la Diable.

Bombe Cléopâtre.

———

Cowes. 7th Août, 1903.

The second *Victoria and Albert*, launched at Pembroke in 1855, was probably the first royal yacht in which formal entertaining was carried out by the sovereign. Queen Victoria's dining room could seat eighteen guests comfortably, and with the galley situated nearby, the food could be served at a reasonable temperature, which made a pleasant change.

Queen Victoria's son, King Edward VII, inherited a new royal yacht, the *Victoria and Albert III*, which was commissioned in July 1901. The dining room was much larger than in her predecessors and could seat thirty guests with ease. There were three magnificent Persian carpets; the curtains were of pure silk and the furniture was by Hepplewhite. The King always took his own servants on board with him, thirty-one in all including one Arab boy whose only duty was to provide His Majesty with a constant supply of coffee.

Edward VII was a stickler for correct behaviour and dress, whether at Court or on board ship. He once sarcastically remarked to a peer who had turned up at a Windsor picnic wearing tweeds: 'Goin' ratting today, Harris?' And when a confused diplomat arrived on board *Victoria and Albert* clad in knee breeches, he was despatched immediately by The King who informed him icily: 'Trousers are always worn on board ship.'

Dinner on board was always a formal affair, the gentlemen wearing full evening dress (this being long before the days when black ties and dinner jackets became fashionable) and ladies in long evening dresses with diamonds and other jewels. The King himself was a living example of the old adage 'Punctuality is the politeness of princes,' and woe betide anyone who was late! He also had a gargantuan appetite and consequently insisted on sitting down at the appointed time. Dinner was usually twelve courses, sometimes as many as fifteen, and despite a gregarious character, The King did not encourage idle chatter at table, where much more important things required his attention. He would start with oysters, perhaps a dozen or more, soup with sherry, caviar, several fish dishes, then on to the serious business of the main courses, fowl, game, mutton, beef, lamb with lashings of vegetables all in rich creamy sauces. He also liked his puddings and finished with ice-cream. But he did not believe in the custom of his mother's day, when at all royal banquets an ice was served between courses to refresh the palate. This was just an interruption so far as he was concerned and he would have none of it. Champagne was his favourite drink and he could consume several bottles during a meal.

Queen Alexandra also enjoyed entertaining on board the yacht and had her own party piece. At the end of each meal she would press an electric switch underneath the table and, much to the surprise of her guests, fire two bronze six-pounder guns which were located outside the royal apartments. It has not been recorded what this unexpected after-dinner treat did for the digestion or blood pressure of unwary guests.

King George V was a sailor King who loved the sea but did not have a high regard for foreign cruises. Consequently he did not use the *Victoria and Albert* as frequently as his father, nor was he fond of entertaining on board. His attitude to sailing was that it was something to be done in a small, fast craft purely as a sport. However, in 1935 he did give a splendid reception on board to celebrate the Silver Jubilee of his reign.

The Queen's father King George VI had also served in the Royal
Navy, but by the time he came to the throne in 1937, the *Victoria
and Albert* had seen her best days and was becoming increasingly
unseaworthy. She was not actually dismantled until 1955 but His
Majesty did not use her for entertainment in anything like the way
that his grandfather had. Besides, the Second World War prevented
any use of the Royal Yacht for purely social purposes, and by
the time the war had ended it was time for a new yacht to be
commissioned.

Britannia was launched in 1953, Coronation year, and ever since
has been used continuously as a floating royal residence. The Queen
has her own bedroom, bathroom and sitting room, as does Prince
Philip. There are suites for other members of the Royal Family and
cabins for the Household. The Ladies-in-Waiting and the Gentlemen
of the Royal Household have their own sitting rooms on board; a
Sick Bay is equipped with an operating theatre; there is a mess for
the Royal Stewards and an office for the royal clerks, even room to
accommodate a royal Rolls Royce in a garage on the boat deck.
Her Majesty is able to entertain on a considerable scale on board the
Royal Yacht, although a lot depends on the weather. In 1984, during
a royal visit to the West Coast of the United States, The Queen had
to cancel a reception and dinner on *Britannia* because the sea was
too rough – even in harbour at San Diego.

An invitation to an entertainment on board is highly prized. It is
likely to be a fairly small reception and provides an opportunity to
see at close quarters a unique royal home.

Britannia is a combination of palace, private yacht and country
house. In The Queen's private apartments and also in the guests'
bedrooms there is an atmosphere of quiet, restrained good taste with
the usual chintz covered furniture found in all the royal residences.
Throughout the royal apartments are relics of previous royal yachts:
a gimbal table designed by Prince Albert on which a glass of whisky
will stand firmly in the strongest swell, and various mementoes
which together make The Queen and her family feel at home, no
matter where they may be in the world.

Unique in a number of ways, *Britannia* is the only ship in the
Royal Navy whose captain is an admiral, and she was the last in

MENU

Mousse de Saumon Ecossaise

Poulet Poêlé au Champagne
Carottes Glacées
Haricots Verts
Pommes Galette

Salade

Bombe Glacée au Cassis

MERCREDI, LE 22 OCTOBRE, 1986
HONG KONG

Even on board ship, Royal menus are written in French and produced on the Yacht's printing press. Guests are given these delightful souvenirs as a reminder of their visit.

which the sailors slept in hammocks – which they did until a refit in 1970. The yacht holds a special place in The Queen's affections because it is a 'home from home'. When she comes aboard *Britannia* at the end of a twenty-seven hour flight, or after a gruelling five-day programme, fulfilled perhaps from the home of a Head of State or Consul-General, she is welcomed by the familiar faces of *Britannia*'s officers and sailors and the comfort of her own apartments. Here she is able to relax before setting forth on the remaining days or weeks of an exhausting overseas tour.

Britannia also happens to be the only royal structure built during The Queen's reign. British monarchs have tended to leave their mark on the country in the form of castles, palaces and cathedrals; the reign of Elizabeth II will be marked in contemporary history by the fact that *Britannia* was created, even though in fifty years she will have been scrapped. Another curious fact about this unusual floating palace is that nowhere on her hull will you find her name. 'Britannia' does not appear anywhere on her exterior – simply the royal cypher, the only ship in the world with this distinction.

At a formal dinner party, the guests sit at a large mahogany table whose principal decoration is a priceless solid gold camel under two palm trees, given to the Duke of Edinburgh by the ruler of Dubai on the State Visit to the Gulf States in 1979. The chairs are reproduction Hepplewhite and there is a story that, when the yacht was first commissioned, the Duke of Edinburgh thought the table too small for the sort of State Banquets he had in mind. To prove his point, he brought servants from Buckingham Palace to the yacht and ordered the cooks to serve a meal. They discovered that the maximum number they could cope with was thirty-two, far too few for a formal banquet. The result of the duke's experiment was that extra wings were added to the table enabling more chairs to be placed.

Formality on board *Britannia* is not quite as rigid as at Buckingham Palace but, as with everything to do with royalty, protocol has to be observed. The guests are greeted at the head of the gangway by an officer who conducts them to the drawing room, where they are presented to Her Majesty once they have all assembled. In the drawing room they are shown some of the interesting mementoes dotted around the ship: a remnant of a White Ensign recovered from the ill-fated last polar expedition of Captain Scott which was presented to King George V in 1912, the afore-mentioned gimbal table designed by Prince Albert, and a satinwood desk which once belonged to Queen Victoria. There is also one other item of furniture not normally found in a drawing room: a kneeling stool for the use of those who are knighted by The Queen on board – surely one of the most romantic settings for such a ceremony in modern history. Her Majesty is a gracious host and as there are only some fifty-six people present, about a third of whom are members of the Household or ship's company, she is able to devote a lot of time to her guests. This is one of the reasons an invitation to dine on board *Britannia* is so highly prized.

Whenever a member of the Royal Family is embarked in the Royal Yacht, the Master of the Household assumes responsibility for all catering and domestic arrangements. He orders the food and drink and is always on board if The Queen and the Duke of Edinburgh are sailing. Servants from Buckingham Palace are brought to the yacht and take over the duties of waiting at table, wearing exactly the same livery as when serving at a State Banquet at the palace or Windsor Castle. Special cabins are allocated to the domestic staff and the only member of the ship's crew who wears any distinguishing insignia is the Steward of the Royal Apartments who is a Lieutenant–Commander. He wears the usual naval uniform but his buttons bear the royal cypher instead of the regulation naval anchor. The kitchens on board are all electric and among the best equipped anywhere at sea.

Visitors in foreign parts are sometimes taken by surprise when they see the abundance of fresh flowers arranged in the royal apartments. The secret is that supplies from the gardens at Windsor are brought on board before every voyage and stored in large refrigerators below decks. The Queen insists on flowers in her rooms wherever she may be and so far *Britannia* has never run short. In foreign ports a steward will go ashore to buy bunches of local exotic blooms to decorate the dining room and drawing room.

Nearly all the food and drink consumed on board is brought from Britain. Before the yacht sails the Master of the Household with his staff will have ordered sufficient supplies of meat, fish, ingredients for desserts, tea, coffee, wine and spirits and of course the cases of Malvern water without which Her Majesty is said never to venture abroad. All these supplies will be checked as they are brought on board; when the voyage is complete, anything left over has to be returned to the kitchens at Buckingham Palace. This can sometimes be something of a problem for the storemen as there may be quite a lapse of time between *Britannia*'s leaving a foreign port and the return of the excess food and drink to London. But now that the catering supplies in all royal residences are computerised, it is possible to keep a tighter control on the use of stores.

A State Banquet held on board *Britannia* is a splendid occasion. The chief guest is usually the prime minister, president or ruler of the host country, accompanied by his family and members of his government. Other guests will include the Foreign Secretary, who usually goes with The Queen on State Visits and stays on board. He will meet his opposite number in the country they are visiting for diplomatic talks; these days State Visits are never allowed to become simply occasions of entertainment. There are practical business reasons behind every one.

Dress at a formal function on board the yacht depends on the climate in whichever part of the world the party finds itself. In the tropics, evening wear is a thin dinner jacket, with decorations. The naval officers wear white mess dress: black trousers, white jacket and black tie. Ladies wear full length evening dresses and The Queen wears a tiara. At sea there is a more informal dress known as Red Sea Rig, which consists of black trousers, cummerbund and an open-necked shirt, but this is only worn when there are no official guests.

On certain celebratory occasions, such as the thirty-first wedding anniversary dinner given by The Queen for President and Mrs Reagan in San Francisco, the guests are photographed by the ship's official photographer (known as 'Snaps') as they come on board. The pictures are developed during dinner and then, having been framed, given to the guests before they depart.

If the weather is really hot, pre-dinner drinks will be taken on the verandah deck under an awning; otherwise the guests assemble in the drawing room with the officers and members of the Household. Footmen from Buckingham Palace have laid the dining table with as much care as they would take at the palace, and for a formal banquet this means several hours' work. On *Britannia*, however, they do not have to walk on the table in stockinged feet.

The menu, a copy of which is given to each guest as a souvenir, shows a coloured drawing of *Britannia* and bears the royal cypher E II R surmounted by a crown. It is in French with the date and name of the port where the dinner is taking place written on the bottom.

After the reception, when The Queen has met all the guests, the doors to the dining room are opened and, with the exception of the royal party, they all take their places. The Queen and her guest of honour remain behind for a few minutes for the official photographs. They then move into the dining room and when all are seated the first course is served. Unless a senior member of the clergy is present, grace is not said. The china, glass and cutlery have been brought from Buckingham Palace and the footmen and under-butlers in their livery move unobtrusively around. Meanwhile the Band of the Royal Marines, which is embarked whenever The Queen is on board, plays in a nearby room. This band of twenty-six players under the baton of a Director of Music reverts to normal duties at the Royal Navy's Home Command in Portsmouth when not

Meals on board 'Britannia' are simple compared to the feasts in other Royal residences, but there is nothing lacking in the service. Everything is as perfect at sea as it is in Buckingham Palace.

touring the world with The Queen. The musicians are all widely experienced in a variety of instruments and can adapt their style from military marching tunes to pure jazz with ease. The string section usually plays during royal meals and one of the highlights of any evening's entertainment on board *Britannia* is when the full Royal Marines Band forms up on the quayside in ceremonial dress to perform the ceremony of Beating Retreat. The Queen loves military music and particularly enjoys inviting her guests to join her on deck to watch the displays of march and countermarch. As President Reagan remarked after seeing this spectacle: 'I thought Hollywood was the entertainment capital of the world, but I don't think they could beat this!'

Another advantage in using the Royal Yacht is that there need be no restriction on the amount of luggage the Household takes on an extended tour. *Britannia* has all the space required – and this is considerable when you remember that, apart from Her Majesty's wardrobe, files relating to every part of the visit are needed, plus the paraphernalia used by the clerks and secretaries on board. Space has also to be found for the hundreds of presents The Queen takes with her whenever she travels abroad.

Her Majesty is very appreciative of her hosts' efforts to entertain her and her husband, and also of the work done by the British embassies in the countries she visits, by the police officers, servants and secretarial staff who do so much to make sure that all goes

A traditional welcome on board 'Britannia' from a native musician from Fiji. Prince Philip is dressed in the tropical uniform of an Admiral of the Fleet.

well. So she always takes a selection of gifts which she hands over personally. There are cuff links and wallets for the men, brooches and powder boxes for the ladies and framed photographs of herself for a chosen few, who can immediately tell how highly they are regarded by the quality of the frames: silver is for Heads of State and ambassadors, blue leather for recipients a little way down the list and brown leather for those who just make it into the 'personal photograph league'. Royal presents have a definite hierarchy.

All the gifts, including the photographs, are paid for by Her Majesty personally.

This is the way the gifts are listed by the royal entourage:

Picture Frame	(A)	Silver – stamped with cypher.
Picture Frame	(B)	Blue leather – stamped with cypher.
Picture Frame	(C)	Blue leather – unstamped.
Picture Frame	(D)	Brown leather – unstamped.
Powder Box	(A)	Square silver box with raised royal cypher in centre in a stamped red leather box.

Powder Box	(B)	Small, round, silver, with cypher engraved in centre. Unstamped box.
Cuff Links	(A)	Gold, with cypher on both links. Red stamped box.
Cuff Links	(B)	Gold, oval, with cypher. Red stamped box.
Cuff Links	(C)	Gold, with cut corners. Cypher in blue enamel, flush. Royal blue box, stamped.
Wallet	(B)	Pigskin, embossed with cypher. Unstamped box.
Wallet	(B)	Brown, pin seal, fitted with gold corners. Cypher in top right hand corner. Unstamped box.

On the final day of a royal visit The Queen's Private Secretary will arrange for all the staff of the host country who are to be presented with gifts to be ready to see Her Majesty. Each one is presented to The Queen who offers a few words of thanks and then gives the present to the recipient. It is yet another example of the thought-fulness of a sovereign who knows and appreciates the extraordinary lengths to which people will go to make her comfortable.

THE ROYAL TRAIN

Queen Elizabeth II is the most widely travelled monarch the world has ever known. With at least two State visits overseas every year since her accession in 1952, and countless journeys throughout the length and breadth of the United Kingdom, Her Majesty spends a major part of the working year on the move.

She has the use of the most exclusive forms of modern transport: private aircraft, the Royal Yacht, luxury limousines, and the not so modern horse-drawn carriages of the Royal Mews. But her own favourite way to travel is by rail. In her case of course it is not an Inter City 125 or a tiny branch line through the Highlands of

Scotland, but the Royal Train which is today the only private railway service in Britain. It is reminiscent of the old days when the great railway barons used their private railway cars as travelling saloons – the ultimate luxury on wheels.

All the members of the Royal Family use the Royal Train but in fact the term itself is something of a misnomer. There is no such thing as *the* Royal Train. There are some fourteen vehicles which can be used to make up a Royal Train and it is possible to see more than one in different parts of the country on the same day. The trains themselves are owned and operated by British Rail and The Queen pays for all her journeys herself.

If The Queen and the Duke of Edinburgh are travelling together, the Royal Train will be what British Rail describes as a Long Train. This means ten carriages consisting of The Queen's personal saloon and sleeping accommodation, the Duke of Edinburgh's saloon and bedroom, a dining car, a vehicle for the Household – the Private Secretary, the Lady-in-Waiting and the Equerry – the Household dining car, the Household sleeping car, an engineering car (engineers and technicians from British Rail accompany every royal journey) and a power unit which is used to supply electricity requirements when the locomotive is not running.

The Prince of Wales is one of the most frequent users of the Royal Train, which is called a Short Train when he is on his own. This consists of five cars including his own lounge, sleeper and bathroom. If the Princess of Wales joins her husband an extra vehicle is attached and there is a nursery car with facilities for the children and their nannies. The atmosphere on board is very relaxed and informal but there is no reduction in the quality of service royalty expects. The dining car can seat twelve people in comfort, and lunch or dinner on board is as perfect as you would expect in any of the royal residences. The food is provided by Inter City Catering and the menus are agreed with the Royal Household beforehand.

The Prince of Wales provides his own crockery and cutlery from the kitchens of Kensington Palace, as did Queen Elizabeth the Queen Mother when she was a regular traveller. (Her dinner set is now on permanent exhibition at the Railway Museum in York, in the vehicles used by her until 1982.) The Queen and the Duke of

Edinburgh have a dinner service that has been on board the Royal Train longer than anyone can remember.

The Queen rarely entertains on board the train, though she did give a small dinner party for other members of the Royal Family when they attended the Investiture of the Prince of Wales at Caernarvon in 1969. She prefers to use the train as the most convenient method of getting to and from engagements and, while on board, usually eats alone or with a Lady-in-Waiting. The Duke of Edinburgh and the Prince of Wales, however, frequently entertain guests to working lunches or dinners.

The first serious user of Royal Trains was Queen Victoria, who had fixed views about rail travel as about everything else. In the first place she would not allow any of her trains to travel at more than 40 miles an hour, which made life rather difficult for the journey planners when ordinary trains were moving at much higher speeds. Her Majesty also disliked eating while travelling so the timetables were arranged so that she could stop for refreshment at various stations en route. Hence the number of elaborate waiting rooms at country stations between Windsor and Ballater – simply to accommodate the royal taste for a formal luncheon or afternoon tea. Another very good reason why Queen Victoria did not favour eating on trains was that at the time trains were not equipped with communicating corridors. It would have been necessary to stop the train every time a meal was served in order to reach the dining car. But Queen Victoria's aversion to eating on the move did not extend to taking a cup of tea and a small kitchen was attached to the rear of her vehicle for this purpose. Even today the Royal Train has no communicating corridor through the royal apartments; but there is a fully automatic telephone system throughout the train with a secret wavelength direct to Buckingham Palace.

King Edward VII had no reservations about eating on the move. He would eat and drink whenever and wherever he could. He enjoyed the Royal Train and used it as often as possible both in Britain and on the Continent. He entertained as generously on the train as everywhere else and commissioned special new carriages with elaborate designs, exotic carpets, magnificent works of art and, for the first time, free standing chairs in the dining cars, commanding a dining room 'as fine as that on the Royal Yacht'. The King's word was law and the resulting saloons were the most luxurious anywhere in the world. They set an entirely new standard for rail travel and have been copied, with allowances for changing fashion, by succeeding generations of royalty. King Edward's Royal Train was the first in Britain to make use of electricity – there were even electric cigar lighters in the smoking salon. The furniture was made of beautiful satinwood inlaid with ivory; the carpets in The King's saloon were in different shades of green, with peacock blue in Queen Alexandra's saloon; while The King's bedstead, embellished with his personal monogram, was in plated silver. Edward VII took an extraordinary delight in inviting his friends to dine on the Royal Train and in displaying his unique decorative talents. He also employed two footmen in the smoking saloon – one just to light his cigars and the other to adjust the curtains.

King George V and Queen Mary inherited this Royal Train and made very few changes, apart from installing a full-length bath for The Queen's use. The driver was instructed to 'slow-down' to a reasonable pace at 6.30 every morning when Queen Mary was travelling because it was at this time that she took her hot bath, and her servants were anxious in case the water spilled over the side. (Today The Queen's compartments have a bath; the Duke of Edinburgh prefers a shower.)

Edward VIII never used the train during his short reign but King George VI made a great deal of use of it, especially during the war when the vehicles were armour plated as protection against bombs.

The latest additions to the Royal Train came into operation in 1986, when the Prince of Wales took a close personal interest in the interior design. In the lounge area of his own saloon a great deal of use has been made of natural woods – sycamore and bird's eye maple. The two-seater sofa and easy chairs are upholstered in dark blue material with large flowery patterns. All the paintings in the royal coaches have come from the Royal Collection and even if these days the Royal Train could scarcely be described as a 'palace on wheels', as were its predecessors, it is still a luxurious, functional 'home from home' for the Royal Family and has become an integral part of many royal programmes.

THE QUEEN'S FLIGHT

The Queen's Flight has been described as the Royal Family's private airline, a description guaranteed to send the man who runs it, the Captain of The Queen's Flight, into an instant rage. Nevertheless, the only people who use it are members of the Royal Family, although in theory ministers of the Crown and senior (very senior) service officers are permitted to use one of the Wessex helicopters, Andovers or the latest additions, two BAe 146 medium haul jets.

The Queen's Flight is based at RAF Benson in Oxfordshire where 180 officers and airmen – and one civilian, a lady receptionist – fly and service the fleet. They are all volunteers, chosen from the cream of the Royal Air Force's aircrew and ground staff. Their proud boast is that they always have an aircraft ready whenever a member of the Royal Family needs it, and they are unique in that they are the only 'airline' in the world in which the passengers do not require tickets. Everyone who flies with The Queen's Flight is known and recognised by all its staff.

Catering forms one of the smallest yet vital elements of the Flight and consists of a Flight Stewards' section manned by four Flight Stewards who look after the well-being of the Royal Family in the air. They join the Flight for a minimum of five years. This is because the Royal Family like to have familiar faces around them and once a Flight Steward has got to know the particular likes and dislikes of the various members of the family, he is able to anticipate their in-flight needs.

The Duke of Edinburgh, the Princess Royal, Prince Charles and the Duke of Gloucester are the most frequent passengers and much of the Flight Stewards' daily routine involves planning and preparing their meals. If the flight is a short journey inside the United Kingdom, the meal will probably be a light lunch or supper, possibly cold. The Prince of Wales often eats only fruit and cheese when flying. He doesn't drink tea, coffee or alcohol but plenty of fruit juices. The Princess Royal often starts her day with an early morning flight and if her Private Secretary, Lieutenant-Colonel Peter Gibbs of the Coldstream Guards, is flying with her, the order will always include sausages, bacon, toast and coffee, but not for her. This full

English breakfast when Peter Gibbs is travelling is a standing joke in The Queen's Flight. Her Royal Highness never eats breakfast either at home or when travelling. A large glass of fresh orange juice with perhaps a little fruit is all she has. The Duke of Edinburgh frequently takes the pilot's seat, though technically the regular pilot remains the captain of the aircraft, and will eat his meal in the cockpit: toast and coffee if it is early morning, something more substantial later in the day.

The general practice is for the Flight Steward to liaise with the Royal Household to find out if anything special is required, but years of experience mean that usually the stewards know the sort of thing that's wanted without constant reference to the Private Secretaries. They will normally ask only whether a full meal should be provided or simply light refreshments. Whatever is needed is then ordered from British Airways' 'in-flight' catering department, whose executive chef is as able as any of his colleagues at Buckingham Palace, with whom he frequently compares notes. The food is collected on the morning of the departure and stored on board in the galley in purpose built 'air-larder' boxes which keep it fresh throughout the day. One of the Flight Stewards described the food served in The Queen's Flight as being 'on a par with British Airways normal first-class cuisine'.

Below is a typical order for a one-day flight for twelve persons: one member of the Royal Family, four members of the Household – Lady-in-Waiting, Private Secretary, Press Secretary and policeman – and seven members of the crew. It is for a flight in one of the Andovers and the royal passenger was Princess Margaret.

Twelve lunch trays complete to gold standards with main course in bulk and eight-inch (20 cm) plates provided empty.
Starters:
   Six guinea fowl terrine. Six smoked salmon.
Desserts:
   Eleven Kirsch gâteaux. One fresh fruit.
Main course:
   Six portions Scampi Alice in foil.
   Six portions veal in foil.

One large foil rice.
One large foil broccoli.
One large foil spinach.
One portion cream on each tray.
One large cheese tray with biscuits and celery.
One large fruit tray.
One foil freshly prepared Melba toast.
Twelve assorted bread rolls.
Forty-eight butter pats.
Two litres fresh orange juice.

A much bigger problem arises when a major overseas tour is planned. The Flight Steward has to keep in very close contact with the Royal Household, not only to find out what sort of food is required but the numbers who will be on board at any particular moment and the part of the world they will be in at the time. Many Queen's Flight journeys are in the tropics – especially when the Princess Royal is on one of her Save the Children Fund tours in Africa or South East Asia – and menus have to be planned up to six weeks in advance. They also have to take into consideration the availability of fresh food locally – in Africa avocado pears are a delicacy enjoyed on many royal flights – and work out the menus around the banquets and official dinners which will be eaten in the countries to be visited.

If the local facilities are not up to the standard required, everything is flown in by British Airways from their depot at Heathrow Airport, London; so airline timetables play a vital role in determining what to send, in order that it arrives while it is still fresh.

The new BAe 146s have resulted in a distinct improvement in the quality of catering on board aircraft of The Queen's Flight. The galleys are of course much larger than those on the Andovers, and the latest kitchen equipment means that anything from a light snack to a full five-course meal can be prepared in flight and served at leisure. The fact that the 146s can fly above the weather also makes life much easier for the Flight Stewards. In the old days they sometimes had to do a precarious balancing act whilst carrying a loaded tray when the aircraft was flying through heavy turbulence.

Her Majesty looks slightly puzzled – is it the food or the fact that she is expected to use chopsticks? – during the first visit to China this century by a reigning British monarch (October 1986).

Happily those days are gone for ever. But it also means that some journeys are much shorter than before, because of the higher cruising speed, so the stewards occasionally have to work a little faster to serve all the meals and drinks. The number of flights they are able to undertake has also increased; in 1988 The Queen's Flight flew a total of 989 journeys in Britain and abroad.

It is worth looking at another food requisition. This time it is for one of the new BAe 146s and the flight took place on 26 May 1988. The Captain was Squadron Leader Laurie and the Flight Steward was Sergeant Coles.

160

Four portions prawn cocktail.
Small foil buttered pinwheels.
One foil two veal steaks in herb butter.
One foil two portions salmon tranche coated in butter.
One small foil French beans.
One small foil leaf spinach.
One small foil parsley potatoes.
One small foil butter pats.
One small foil carrot batons.
Six bread rolls.
Small container fresh fruit salad.
Pint single cream.
One small cheese board.
One packet cheese biscuits.
Small fruit tray.
Small foil petits fours.
Two first-class lunch trays to HMC 302A.
Nine crew hot lunch trays to include alternative for First Officer.
Nine crew breakfast trays fully laid up to include alternative for
    First Officer.
Twelve fresh eggs.
Three pints of milk.
One tray sandwiches.
Two lemons.
Dry ice.

Note the instruction to the in-flight caterers for alternative meals for the First Officer or co-pilot. As with all commercial airlines, the pilot and co-pilot are never allowed to eat the same food in order to lessen the chance of food poisoning. This is standard practice in aviation throughout the world.

Can you guess from the menu which member of the Royal Family is travelling on this flight? Perhaps the leaf spinach and fruit salad would make you think it was the Prince of Wales. In fact the royal passenger was the Duke of Gloucester, one of the most regular users of The Queen's Flight. He was returning from Gibraltar to Northolt Airport, London.

When The Queen and Prince Philip paid a State visit to Morocco they joined King Hassan in a traditional feast – eating with their hands while seated on the floor.

The Queen's and her family's travel arrangements are interesting to outsiders not only because they journey in far more comfort and luxury than the rest of us, but also because they give us a unique insight into another aspect of the working of monarchy – and also a glimpse, perhaps, of the attitude of the Royal Family to the people. At The Queen's insistence all journeys by the Royal Train are programmed so as not to interrupt normal schedules; similarly,

162

although a 'Purple Airspace' is declared whenever an aircraft of The Queen's Flight is carrying a member of the Royal Family (which means that no other aircraft can enter that airspace for fifteen minutes before and after the flight — a little like a royal 'red carpet'), the flights are all arranged with commercial timetables in mind. When *Britannia* sails on a royal cruise, the dates are always arranged so that the vessel can also be used by British trade missions overseas. Royal Yacht 'Sea Days' have become one of Britain's most successful aids to export drives.

Travel is as important to The Queen as to any international business tycoon. The ship, aircraft and trains she uses enable her to see and be seen by more of her people than all her predecessors put together. Nobody expects Her Majesty to reduce in any way the manner in which she lives, works and entertains simply because she is not at home. Her style of monarchy has been to maintain the magic, but never to keep her subjects at too great a distance.

7

Victoria to George VI

British sovereigns have always been generous hosts, seizing almost any opportunity to stage spectacular banquets, balls and receptions. So if today The Queen is considered the world's most lavish host, she is only continuing a tradition practised by nearly all her predecessors. Even so today's arrangements, menus and guest lists for a State Banquet or formal dinner party at Buckingham Palace or Windsor Castle, elegant as they are, seem almost pale in comparison with those of previous reigns.

QUEEN VICTORIA

This historic photograph was taken at Balmoral in September 1896. It shows Queen Victoria with the Prince of Wales standing behind her and Tsar Nicholas II of Russia with his wife, Empress Alexandra, and their first child, Grand Duchess Olga. Altogether there were four daughters and one son, Alexei, who was born in 1904. The entire family was shot at Ekaterinburg in July 1918, a year after the Tsar's abdication.

Queen Victoria's reign of sixty-three years and seven months was the longest of any English monarch and her name has lived on as the personification of the greatest period in British history. Yet the public image was of a Queen who rarely smiled and who, after the death of her beloved husband, lived the life of a recluse. The facts are that Queen Victoria entertained on a massive scale which has never been equalled, and was herself entertained by a wide variety of artists, musicians, actors, poets and writers throughout her life.

Court records of the latter part of the nineteenth century show a veritable procession of entertainers to Windsor Castle. They ranged from Welsh Male Voice Choirs to singers from the Royal Opera House; every soloist of note performed for The Queen, and Sir

Arthur Sullivan, who was a personal friend of Her Majesty, brought members of his D'Oyly Carte Company to sing excerpts from *HMS Pinafore*, *The Mikado* and The Queen's favourite operetta, *The Gondoliers*.

At home The Queen enjoyed the good things of life. She was surrounded by family and friends and every evening began with a sumptuous meal. Her Majesty never compromised. Each dinner was laid out as for a banquet and the pick of the Royal Plate was used. Frequently the royal party dined off solid gold, even if the occasion was no more than a performance by a local amateur dramatic group. Queen Victoria was renowned for her fondness for gold, and even when alone often ate from gold soup bowls and plates or, occasionally at breakfast, a gold egg-cup. At some meals the only items on the table not made of gold were the cups and saucers.

Queen Victoria had one rule which was inflexible, and which is enforced to this day by her great-great-great-grandson Prince Charles: no smoking. The Queen hated smoking more than almost anything else and had NO SMOKING signs put up in every room of Windsor Castle. She knew at once if someone had been smoking and the culprit was sought out and told in no uncertain terms what she thought of him, no matter what his rank.

The formal occasions when The Queen entertained fellow royalty were splendid in every way. Servants wearing State Livery and with powdered hair stood behind every chair. It was usual for each guest to be waited on by at least three servants, sometimes more. One such occasion was the State Banquet to celebrate the christening of Queen Victoria's eighth child Prince Leopold on 28 June 1853. It was held in the State Ballroom of Buckingham Palace and the 115 guests included the King and Queen of Hanover, the Prince and Princess of Prussia, the Duchesses of Gloucester, Kent and Cambridge, the Duke and Duchess of Saxe-Coburg-Gotha, the Duke and Duchess of Mecklenburg with Princess Caroline, Prince Edward of Weimar, the Prince of Hohenlohe, the Duchess of Sutherland and the hero of Waterloo, the Duke of Wellington. The tables groaned under the weight of four sirloins of beef, four sides of mutton and four haunches of venison. There was a choice of sixteen soups, twelve fish dishes and forty-eight entrées.

Earlier in the day the Royal Family had staved off the pangs of hunger with a light lunch consisting of salmon mousse with Kirsch sauce, casserole of capon, fricassee of chicken garnished with mushrooms, together with asparagus and new potatoes, followed by cream caramel, ice-cream and biscuits. The Queen's eldest son, the Prince of Wales (later King Edward VII), who was twelve, was served a single course of boiled chicken and rice.

Members of the Household were also invited to celebrate the christening with a number of special luncheons – each served in a separate room to preserve the dignity of the rigid class system within the Royal Household. The numbers and menus were as follows:

16 Gentlemen-at-Arms

Beef, Pigeon Pie, Ham, Fowl, Jellies and Pastries.

24 Singers and Musicians

Beef, Ham, Tongue, Fowl, Lobster, Lamb Cutlets, Jellies.

22 Choristers

Beef, Lamb, Ham, Fowls, Jellies and Pastries.

11 Singing Boys

Beef, Lamb, Jellies and Pastries.

30 Yeomen of the Guard

Beef and Mutton.

8 Marshalmen and 4 Porters

Mutton.

8 Police

Beef.

20 Military Band

Beef and Mutton.

20 Silver Pantry and 16 Kitchen Maids

Beef and Mutton.

7 Nursery [*Staff*]

Mutton and Stewed Steak.

The Princess of Prussia's Dresser

Soup, Fish, Beef, Lamb Cutlets.

After the banquet to celebrate the christening Queen Victoria retired to her suite and the Royal Menu Book reveals that Her Majesty's supper that evening consisted of ham and chicken sandwiches.

The Master of the Household kept a record of every meal served in all the royal residences and also the exact amount of food and drink consumed. For the month of August 1853 a total of 6,723 persons, including the Royal Family, their guests, the Household, domestic staff, police, bandsmen and even upholsterers were listed as having eaten meals in Buckingham Palace. In descending order of precedence the list reads:

Royal Table	341
Royal Luncheons	257
Household Table	120
Household Luncheons	364
Suppers	30
Artists	47
Musicians	4
Concert Singers	5
Nursery	272
Stewards Room	1006
Servants Hall	2694
Sick Persons	9

Kitchen	. . . .	314
Kitchen Maids	. . . .	74
Coffee Room	. . . .	67
Silver Pantry	. . . .	77
Stewards Room Men	. . . .	54
Upholsterers	. . . .	8
Night Porters	. . . .	24
Stablemen	. . . .	54
Bands	. . . .	240
Sailors, Labourers	. . . .	506
Police	. . . .	156
Total	. . . .	6723

It is perhaps worth while to leap forward some twenty-nine years and look at two other functions involving Prince Leopold. They are both concerned with his wedding on Thursday, 27 April 1882.

The wedding breakfast of Princess Beatrice, the youngest child of Queen Victoria. She married Prince Henry of Battenberg in 1885 at her mother's house, Osborne, on the Isle of Wight. The wedding breakfast was held in a marquee erected in the grounds.

The bride was Princess Helena of Waldeck-Pyrmont, a sister of Queen Emma of the Netherlands and thus a great-aunt to the present Princess Juliana, the mother of Queen Beatrix. Prince Leopold had been created Duke of Albany in 1881, the year before. The ceremony took place in private (as was the custom with all royal weddings until the twentieth century) in the Chapel Royal at Windsor Castle. However, the wedding breakfast, which began at noon, was held in the splendour of St George's Hall, and the guests, most of whom were members of Europe's reigning families, and as such were all related in some way to Queen Victoria, sat down to a seven-course banquet. This is the menu:

The wedding group of Princess Beatrice and Prince Henry of Battenberg at Osborne on 23rd July 1885. The bridegroom was an uncle of Earl Mountbatten of Burma. Princess Beatrice survived her husband by fifty years – dying in 1944.

The Royal Wedding Breakfast

POTAGES
À la Brunoise
À la Crème de Riz

ENTRÉES
Les Côtelettes d'Agneau, Panées et Sautées
Les Filets de Poulets Bigarres aux Truffes
Les Escalopes de Ris de Veau à la Chicorée
Les Filets de Canetons aux Pois

RELEVÉS
La Pièce de Boeuf Braisée Sauce Raifort
Les Poulardes à la Jardinière

ENTRÉES FROIDES
La Salade de Homards
Les Oeufs de Pluviers

RÔT
Les Poulets Gras au Cresson

ENTREMETS
Les Pois Sautés au Beurre
Les Artichauts à la Lyonnaise

Le Gâteau de Genoise au Chocolat
La Crème à la d'Orléans
La Gelée Garnie d'Oranges
La Meringue Suisse à la Chantilly

RELEVÉS
Le Pudding à la Diplomate
Les Soufflés à la Canelle

The wedding breakfast lasted until nearly four o'clock in the afternoon, which meant that the guests had just time to rest briefly before changing and joining Her Majesty for dinner at 8.30 pm. Once again there was a choice of seven courses, each accompanied by the finest wines the Yeoman of the Cellars could find.

Her Majesty's Dinner

Thursday, 27th April, 1882

POTAGES
À la Tortue – À la Crème d'Orges – Au Printanier

POISSONS
Le Saumon, Sauce Homard et Persil
Les Filets de Sole Frits

ENTRÉES
Les Rissolles à la D'Artois
Les Côtelettes d'Agneau aux Haricots Verts
Les Suprêmes de Volaille aux Pois
Les Filets de Boeuf à la Financière

RELEVÉS
Roast Beef, Haunches of Venison, Roast Mutton

RÔTS
Les Poulets Gras – Les Cailles Bardées

ENTREMETS
Les Asperges à la Sauce

Princess Beatrice's wedding cake which was baked in the Royal kitchens at Windsor Castle. Only the bottom tier was eaten at the wedding breakfast – the others being stored until they were used at the christenings of her four children.

THE ROYAL WEDDING BREAKFAST
SATURDAY 27TH JULY 1889

POTAGES.
Aux Quenelles au Consommé.   A la Crème de Riz.

ENTRÉES.
Les Côtelettes d'Agneau Sauce Italienne.
Les Filets de Volaille bigarrés aux Truffes.
Les Aiguillettes de Canetons aux Pois.

RELEVÉS.
Les Poulardes à la Jardinière.   Les Truites à la Norvège.
Le Filet de Bœuf braisé à la Gelée.

ENTRÉES FROIDES.
Les Aspics de Gibier en Belle Vue.
Les Chauds Froides de Poulets aux Légumes. Les Salades de Hômard.
Les Mayonaises de Volaille.

RÔTS.
Les Poulets Gras aux Cressons.   Les Ortolans.

ENTREMÊTS.
Les Pois à la Française et Epinards au Velouté.
Les Gelées de Fruits et Champagne. Les Crèmes à la d'Orleans.
Kälte Schaale Von Früchten.   Les Puddings Diplomate.
Les Meringues à la Moderne.
Les Babas au Kirsch   Les Gateaux au
et Vanille.   Chocolat et Moka.

Les Escalopes de Fois Gras à l'Aspic
La Gelée au Vin de Champagne
Les Choux Glacés à la Duchesse

RELEVÉ
Les Savarins au Curaçao Sauce Abricot

There is no indication in the Court records as to whether the bride and groom joined the rest of the guests for dinner that evening, or whether discretion was the better part of valour on that occasion and they left for their honeymoon immediately after the wedding breakfast. Prince Leopold and Princess Helena enjoyed only a short married life. He died of haemophilia within two years though his wife survived him until 1922. They had two children, one of whom was Princess Alice, who lived until 1981 and was the last of Queen Victoria's grandchildren to survive.

When Prince Albert the Prince Consort died in 1861 Queen Victoria had retired into premature and permanent widowhood, spending most of her time at Windsor. She was never seen dressed in anything other than black, even at official functions, but contrary to what has become the public's conception of her, she was not a morbid person and was frequently 'amused', sometimes by slightly risqué humour. As late as 1890, she recorded in the Journal which she religiously kept up every day of her life, that she had enjoyed dancing a quadrille with Eddy (Prince Albert Edward, eldest son of the Prince of Wales) at Balmoral. One of the last public entertainments Her Majesty attended was a Garden Party in the grounds of Buckingham Palace on 11 July 1900. She was by then very old

One of the rare occasions when commoners were invited to Windsor Castle during the reign of Queen Victoria. This was a special garden party given by Her Majesty in 1897 for members of the House of Commons. Queen Victoria can be seen beneath the white parasol as she is driven to the Royal marquee for tea.

and infirm and on a blazing hot summer's day she rode in an open carriage, drawn by two tiny white horses, across the lawns of the palace. She was too ill to walk but all the other members of the Royal Family followed on foot with the exception of Alexandra, the Princess of Wales, who sat beside her mother-in-law.

The gardens of the palace were at their best and in those days an additional attraction was the presence of the royal watermen in their brilliant scarlet uniforms, who rowed the visitors about the ornamental water. This was of course long before the days when outside caterers provided the refreshments, and the palace staff had brought everything they needed from the kitchens in huge hampers. Such were the appetites in Victorian times that three servings were allowed for each guest. If any was left over it was given to the poor and needy in the East End of London at the end of the afternoon.

Five thousand guests sweltered in the London heatwave and applauded The Queen as she rode to the Royal Tea Tent for what would prove to be the last Garden Party of her reign. *The Times* published the full list of guests the following day under the headings of: Dukes, Duchesses, Marquises & Marchionesses, Earls, Countesses, Viscounts and Viscountesses. There were not many untitled people in the list. As a finale of Victorian garden parties, the occasion was unequalled.

Queen Victoria died peacefully at half past six in the evening on Tuesday, 22 January 1901.

KING EDWARD VII

When 'Bertie' succeeded his mother he already had a reputation as a *bon viveur*.

His appetite for all the good things in life was legendary, and he surrounded himself with the best food, the finest wines, the most beautiful women and the most amusing men.

He had waited sixty years to ascend the Throne and when his time came he made the most of it. The Edwardian age was brief – only nine years – but with Edward VII the Court took on a glamour and brilliance that reflected the optimism of the new century and has never been surpassed.

His Majesty also continued the custom of including his staff when there was a special occasion to be celebrated. On 9 November 1903, in honour of his sixty-second birthday, he not only gave a luncheon party for fourteen guests at which they ate ten courses, followed by a dinner party that evening for thirty-four guests with sixteen courses, but also provided all the workers on the Sandringham Estate with a Labourers' Dinner held in a massive tent in Sandringham Park. Five hundred workers and their families were invited and between them they consumed:

> 8 sides of roast beef
> 8 sides of beef sate
> 8 gigots of roast mutton
> 8 pieces of steak Anglaise
> 40 plates of purée of carrots
> 40 plates of potatoes
> 48 plum puddings
> 600 bread rolls plus
> 1 gallon (4.5 l) of vinegar
> 2 lbs (1 kg) of pepper
> 2 lbs (1 kg) of mustard
> 1 lb (450 g) of black salt

The following day The King held his usual shooting party and thirty hungry guests returned to Sandringham House for a lunch which consisted of ten courses. It was unusual for the shooting party to return to 'The Big House' for lunch; normally a large tent was erected out in the field, and the servants carried everything that was needed from the Sandringham kitchens in order that the day's sport would not be interrupted for too long. The number of people was reduced to twenty-four for dinner, but the number of courses was increased to fourteen.

Sandringham House took on its most glamorous aura at night. All the lights were on; fires blazed in every room. The massive central hall decorated in red, blue and gold (the royal racing colours),

One of King Edward VII's famous shooting parties at Sandringham in 1902. Guests said the weekend passed in a haze of continuous gunfire and the sound of falling birds. The King used to boast that he would shoot 'anything that moves'.

and called the Saloon by the Royal Family, was filled with artists, bankers, diplomats and statesmen all enjoying brilliant conversation. Throughout the evening Gottlieb's, one of the most fashionable German orchestras, which had come down from London specially for the event, played selections from the popular music of the day. After dinner the company split up into several groups – some playing bridge or other card games while others were content to catch up on the latest gossip. This was Society with a capital S, enjoying itself with the man who was its undisputed leader, the guest list changing every week.

Meanwhile in the Stewards' Room, sixty-three senior members of the domestic staff enjoyed a seven-course dinner and in the Servants' Hall, 148 lesser mortals made do with four. Outside in the park twenty-eight loaders and eighty beaters were fed cold beef, bread and cheese and each was given a pint of beer.

A few weeks later Queen Alexandra celebrated her fifty-eighth birthday. The date was Tuesday, 1 December 1903, and to mark the occasion Her Majesty decided to give a tea party for all the schoolchildren in the area. She was advised that it would not be practical to invite the youngsters to Sandringham, so instead she sent the party to them at their schools. Five schools – West Newton, Sherbourne, Wolferton, Dersingham and Anmer – received a total of:

18 lbs (8 kg)	Tea
145 loaves	Bread (cut)
38 lbs (17 kg)	Butter
40 quarts (23 l)	Milk
110 lbs (50 kg)	Sugar
580	Buns
130 lbs (59 kg)	Cake
49 lbs (22 kg)	Biscuits
580	Oranges
580	Apples

The goodies were all delivered by Sandringham's coal porter in a horsedrawn carriage, and even in those leisurely days, the royal timetable was such that every school received its supply at the appointed hour so that at four o'clock precisely (so as not to interfere with lessons) the children all sat down to a splendid feast.

Both as King and for most of the sixty years he spent as Prince of Wales, Edward VII was regarded as England's outstanding host, a reputation he enjoyed and jealously guarded. In London, at Marlborough House, or at Sandringham, the place he considered to be his home, nothing was left to chance. There were the finest foods, wines and diversions, and the guests were required in turn to maintain the highest standards as laid down by their royal host.

Dress had to be absolutely correct: full evening wear for dinner and everyone was expected to be on time. 'Bertie' himself was never late for anything and woe betide any guest, male or female, who arrived a minute late for cocktails, lunch or dinner. The King would rebuke them in no uncertain terms, in the loudest of voices and in front of everyone else. Afternoon tea was served promptly at five and dinner at eight thirty. Nobody was permitted to retire before the royal couple, even when this meant staying awake until two or three in the morning. One elderly guest, nearly eighty, simply could not keep awake after midnight and, thinking he would not be missed, quietly went to bed. Hardly had he settled under the covers when there was a knock at his door. It was a footman with a message from The King summoning him back to the drawing room, where he was scolded for his lack of manners.

Alexandra was an exemplary hostess. Just as today The Queen personally inspects every suite and bedroom before guests arrive at one of her homes, so too would Alexandra as Princess of Wales (and later as Queen) make sure everything was in order before the houseparty assembled. She was also aware of her husband's insistence on protocol, so would call on those guests who were staying for the first time and put them in the picture. They were told of The King's likes and dislikes and also advised which topics of conversation to avoid. It was always safer, she said, to talk about things rather than people; one never knew whether the person one had mentioned was in favour at the time.

Edward liked people about him that he knew – members of his own 'set'. Most of the men were upper-class Englishmen who shared their host's interests: hunting, shooting and cards. There was a sprinkling of leading bankers and financiers (as the Prince of Wales he was always in debt) and the odd bishop or two. The Queen preferred the company of men who were 'achievers': successful politicians, musicians such as Sir Arthur Sullivan (but not his partner Mr W. S. Gilbert for some unknown reason) and clergy who were known for their liberal views. Alexandra was a brilliant hostess who could mix with her guests quite happily no matter where they came from. She was the least snobbish of women and, although fully aware of her own position, had a refreshing honesty about titles and the type of people who sought them. At one dinner party she noticed that her neighbour Mr Disraeli was wearing no decorations, the only person in the room with none. As a joke she pinned her menu on the statesman's lapel, saying, 'It's a pity you have no decorations so I will bestow this one on you.'

Queen Alexandra was Danish and most of the food consumed in

the royal dining rooms was *cuisine classique*, but her favourite dish was that most English of foods, Yorkshire pudding. When she and her husband came to the Throne they began a custom of Sunday evening suppers at which the main course was invariably roast beef and Yorkshire pudding.

Without exception all weekend visitors to Sandringham were expected to ride. Both The King and Queen were expert horsepeople and His Majesty had little patience with any guest who could not keep up. It was occasionally left to the Queen to guide diplomatically those who were not completely at home in the saddle, back to the safety and comfort of Sandringham House, out of sight of her active and enthusiastic husband.

Both Edward and Alexandra were fond of dancing and again The King expected everyone to know the right steps. If one of his partners made an error in the quadrille or an eightsome reel, he would storm off the floor in an instant rage. Four annual balls were held at Sandringham: the County, the Farmers', the Ball held every December to celebrate Alexandra's birthday and the Servants' Ball. Between two and three hundred people would be present at each of these and although The King liked the servants to remain below stairs, The Queen openly admitted that the Servants' Ball was her favourite. Everyone was invited: tenant farmers, estate workers, and servants from the head butler to the humblest scullery maid, and the royal couple danced with as many as they could.

One of their tenants recorded his version of a Servants' Ball during the time when Alexandra and Bertie were still Prince and Princess of Wales:

The Ball opened with a country dance, the Prince and Princess leading off with the heads of the respective departments. The house-party, equerries, ladies-in-waiting, and all invited from the neighbourhood, were ordered to join in, no shirking or sitting out allowed, and when the sides had been made up, the Prince and Princess set off with their partners, round and round, down the middle and up again, and so on to the end, the Prince the jolliest of the jolly ... His own Master of Ceremonies ... sending messages to the band, arranging every dance ...

noticing the smallest mistake in the figures and putting every-body in their places ... Then a jig was started and it was so pretty to see the way the Princess danced it, while the State liveries of the footmen and the green velvet of the gamekeepers and Highland costumes, mixed up with the scarlet coats of the country gentlemen, and the lovely toilettes and the merry tune, made a sight to be seen or heard. Almost before one dance ended, the Prince started another, and suddenly the Scotch pipers would screech out and the Prince would fold his arms and fling himself into a Highland fling, and so on fast and furious until the small hours of the morning ...

When the Prince of Wales entertained, everyone had a good time – or else!

The Royal Family has always enjoyed its Christmas festivities but it wasn't until King George V came to the Throne in 1910 that turkey appeared on the menu on Christmas Day. When King Edward VII and Queen Alexandra sat down to lunch at Sand-ringham on Christmas Day 1903 the only concession to festive fare was in their choice of pudding. They began with Scotch broth; the main course was roast beef with salad, braised celery and boiled potatoes, followed by plum pudding. An intriguing footnote to the Royal Menu Book of that day indicates that among the Household in attendance was '1 Russian Messenger'.

KING GEORGE V

So far as being the host at Buckingham Palace was concerned, King George V did not relish taking over the Throne from his father. He was a family man who enjoyed country pursuits and his idea of a perfect evening's entertainment was to sit alone with his stamp collection or perhaps reading aloud to his wife. But he recognised that Society would expect him to assume the responsibilities of its leader and, albeit reluctantly, brought to those social functions a stature and aura which left nothing to be desired.

And even if his domestic arrangements were considered to be

simple, this was really only so in comparison to the lifestyle of his gregarious father. In fact his home life was the perfect example of well-ordered, unostentatious elegance and if he appeared to accept everything that was offered, it was because only the very best of everything was placed in front of him. Nothing ever went wrong, whether at Buckingham Palace or Windsor Castle or out in the field for one of his famous shooting lunches. The same attention to the finest detail and expert care was lavished on the entertainment of his guests, be it in a tent or the State Ballroom.

The late Duke of Windsor in his book *A King's Story* tells of the ritual surrounding dinner during Ascot Week at Windsor Castle:

A few seconds before 8.30 my father and mother with the other members of the family present would start down the corridor towards the Green Drawing Room. At the door we would be met by the Master of the Household who, as he backed across the threshold, would bow the King and Queen in. The ladies in evening gowns and sparkling jewels formed a quarter circle on one side of the room. The men were similarly drawn up on the other. The King, his sons, a few close friends, and members of the Household would be in the Windsor uniform. The rest of the men would be in black tail-coats. All would wear knee-breeches. While my mother shook hands with the men, my father would repeat the same formality with the curtsying women. Then the man who had been commanded to sit on my mother's right would bow and, offering her his arm, escort her to the table while the strains of 'God Save the King' issued from a grille in the dining-room behind which was concealed a Guards string band that played during dinner. One evening the gilt service would be used, on the next an equally magnificent silver one. The courses would be served by pages in blue livery and footmen in scarlet ... At the end of dinner, which never lasted more than an hour, my mother would catch my father's eye as a signal that she was about to leave with the ladies. The latter as they withdrew would each curtsy to my father.

Then he would motion to two of the men to take the empty

chairs beside him. Over the port, coffee and liqueurs the day's racing and current politics would be discussed. My father never sat more than twenty minutes – there was barely time to smoke even the shortest cigar. Abruptly, as if controlled by a hidden time-clock, he would rise and lead his guests back to the Green Drawing Room to join my mother. At 11 o'clock as if by magic the company would resume the same half-circle in which we had found them, the ladies on one side the men on the other. Bidding their guests good night, my parents would withdraw with the members of the Royal Family. The door would close silently behind us. The evening was over.

It was not the most exciting entertainment for the younger members of the Royal Family, but all their efforts to enliven the proceedings, even after their parents had retired for the night, seemed doomed to failure. The only people who were pleased that the evenings came to an early end were the musicians. They were trapped in a tiny, windowless cell from which there was no escape throughout the evening. On one occasion Queen Mary peeped in to see how they were getting on and was horrified at the conditions, which she likened to the 'Black Hole of Calcutta', the men sitting drenched in sweat, wearing heavy uniforms and with no opportunity even to go to the lavatory.

The catering arrangements for the Royal Family give us a few clues about the tastes of the new King and his Queen. Looking at the menu for Christmas Day 1910, the first in the reign of King George V, one can see signs of the true Christmas spirit:

Mutton Broth
Oeufs Brovilles aux Pointes d'Asperges
Dindonneau Rôti aux Marrons
Les Viandes Froides à la Gelée
Salade
Plum Pudding au Sabayon

The Palace Steward was also instructed to provide eight boxes of crackers for the royal table.

The residents of the Servants' Hall did quite well on that Christmas Day also. They received a wine allowance for lunch of six bottles of port, two of sherry, one of gin, one of brandy and four of whisky from the royal cellars.

King George V was known to dislike fancy foods and, particularly when he was shooting, he enjoyed plain cooking – but perfectly prepared of course. On Tuesday, 1 November 1910 The King was staying at York Cottage, the house he and Queen Mary had occupied for many years before they became King and Queen. For his Shooting Lunch on that cold, brisk Tuesday he ordered hot Scotch broth, kidney and oyster pudding, beef steaks, cold chicken and ham, with cold pudding and gateau for dessert.

Similarly there was not a great deal of mollycoddling in the nursery with regard to food. It was good, old fashioned plain fare and you ate everything that was put in front of you. When the Prince of Wales (later Edward VIII and later still Duke of Windsor), his sister Princess Mary (later the Princess Royal) and their brother Prince George (later the Duke of Kent) had lunch in the schoolroom on 28 December 1910 there was no sign of any left-over Christmas fare. They were given mutton broth, cottage pie, cold meat and apple pudding. King Edward VIII was to say many years later that if he never saw or tasted mutton again he would be very pleased.

King George V's second son Prince Albert (later King George VI) was allowed a special treat on Thursday, 18 April 1912. It was on that day that he was confirmed in Sandringham Church and at the age of sixteen was allowed to join his parents at the royal dinner. There were twelve persons present, including the Archbishop of Canterbury, and the seven-course meal was considered a celebration even though the young guest of honour was not permitted to taste any of the exquisite wines or liqueurs. They began with Consommé à l'Indienne – a clear soup first enjoyed by The King and Queen a year earlier at the famous Delhi Durbar of 1911. Then came Filets de Sole Frits which even the nervous and unsophisticated Prince Albert could relish, and Jambon de Prague aux Épinards, wafer thin slices of lean ham with spinach. The main course was Longe d'Agneau with Sauce Menthe (lamb with mint sauce), Oilles Rôties and Asperges en Branches. Then came Farola Pudding or Glace

Anna with, to finish, Oeufs de Pluvier, a delicacy still enjoyed at many royal meals.

The following day Prince Albert joined his younger sister and brothers in the schoolroom for lunch and a return to the more prosaic fare of cold cottage pie and apple tart, which, according to those who knew him at the time, he welcomed with undisguised relief.

If King George V expressed a preference for simple food he also had an unsophisticated palate when it came to drink. The King drank whisky with anything and The Queen liked only the lightest of white wines. The Royal Menu Book for 26 May 1924 includes the following passage:

Wines drunk by T. M. The King and Queen. Lunch and Dinner.

Lunch	–	The King	–	Bottled Ale (McEwans Red Label)
				Royal Tawny Port
		The Queen	–	Malvern Water
Dinner	–	The King	–	Whisky and Brighton Seltzer
				Royal Tawny Port
		The Queen	–	Sparkling Moselle

Earlier that same year, on 13 March, Their Majesties gave a dinner for thirty-nine people in the State Dining Room at Buckingham Palace. After meeting their guests in the State Apartments they sat down at eight thirty to a menu which, though maybe not to the complete taste of The King, had been chosen by Queen Mary with, perhaps, the culinary reputation of Buckingham Palace in mind. In fact, throughout his reign of twenty-six years, The King was content to leave all matters concerning menus to his wife. She became an authority on cuisine and dealt with the royal chef every week so far as the Royal Family's meals were concerned and also made the final decisions when the menu for a State Banquet was proposed. The only time The King involved himself was during the First World War, when he insisted that all meals for family and Household should conform to the rationing restrictions of the day, and he personally issued orders that no wine was to be served with meals for the duration of the war. This was one of the most unpopular orders ever received in the Royal Household, where servants of every rank had become used to drinking whatever they wanted with their meals. For the State Dinner mentioned above, this was the menu chosen by Queen Mary:

Torte Clair
Médaillons de Saumon à la Reine
Aiguillettes de Canetons à la Beauvilliers
Selle d'Agneau garnie aux Princesse
Cailles roties sur Canapés
Asperges, Sauce Bernaise
Soufflé Glace Jacqueline Gaufrettes
Croûtes Laponiennes

The pages waiting at table wore blue coats and breeches while the footmen wore epaulettes and breeches. The floral decorations were provided by Messrs Goodyear, whose Mayfair shop is still in Brook Street as part of Claridges Hotel, and there were also tulips and violets from the royal gardens. It took eight people to arrange the flowers and afterwards they were given refreshments in the form of a bottle of port and biscuits.

The programme of the evening indicates that 'Mr Forsyth played during Dinner' and that the bandmaster's dinner was served at 7.15 pm in Lady Barrington's room. Presumably Her Ladyship was absent at the time. Henry Forsyth had been a Pipe Major in the Scots Guards and was a veteran of the Boer War. When he joined the Royal Household on his discharge from the army, his main task was to parade in the garden just below the window of The King's bedroom. As the hour of eight o'clock struck, the morning silence would be rent with the skirl of the bagpipes as Mr Forsyth marched up and down playing a medley of Scottish tunes. He was also the man who taught the royal children how to salute.

During the function, members of the band were allowed one pint of beer each for the time they were playing and one further pint with their supper when they had finished for the evening. The

Household staff who were on duty did rather well for liquid refreshment, as the accounts show:

Pages on duty .... 4 bottles whisky
Footmen .... 2 bottles whisky
Silver Pantry .... 1 bottle whisky
6 Coal Porters .... 6 pints of beer
13 L.C. [Lower Coal] Porters ......13 pints of beer
(including supper)
Housemaids (cloakroom) .... $\frac{1}{2}$ bottle port
Police .... 1 bottle whisky

By all accounts the evening was a great success!

In May 1924 Their Majesties the King and Queen of Roumania made a State Visit to England. There was the usual arrival ceremony with a full Guard of Honour, which was inspected by His Majesty, drawn up in front of Victoria Station. The route of the carriage procession to Buckingham Palace was lined by soldiers in dress uniforms and another guard of honour was present for the arrival in the forecourt of the palace itself. The four-day programme was filled with lunches, banquets and even a State Ball on the evening of 14 May when some 2,000 guests enjoyed the splendour of Buckingham Palace's State Apartments. As usual the servants also had occasion to toast Their Majesties. This they did in style:

28 Yeomen of the Guard .... 7 bottles of port
14 Pipers .... 1 pint of beer each
Under Butlers .... 1 bottle of whisky,
36 pints of beer
Kitchen Maids .... 1 bottle of port
Coal Carriers ....20 pints of beer
Police ....24 pints of beer
Mrs Clark (Housekeeper) .... 2 bottles of port

When the account for the floral decorations for the State Banquet arrived from Messrs Goodyear it was discovered to be £110, a sum that would have paid the wages of four charwomen at the palace for a year.

State Visits mean a great deal more work for the staff in the Royal Household. This one was no exception, and the consumption of beer in the Servants' Hall went up accordingly. For the duration of the State Visit of 12–15 May a total of 184½ gallons (837 l) of beer was supplied to the Servants' Hall. However only 165 gallons and 3 pints (750 l) were actually drunk so at the end of the visit they were required to return 19 gallons (86 l) to the Yeoman of Wine and Spirits. There must have been a miscalculation somewhere! One reason for the increased consumption was that to help with the extra work a number of additional staff is usually hired on a temporary basis – some for the duration of the State Visit, others just for the evening of a banquet or State Ball. This is the full list of Hired Persons required for the State Visit of the King and Queen of Roumania 12–15 May 1924:

FOOTMEN'S ROOM

4 Footmen	@ £1 a day		Duration of Visit
12 ,,	@ 25/-	,, (£1.25)	State Banquet
11 ,,	@ 25/-	,, ,,	State Ball

EXTRA WAITERS

Mr Sayer	@ 30/-	,, (£1.50)	State Banquet
29 men	@ 25/-	,, (£1.25)	,, ,,
20 ,,	@ 25/-	,, ,,	State Ball

GLASS PANTRY

4 men	@ 10/-	,, (50 p)	Duration of Visit
3 ,,	@ 10/-	,, ,,	State Ball

SERVANTS' HALL

1 woman	@ 4/-	,, (20 p)	Duration of Visit
1 ,,	@ 4/-	,, ,,	,, ,,

STEWARDS' ROOM

2 men	@ 10/-	,, (50 p)	,, ,,
1 man	@ 7/6	,, (37½ p)	,, ,,

CELLARS

6 men	@ 10/-	,, (50 p)	State Banquet

12 men	@ 15/- a day (75 p)	State Ball
2 ,,	@ 10/- ,, (50 p)	13th & 14th only
KITCHEN		
9 chefs	@ 30/- ,, (£1.50)	Duration of Visit
4 kitchen porters	@ 7/6 ,, (37½ p)	,, ,,
5 charwomen	@ 4/- ,, (20 p)	,, ,,
SILVER PANTRY		
6 men	@ 10/- ,, (50 p)	11–13th only
18 ,,	@ 10/- ,, ,,	12–13th only
16 ,,	@ 10/- ,, ,,	12–15th
3 women	@ 4/- ,, (20 p)	12–13th only
3 ,,	@ 4/- ,, ,,	14–15th only
1 ,,	@ 4/- ,, ,,	16th only

In effect this meant that 174 men and women worked a total of 315 days for the princely sum of £250.70.

It is perhaps worth noting that in the hierarchy of the kitchens the chef, then as now, reigned supreme. The sum of £1.50 a day, giving a total of £7.50 for a five-day working week, was in those days at least three times as much as the average weekly wage in Britain. Housemaids were delighted to receive £30 a year plus their room and board and butlers in the most stately of homes were fortunate indeed if their yearly salary topped £200.

On the day The King and Queen of Roumania left London at the end of their State Visit, King George decided to relax after the rigours of four days' formality, and with a group of his close friends he organised a shooting party at Windsor. The royal guns were supplied by Messr Purdey & Sons of Mayfair, as indeed they are to this day. A footnote in the Royal Menu Book of the day, written in the hand of the then Master of the Household, instructs: '1 extra bottle of Port if Mr Purdey goes.'

KING EDWARD VIII

Born in 1894, King Edward VIII was the eldest son of King George V and Queen Mary, who were then Duke and Duchess of York. His grandfather, King Edward VII, conferred the title Prince of Wales on his father in November 1901, and he succeeded his father as Prince of Wales in 1910 after the latter's accession as King George V. Upon George V's death on 20 January 1936, he succeeded as King Edward VIII, but his reign was to last less than a year and he was never crowned. A constitutional crisis followed his announcement of his intended marriage to an American divorcee Mrs Wallis Simpson, and at the end of 1936 Edward VIII abdicated in favour of his brother Prince Albert, who became George VI.

During the short reign of Edward VIII there was not a great deal of formal entertaining at Buckingham Palace or any of the other royal residences because of the six months' Court mourning imposed after the death of King George V. However, the new King gave a number of small intimate dinner parties at Buckingham Palace and Windsor and he also invited a number of friends and relations to join him for a house-party at Balmoral, the private Scottish home bought for the Royal Family by Prince Albert, Prince Consort to Queen Victoria.

The party lasted for two weeks in September and was notable for guests whose names appeared in the guest-book for the first (and only) time. Gone were the prime ministers and politicians of cabinet rank, the archbishops and senior officers from the services. Instead the King had decided to ask his personal friends, most of whom would never have been invited by his father and mother. Mrs Simpson was included and her name was recorded in the Court Circular on the specific instructions of The King himself. She became his hostess for the duration of the house-party and took a pro-prietorial role in all the domestic arrangements at Balmoral. There were deer-stalking and grouse shooting every day, games of bridge after dinner in the evenings and His Majesty ordered all the latest films from London and Hollywood for the amusement of his guests. There was also one other item of entertainment that was unique to this unusual gathering. Every evening after dinner and before the coffee and liqueurs were served, The King, clad in Highland evening dress complete with kilt of Royal Stuart tartan (the special Balmoral tartan is only worn during the daytime), would lead the Balmoral Pipe Band around the dining room. His Majesty certainly managed

Polo was a royal favourite as far back as 1921. Here the Prince of Wales (later Duke of Windsor) introduces King Alfonso of Spain to players in an international match. This was, of course, long before the days when a Prince of Wales would appear anywhere in public in anything other than formal attire.

to play a few tunes on the bagpipes; the quality of his musicianship was questionable – but only in whispers behind closed doors!

Back in London The King continued to entertain his friends and exotic cocktails began to appear at royal receptions for the first time. In his father's and grandfather's time, pre-dinner drinks consisted solely of whisky for the men and gin for the ladies.

His Majesty gave two dinner parties at St James's Palace, both formal affairs planned with the obvious intention of introducing Wallis Simpson to influential members of the government and Court. Her name was included in the Court Circular each time. At the first dinner the Prime Minister, Mr Stanley Baldwin, was formally introduced to Mrs Simpson. It was the first and only time the Prime Minister would acknowledge the lady who was to be the cause of the abdication.

The events leading up to the abdication overshadowed all other items in the royal calendar that year, but The King carried out his public duties and as host to the nation went through the formalities of allowing debutantes to be presented to him at Court, though he did draw the line at the more formal 'Drawing Room' presentations; instead, they were to curtsey to him at the Garden Party in the grounds of Buckingham Palace. On that occasion more than 600 young ladies in expensive dresses and summer hats were soaked during a freak storm. The rains came half way through the first session and after sitting in a gilt chair under a silk canopy for more than an hour, The King realised what a ridiculous spectacle they all presented as the girls became more bedraggled by the minute. So he sensibly called a halt to the proceedings and, bowing to the waiting queue, returned to the comparative comfort of the palace. Apparently, the mothers of those unfortunate enough not to have been formally presented never quite recovered from the social stigma.

Edward VIII was a gregarious and fun-loving person who loved being entertained. Throughout his short and unconventional reign he liked nothing better than to visit the fashionable home of one of his cronies for a long, elegant dinner party – usually insisting that Mrs Simpson was invited too. One of the last he attended as King was on the evening of Thursday, 19 November 1936 at number 5 Belgrave Square, a mere five minutes from Buckingham Palace. It was the home of an old friend, Sir Henry 'Chips' Channon, and his wife. Channon was a member of the ultra wealthy Guinness brewing family and consequently money was no object when it came to entertaining the sovereign. It was just as well, for the ability and willingness to spend more on a single night's entertainment than the average working man earned in a year was a prerequisite when it came to acting as host to the cream of Society.

In his book *Chips – The Diaries of Sir Henry Channon* he recalls from his journal of the day the details of what was apparently a most successful evening:

> ... all morning I rushed about getting a film, as the King, most kindly, had put his apparatus at our disposal. It came from Buckingham Palace, and was put up in the Drawing Room. It was enormous and enclosed in a steel cage, and was formerly the possession of the late King.

I thought that our dining room looked a cascade of beauty, for the table seemed literally to swim with Dresden. Then at 8 o'clock, I read that Don Alfonso, second son of the Infanta Beatrice of Spain, had been killed in an aeroplane accident while fighting with the Insurgent forces in Spain. Bang goes our royal evening, I thought, and how ridiculous and manqué we shall appear. Then Princess Olga rang up ... but she only said she would be late as she was rushing to Claridges to console the Infanta. At 8.30 the guests gradually arrived ... at 9.20 I went to the front door to await the Kents and Yugoslavs, who were late. Two minutes later the King's car drew up, and he got out breezily, followed by Perry Brownlow, his Lord-in-Waiting. At once I saw he was in a gay mood ... I led him in and he spoke to everyone, and I then went back to the front door to meet the Kents. [The Duke and Duchess of Kent lived next door.] Paul of Yugoslavia followed, and for a moment I hestitated. Should we go into dinner or wait for Princess Olga? We decided to go in. Dinner was announced and Princess Marina, in a trailing black velvet tea gown which half hid her pregnancy, led the way. [The Duchess of Kent's daughter Princess Alexandra was born on Christmas Day 1936.]

The King said: 'Who is that man? Is he on your list?' It was Pierre de Monaco, whom I had asked at 8 o'clock, so he had not been on the King's list which I had sent him, and which he was clutching in his hand. But nothing could mar his excellent temper and we marched into dinner, the ladies leading. The King will never precede the ladies and dislikes being asked to do so. There was an awkward pause at first as Princess Olga had not yet arrived, and soup was served before she finally appeared, in a vast tiara and wearing two ropes of diamonds. She greeted Honor [Channon's wife] and curtsied to the King and then dinner proceeded ... Honor got on famously with the King, who ate a lot, drank claret and laughed much ... Tiaras nodded, diamonds sparkled, the service was excellent and conversation flowed ... the ladies rose, each one curtsying to the King as they left the dining room. The King called to me 'Sit on my left Chips. Come next to me Paul.'

We thus had a three handed conversation – two reigning sovereigns and Chips ... Then we went up to the drawing room which I had converted at endless trouble into a cinema. The King however, said, 'It's too late for a long film now.' So I cancelled it and only the topical budget, showing the King at Portsmouth, etc., were shown followed by a short Mickey Mouse ... On my return the room seemed to sway with jewels, and at 12.30 the King ... rose, and I escorted him downstairs to the front door, where he thanked me warmly ... They all left about 1.30, exalted and impressed, and, exhausted, I crept up to bed. The atmosphere had been terrific; so many royalties, so many jewels: the King told Honor that he approved of splendour.

Once the abdication had been announced and the ex-King had departed for France, his life and that of the woman he subsequently married continued on a royal scale. For more than half a century they remained one of the world's most glamorous couples. It was a lifestyle of unashamed luxury with parties almost every night, meals in the world's most expensive restaurants, charity balls and Caribbean cruises on private yachts. This continued until the day the Duke of Windsor died at his home in Paris on 28 May 1972.

KING GEORGE VI

When King George VI came to the Throne in 1937 he brought with him the image of 'Bertie the family man'. As Duke and Duchess of York, he and his wife had established a reputation as home loving, doting parents to the two young Princesses Elizabeth and Margaret. The new King was known to be at his happiest in his own home surrounded by his family and, because of a slight speech impediment, caused, some said, through efforts to correct his natural left-handedness as a child, he was not an enthusiastic party goer. Although the new Queen was regarded as one of the outstanding beauties of her day and consequently her company was sought by the cream of London Society, the Yorks had not entertained on the same scale as the Duke and Duchess of Kent, at least not until the move to Buckingham Palace. The Duke of York's younger brother, George, had married the glamorous Princess Marina in 1934 and they had become one of London's most attractive couples.

Nevertheless the early part of King George VI's reign saw a partial return of glamour to the Court. Queen Elizabeth reintroduced a number of gala occasions to the royal calendar and although The King was a reluctant host, he nevertheless went along with his wife's suggestions and wisely left all the arrangements to her. She was a brilliant organiser, just as she remains today, her dinner parties at Clarence House being the most elegant and enjoyable occasions.

In his book *Diaries and Letters 1930–39* Sir Harold Nicolson gives a revealing description of a private dinner party at Buckingham Palace on St Patrick's night 1937. Nicolson had been a Member of Parliament for two years and would eventually become a Junior Minister in Winston Churchill's wartime government. He was on friendly terms with many members of the Royal Family, including the ex-King Edward and Queen Mary, who co-operated with him on his authorised biography of her late husband King George V.

Diary   March 17, 1937

It is quite possible, without undue shame, to arrive at Buckingham Palace in a taxi even though one's taxi driver (in an orgy of democracy) insists on throwing his cigarette down on the red carpet of the steps; but it is difficult when the outer hall is filled with Beefeaters [sic], Gentlemen at Arms, and Royal Watermen to dash past duchesses in their tiaras and to say to someone (who, for all one knows, may be the Lord Chamberlain or the Master of the Horse) 'please, do you think I could get a taxi?'

I then go upstairs a little alarmed by the fact that upon each fourth step stands a footman dressed in scarlet and gold epaulettes and powdered about the hair.

In the first Drawing Room the equerries and ladies-in-waiting are in attendance as the guests arrive and a very distinguished gathering it is – Baldwin, the Prime Minister, Lloyd George, a former Prime Minister, Lord Halifax, a former Viceroy and future Foreign Secretary, Montague Norman, Governor of the Bank of England, the Duke of Rutland, the Duke of Buccleuch, Lord David Cecil and a cabinet minister or two. Their wives are in full fig, some with tiaras glittering in their coiffures.

The guests are then ushered into another Drawing Room and arranged in appropriate order. At 8.45 the King and Queen enter silently and shake hands all round. The equerries then approach the Duchess of Rutland and Mr Baldwin and lead them to the King and Queen who are now waiting to lead the procession to the State Dining Room. The King escorts the

The formal wedding photograph of the Duke and Duchess of York (later King George VI and Queen Elizabeth) taken in the Music Room at Buckingham Palace on 26th April 1923. The eight bridesmaids were Diamond Hardinge, Betty Cator (an old school friend), Lady Catherine Hamilton, Lady Mary Thynne, Lady May Cambridge and her cousin, Lady Mary Cambridge, Cecilia Bowes-Lyon and Mary Elphinstone, both nieces of the bride.

Duchess. The Queen extends her arm to the Prime Minister. As the party approaches the Dining Room the band of the Grenadier Guards in the room beyond strikes up 'God Save the King' and we, who are not in the know, wonder whether we should halt and stand to attention.

The dining table is one mass of gold candelabra and scarlet tulips. Behind us the whole of the Windsor Plate is massed in tiers. The dinner has been unwisely selected since we have soup, fish, quail, ham, chicken, ice and savoury. The wine on the other hand is excellent and the port superb. I discuss with David Cecil the reason why we have been asked. He says, 'I know why I have been asked. I have been asked as a younger member of the British aristocracy.' I say I have been asked as a rising politician, and I regret to observe that David is not as convinced by this explanation as I might have wished.

Afterwards the Queen goes the rounds. She wears upon her face a faint smile indicative of how much she would have liked her dinner party were it not for the fact that she was Queen of England. Nothing could exceed the charm or dignity which she displays, and I cannot help feeling what a mess poor Mrs Simpson would have made of such an occasion. It demonstrated to us more than anything how wholly impossible that marriage would have been. The Queen teases me very charmingly about my pink face and my pink views in exactly the same words as Mr Baldwin [Prime Minister] had used previously, so that I felt sure that during dinner he had told her of the remark that he cast at me from the Front Bench.

I go back to [Oliver] Stanley's [Cabinet Minister, later Secretary for War] house and have some beer while we discuss the strange legend of monarchy.

Of course within two short years the Second World War interrupted all social life at Court, and for six years Their Majesties' entertaining was controlled by the ration book. State Balls and banquets were replaced by the occasional dance at which nearly everyone was in uniform. If The King and Queen invited the prime minister to lunch or dinner it was invariably a working meal and most of the priceless china and gold plate was removed from the palace cellars to secret hiding places outside London. The people of Britain were suffering and The King and Queen were determined that they would share the hardships of their subjects as much as possible.

By Christmas Day 1944 the end of the war was in sight and the Christmas Luncheon menu shows a partial return to pre-war days, although everything on the royal table had come from the estates at Windsor and Sandringham. (During the first years of the war, The King had ordered the lawns on either side of The Long Walk at Windsor Castle to be dug up and planted with vegetables.) The royal luncheon menu was as follows:

Dindonneau farci Charcutière
Le Buffet
Fête de Porc Jambon Langue
Terraine de Gibier à la Gelée
Salade
Christmas Pudding
Brandy Butter
Mince Pies

The dinner menu for that evening was:

Crème Dubarry
Mousse de Perdreau à la Gelée
Salade
Compote de Fruits
Mince Pies
Sardine Diablée

Members of the Household who in pre-war days had enjoyed a gastronomic paradise in the royal residences were offered identical menus to those of the Royal Family for their Christmas meals.

Wednesday, 8 May 1945 was a red-letter day in all the Allied countries. It became known as VE (Victory in Europe) Day because that was when Germany surrendered and the war in Europe ended. There was celebrating in every corner of Britain and long-hidden stores of pre-war food and drink were brought out for the first time in six years. At parties in every London hotel the chefs competed to create the most outstanding dish. Ice-cream appeared in shops for the first time since 1939 – some of the youngest children could not even remember how it tasted.

The King and Queen appeared on the balcony at Buckingham Palace accompanied by their daughters, Princess Elizabeth wearing her ATS uniform, and alongside Their Majesties stood the Prime Minister, Winston Churchill, acknowledging the cheers of the ecstatic crowds. Mr Churchill was invited to stay for lunch, a modest meal of salmon kedgeree, cutlets of lamb, ham and tongue, salad and crème caramel. But in honour of the occasion The King decided to open the palace cellars and sample some champagne and vintage port.

Mr Churchill left the palace shortly after lunch but with an invitation to come back for dinner. In the meantime, life at Buckingham Palace returned to its normal routine, with afternoon tea being served in the Private Apartments at four o'clock. The Queen presided as usual, pouring the tea herself while the family tucked in to tiny cucumber sandwiches (with the crusts cut off), fruit cake, Swiss roll and currant buns.

Dinner on VE Night was a festive occasion. Queen Mary, The King's mother, was driven to London from her wartime home at Badminton and Winston Churchill wore his decorations, some dating back to the Boer War. The royal chef had excelled himself in producing, despite the food rationing still very much in force, a meal which was simple yet perfect for the occasion. The first course was poached turbot accompanied by a Niersteiner Riesling. Then came a casserole of partridge (the birds all coming from the royal estates) with broccoli and new potatoes, washed down with Château Mouton Rothschild, and between the main course and the dessert a green salad was served along with the first of several bottles of Heidsieck champagne. The pudding chef had concocted a delightful dessert out of vanilla ice-cream and cherries (one of the first houses in Britain to serve ice-cream at the time) and to finish there was the lightest of cheese soufflés. After the Allied victory had been toasted in the finest Graham port, Mr Churchill was invited by The King to light one of his famous long cigars. His Majesty also accepted a cigar although his preference was for Senior Service cigarettes, of which he smoked up to sixty a day.

It was one of the most enjoyable evenings ever spent at Buckingham Palace with The King and Queen entertaining only their immediate family and a few close friends. There was no official guest list; it was a spontaneous celebration and the talk lasted long into the night.

8

Royal Recipes

In the days of Queen Victoria and King Edward VII, fourteen-course meals were the norm at all the royal residences. In some ways it is strange to realise how little they have in common with the meals served at Buckingham Palace and Windsor Castle today.

The age of the freezer and microwave has arrived in the royal kitchens as much as in any other modern household, and with computers monitoring supplies of food and drink, everyone has to be cost conscious and every item accounted for.

In previous reigns royal catering was a labour intensive affair; no one cared if another pair of hands was needed to peel the potatoes or scour the pots. There was a plentiful supply of willing bodies, all anxious to serve the monarch for a pittance. Today the kitchens are unionised, overtime is claimed and paid for all extra hours, and the prestige of working for The Queen is balanced against the wages she pays, and the fact that employment in royal service is an 'open sesame' to more lucrative areas of domestic service in the homes of the new multi-millionaires of the technological age.

In King George V and Queen Mary's Household meals were an occasion to be celebrated. The first plover's egg was delivered with all due ceremony and dinner on the 'glorious 12th' of August invariably included the first grouse of the season. Strawberries were served only during the months they could be picked in Britain and when the menu said 'Fresh vegetables' they really were fresh: picked that morning and delivered direct to the kitchen by the royal gardener. Their Majesties had little time for modern labour saving devices like refrigerators, and deep-freezing meat was unheard of in the Royal Household.

Today it would be impossible to run a large house in the same way. The cost of labour would be prohibitive if every facility kitchen designers have manufactured to make life easier were not employed. While 'junk' food is still barred from royal menus, no one from The Queen down is averse to eating dishes that have come from the deep freeze. Here are some favourite recipes from the time of Queen Victoria until the present reign.

Queen Victoria

Bavarois au Chocolat

Put in a stewpan 8oz (225g) of sugar and 1 quart (1.14l) of milk, gradually stirring in 8 egg yolks and 4oz (110g) of grated cooking chocolate. Allow to thicken as with a custard, stirring constantly, but do not allow to boil. When cold stir in 1 pint of whipped cream and 6 sheets of melted gelatine. Pour into moulds and freeze. Serve in individual glass dishes with petits fours.

This was a great favourite of Queen Victoria and it was served in the Royal Tea Tent at the last Garden Party she attended at Buckingham Palace on 11 July 1900.

Each Christmas Her Majesty would give every one of her servants a plum pudding weighing 2lbs (900g). It was made to a special recipe known as:

Buckingham Palace Plum Pudding

Ingredients: 60lbs (27kg) flour, 30lbs (13.6kg) Lisbon sugar, 40lbs (18kg) currants, 40lbs (18kg) raisins (seeded and chopped), 30lbs (13.6kg) candied peel, 50lbs (22kg) chopped beef suet, 4 gallons (18l) strong ale, 150 eggs, 1lb (450g) mixed spice, 1 bottle rum, 1 bottle brandy. Method: Mix together the dry ingredients, then stir in beaten eggs, then ale, then rum and brandy mixed. Place each 2lb pudding in a cloth, and boil for 8 hours in a saucepan of water.

The ingredients shown above are sufficient for 150 puddings.

Another Christmas special was the mince pies made for the Royal Family and the Household at Windsor. The ingredients shown were for the entire Household and produced some 675lbs (306kg).

Mincemeat

Ingredients: 82lbs (37kg) currants, 30lbs (13.6kg) orange peel, 30lbs (13.6kg) lemon peel, 30lbs (13.6kg) Cedrat peel (another kind of lemon), 2lbs (900g) cinnamon, $1\frac{1}{2}$lbs (1.35kg) allspice, $1\frac{1}{2}$lbs (1.35kg) cloves, $1\frac{1}{2}$lbs (1.35kg) nutmeg, $\frac{1}{2}$ sugar loaf (about 7lbs/3kg), 24lbs (11kg) Lisbon sugar, 120lbs (54kg) minced beef, 120lbs (54kg) suet, juice of 25 lemons, 4 bushels russet apples, peeled and cored (a bushel was an 8-gallon/36l measure), 4 bushels Bramley apples, peeled and cored, 24 bottles brandy.

Method: Pass all the dry ingredients through a coarse sausage machine after mixing, then stir in the lemon juice and brandy.

KING EDWARD VII AND QUEEN ALEXANDRA

Both Edward VII and Queen Alexandra enjoyed entertaining and trying new dishes on their guests. But they also had their favourites which would appear on the menu time after time. The King knew exactly how each dish should taste when cooked to perfection, and also how important it was for a particular dish to be served at exactly the right moment. So when he had finished his portion, his plate was removed immediately, ready for the next, and that went for everybody at the table – finished or not.

The Coronation Banquet for King Edward VII was held in the State Ballroom at Buckingham Palace on 9 August 1902. Originally it had been planned for 26 June but the ceremony had to be postponed at the last minute when The King underwent an emergency operation for inflammation of the appendix. However, the delayed Coronation went without a hitch (with Queen Alexandra's Ladies-in-Waiting secretly nibbling bars of chocolate during the five-hour ceremony in Westminster Abbey) and by the time they returned to the palace everyone was more than ready for the banquet which followed. The recipe for one of the fourteen courses follows.

Cotelettes de Bécassines à la Souvaroff

Take 8 snipe, bone except for the leg bones, and put the two cutlets each makes on a dish. Season with pepper and salt, pour a drop of brandy on top of each, spread with a little farce of game about half an inch thick, then more forcemeat. Gently place each cutlet in a pig's caul, wrap and brush over with yolk of egg and breadcrumbs. Grill both sides until brown.

Serve on a silver dish bordered with potatoes and forcemeat, heaping in the centre beans, truffles and mushrooms. Serve with madeira sauce made with small slices of truffle. (Sufficient for 16.)

Edward VII liked the theatre in all its forms: musicals, plays and opera. When he went to the Royal Opera House at Covent Garden, he would take his own supper, as The Queen does today. The Palace Steward would prepare the meal in a room adjoining the Royal Box with silver and china brought from Buckingham Palace. It would usually be a cold meal but lacked nothing in terms of splendour and elegance. Liveried footmen were on duty to serve at table; the floral arrangements were always magnificent and the finest wines were brought from the royal cellars.

This is the recipe for a dish made with quail, one of The King's favourite foods, served at a supper party at Covent Garden in 1903.

Caille à la Diplomate

Take 16 quail, each weighing about 5 ounces (140g); clean and stuff with foie gras. Truss and cook for 12 minutes in 2 quarts (2.5l) of good stock which must be at the boil. Remove quail to a pan, pour boiling stock over and leave to stand until cold. Wash and clean the quail, removing all fat, then brush with meat glaze and dip in jelly made from the stock flavoured with sherry. It may be necessary to dip in jelly six or seven times until a good coating is obtained.

Serve cold on a silver dish with jelly, croutons and a Russian salad. Garnish with asparagus tips and serve with horseradish sauce. (To serve 16.)

Another occasion when King Edward VII liked to display his expert

BUCKINGHAM PALACE

Consommé

Sole Souchet

Devonshire Junket, Sauce aux Fraises

6 Mai 1910.

culinary tastes was at Royal Ascot. The race meeting in June is still one of the 'fixed feasts' in the royal calendar and The Queen's annual house party one of the highlights of the London Season – for those lucky enough to be invited.

The recipe below is taken from one of King Edward VII's luncheon parties during the Ascot Meeting of 1908.

Mousse de Crabe, Sauce Remoulade

Take a large crab, remove the meat, putting the claws to one side. Mix meat with a little mayonnaise sauce, pound in a mortar and pass through a very fine sieve, seasoning with pepper, salt and paprika.

Add 6 sheets of gelatine or strong fish stock, $\frac{1}{4}$ pint (120ml) of whipped cream, and set in a mousse mould coated with jelly. When turned out of the mould garnish the hollow centre with meat from the claws.

Sauce Remoulade

Mix 2 teaspoons of French mustard, a little tarragon and chervil chopped together and a little grated lemon peel with 5 tablespoons (75ml) of mayonnaise. Serve in sauceboat.

The next year, 1909, the following dish was served at The King's Epsom luncheon party.

Truites Froides au Rubis

Take 2 good pink salmon trout, each weighing about $1\frac{1}{2}$lbs (675g), and cook in a court-bouillon (water, white wine, carrot, onion, parsley, salt, bayleaf, peppercorns).

Simmer for half an hour, and when cold skin, bone and reform with a napkin. Save the head and tail and replace on a dish after skinning. Sieve court-bouillon, clarify with white of egg and make into a jelly, adding a little claret. Cover trout with jelly, garnish with stuffed eggs, diced tomatoes, cucumbers and prawns.

To make the stuffed eggs for garnishing: hardboil, scoop out yolks, mix with mayonnaise sauce and pass through a sieve before replacing.

Throughout her long life Queen Alexandra loved to celebrate her birthday in the traditional manner, with cards, presents and an enormous birthday cake. Below is the recipe for the 36lb (16kg) cake that the royal chef at Buckingham Palace made for 1 December every year that she was Queen.

Queen Alexandra's Birthday Cake

Ingredients: $3\frac{1}{2}$lbs (1.6kg) butter, 4lbs (1.8kg) Lisbon sugar, 5lbs (2.3kg) flour, 6lbs (2.7kg) currants, 2lbs (900g) sultanas well washed and dried, 1lb (450g) filleted almonds, $1\frac{1}{2}$lbs (675g) orange peel, $1\frac{1}{2}$lbs (675g) lemon peel, 3lbs (1.4kg) Cedrat peel, all cut small, 40 eggs well beaten, grated rind of 8 lemons, $\frac{1}{2}$ bottle brandy, $\frac{1}{2}$ bottle rum and the following spices mixed well together: $1\frac{1}{2}$ tablespoons allspice, 2 tablespoons cinnamon, 1 tablespoon mace, 1 tablespoon cloves, 1 tablespoon nutmeg. Method: Mix together dry ingredients, then stir in eggs, brandy and rum. Bake for 11 hours in a medium oven. Top with almond paste and sugar icing with orange-flower water flavouring.

KING GEORGE V AND QUEEN MARY

When King George V succeeded to the Throne in 1910 it made very little difference to his preference for what he called good, plain food such as mutton pies and Irish stew. However, service in the Royal Navy had given him a taste for the more exotic dishes of the east, for example Bombay Duck, and he also liked curry to be included in the menu from time to time.

Curry Sauce and Bombay Duck

Ingredients: 3 large onions, 2 cooking apples cored and skinned, 8 large tomatoes peeled and seeded, 1 clove garlic, 1 bay leaf, 4oz (110g) desiccated coconut, 1 quart (1.14l) good chicken stock, 3 tablespoons curry powder, 1 tablespoon curry paste. Method: Chop onions, apple, tomatoes. Melt 2oz (55g) of butter in a stewpan and fry onions, then apples and tomatoes, until cooked but not browned. Mix in curry paste and powder. Boil coconut with stock, strain and add, cooking for 10 minutes.

Cut chicken into small pieces, cook quickly in butter without colouring and add to sauce. Bake in a stewpan for 45 minutes. Take out meat and clean. Pass sauce through a fine sieve, boil, add juice of $\frac{1}{2}$ lemon and a gill of fresh cream until it reaches a good thickness. Return meat, heat and serve with plain white rice and a macedoine of vegetables (boiled and cubed carrots, turnips, potatoes, tomatoes, pimentoes and a few peas).

Bombay duck, a fish caught in the Indian Ocean and dried in the sun, is split and grilled and served with the curry.

King George V's Irish Stew

Ingredients: 2lbs (900g) neck of mutton, 2lbs (900g) potatoes, 1lb (450g) onions, $1\frac{1}{2}$ pints (800ml) water.

Method: Cut mutton into thick cutlets and blanch. Put in stewpan in layers, one of onion cut very thin, one of potatoes, then one layer of mutton, seasoning with salt and pepper. Add water and cook gently for $1\frac{1}{2}$ hours. Take meat out, pass potatoes and onions through a coarse sieve, making a purée of medium thickness. Arrange mutton in a deep dish with some plain boiled potatoes, olive shaped, and small boiled button onions. Pour purée over and serve very hot. Garnish with chopped parsley and freshly ground black pepper.

Mutton pies have been made to a special recipe for the Royal Family since the reign of Queen Victoria and are still made the same way today. King George V was very fond of them, either when lunching at the Palace or out in the field during a day's sport.

Buckingham Palace Mutton Pies

Make a number of tartlet cases about the size of mince pies from short paste, and from puff paste cut out two circles, one smaller than the other, for the tops of the tartlets. Cut a small hole in the smaller of the circles, and cook in the oven with the cases.

Cut slices from a cooked leg of mutton into small squares without fat or sinew; cook two finely chopped shallots in butter and mix with the meat in a pan with enough good stock to cover it. It should then be cooked slowly for about an hour until the meat is very tender. Remove the meat, cover with a rich brown sauce seasoned with salt and pepper and a dash of Worcester sauce, and fill the cases with this mixture. Put a little meat jelly on the top, cover with the puff paste circles, one on top of the other, and fill the small hole with a little beef jelly. Serve cold.

Grouse à la Balmoral

Take 8 grouse and boil until tender in good strong game stock for about 3 hours.

When cold slice meat from breast, clean and arrange the pieces on a silver dish. Make a thick jelly with the stock, flavouring it with sherry and brandy, and when set, pour it over the grouse. Serve ungarnished with a plain green salad. (Serves 16.)

On 12 December 1928 King George V underwent a serious operation for a streptococcus infection which resulted in a convalescence which lasted over a year. Queen Mary personally supervised his diet during this period and together with the royal chef decided on a number of special dishes which were served only to him.

Pommes de Terre Danoise & Oeuf Suzette

Bake a very large potato in the oven after scrubbing and removing the eyes, and when cooked, slice off the top and scoop out the inside. Pass it through a sieve, mix with a little hot milk, cream, butter and salt into a purée, and return. Serve the potato very hot, dotted with butter. For the Oeuf Suzette, follow the same procedure but line the inside of the potato with thin slices of ham in bechamel sauce, replace half the purée, and top with one or two poached eggs surrounded by bechamel sauce and sprinkled with grated cheese. Heat in oven until very hot, and brown the cheese under a grill.

Beef Jelly

Take tiny cubes of raw fillet of beef, set in a clear chicken or beef jelly and allow to cool.

Of all the food served in the Royal Household when The King was an invalid there was one dish which he liked above all others and which also became a favourite with Queen Mary.

Chicken Mousse

Take several fillets of chicken, remove all sinews and pound with the whipped up white of 1 egg and a tablespoon of very thick bechamel or chicken sauce. Then pass through a very fine sieve and stir in $\frac{1}{4}$ pint (120ml) of whipped cream until it reaches a firm consistency. This can be tested by dropping small pieces into boiling water. When sufficiently firm to hold its shape put the mixture into a buttered copper mousse mould and poach in a covered stewpan on a hot plate for 15 minutes. It should not be allowed to boil. Turn out on a silver dish and serve with plain white chicken gravy. (Serves 4.)

Queen Mary enjoyed a 'sweet tooth' throughout her long life and even in old age would urge her chef at Marlborough House to concoct one of his specialities such as:

Coupes Montreuil

Make a vanilla cream from 8oz (225g) of sugar boiled with 1 quart (1.1l) of milk, into which is stirred gradually the beaten yolks of 8 eggs. Allow to thicken but not to boil. When cold, stir in $\frac{1}{2}$ pint (240ml) of fresh cream, and freeze.

Slice 4 raw peaches and arrange in dessert glasses, allowing half a peach per person. Squeeze a little lemon juice over each so the fruit will not turn brown, sprinkle with caster sugar. Top with vanilla cream and serve plain. (Serves 8.)

Coupes Malmaison

Use the same vanilla-cream recipe. Peel and pip some large white grapes, allowing 6 or 8 per person, and arrange in dessert glasses. Pour over a little champagne and sprinkle with little pieces of ice. Top with vanilla cream. Serve with biscuits or wafers.

Bavarois au Sauce Cassis

Make the vanilla cream as above. In a copper sugar boiler put 3lbs (1.4kg) blackcurrants, 1 pint (560ml) water and $1\frac{1}{2}$lbs (675g) sugar, granulated, lump or caster. Boil for 30 minutes, until currants are well cooked and tender. Thicken with arrowroot, and strain. Serve sauce over vanilla cream in glass serving dishes.

Every year on Good Friday King George V and Queen Mary would eat a traditional meal of fish which was always prepared to the same recipe.

Cod with Egg Sauce

Take a few fillets of cod, salt and leave overnight. Cut into small portions, wash well and simmer for 10 minutes.

Egg Sauce: Make a roux of 2oz (55g) of butter and 4oz (110g) of flour; stir in gradually $1\frac{1}{2}$ pints (850ml) milk and bring to boil until it thickens. Add 3 hardboiled eggs, diced and chopped, and a little chopped parsley. Pour over fish fillets arranged on a dish. Serve with boiled parsnips and potatoes.

KING EDWARD VIII

In the days leading up to the abdication crisis The King lunched frequently with his mother Queen Mary at Marlborough House, though, because of her innate horror of anything approaching scandal, they never once mentioned the name of the lady who was at the centre of all the trouble. His Majesty was always very fussy about his food, demanding to know well in advance from all would-be hosts what was being offered for lunch or dinner. When the time came he rarely ate very much at all, preferring to pick at his food, and pushing it around the plate throughout the meal. There was one special dish that he always asked for whenever he visited his mother at Marlborough House, and it was always provided, but there is no record of whether he ate it or indeed, if he did, whether or not he enjoyed it.

Saumon à la Marlborough House

Take a firm fresh salmon, pink and well coloured, and cut into very thin slices or cutlets. Grill for a few minutes each side under a hot grill. Serve plain and ungarnished with mashed potatoes and croquettes.

KING GEORGE VI

When Bertie, the second son of King George V, succeeded his brother as George VI, he became the third monarch to reign over the British Empire in one year (1936). A man of simple tastes, this 'reluctant monarch' had very little interest in food. So long as his meals were well prepared and served at the right time, he was usually happy to leave the choice of menu to The Queen. But he did have one particular favourite which was served very often for lunch at Buckingham Palace throughout the Second World War. It was a simple omelette.

King George VI's Omelette

Ingredients: 3 egg yolks, 2 tablespoons rich cream, 2 egg whites, salt and pepper.

Method: Whisk together lightly egg yolks and cream, strain, then whip in whites not too stiffly, season, and cook quickly on one side in clarified butter.

QUEEN ELIZABETH II

Lamb is one of Her Majesty's favourite dishes, served in almost any form. Lamb cutlets with artichokes is one of the many combinations tried at Buckingham Palace and Windsor Castle.

Lamb Cutlets and Artichokes

Boil whole artichokes for 40–45 minutes in salted water. Serve hot with melted butter or hollandaise sauce alongside grilled lamb cutlets.

BUCKINGHAM PALACE CHRISTMAS PUDDING

One Royal Family tradition that has not changed over the years is that of having its Christmas puddings made in the royal kitchens. The recipe used by the King who taught the English to eat Christmas pudding – the Hanoverian George I – is still the basis of the puddings which grace the table at Sandringham and Windsor, with a little variation to give them a lighter texture. Ground almonds are now included and the golden colour comes from mixing in beer with the other ingredients.

The puddings are made in this way:

To each $1\frac{1}{2}$lb finely shredded suet add 1lb breadcrumbs, $\frac{1}{2}$lb sifted flour, $\frac{3}{4}$lb ground almonds, 1lb each demerara sugar, stoned raisins, currants and sultanas, 4oz each thinly sliced candied citron, lemon and orange peel, 1 teaspoonful mixed spice, scraping of nutmeg, pinch of salt, 1lb eggs (weighed in their shells), $\frac{1}{4}$ bottle sherry, 1 wine glass brandy, $\frac{1}{2}$ pint beer. Ingredients to be mixed in the usual way and allowed to stand for 12 hours in a cool place, then fill the basins and boil for eight hours.

THE DUKE OF EDINBURGH

His Royal Highness enjoys poultry and game, particularly if he has shot it himself. Partridge is a regular feature on royal menus and was even served at the wedding of the Duke and the then Princess

Elizabeth, possibly because with food rationing game was one of the few forms of meat available in quantity at the time.

Casserole of Partridge

Cut birds into joints and coat with seasoned glaze. Brown in hot fat in a pan. Remove from pan and place in a casserole dish. Rinse pan with a quarter pint (140ml) of dry red wine. Add liquid to casserole and cover with lid. Cook in centre of oven at 325°F/170°C/Gas Mark 3 for one hour or until meat is tender.

THE PRINCE AND PRINCESS OF WALES

Some of the dishes served at Highgrove and Kensington Palace reflect the modern tastes of the Princess of Wales perhaps more than her husband's conventional appetite.

Quails' Eggs Tartelettes

8 hard-boiled quails' eggs, parsley leaves, $\frac{1}{2}$ pint (280ml) aspic jelly. For the pastry: 4oz (110g) plain flour, 2oz (55g) butter, pinch of salt. Make the pastry. Use to line 8 boat-shaped tartelette tins. Prick the bases with a fork and chill for 10 minutes. Bake blind at 375°F/190°C/Gas Mark 5 for 10–15 minutes. Remove paper and return to oven for 5 minutes. Cool on a wire rack.

Halve the quails' eggs and arrange in pastry shells with parsley leaves; spoon over setting aspic jelly. Serve with garnish of watercress or parsley. (Sufficient for 4.)

THE PRINCESS ROYAL

The Queen's only daughter claims not to care too much about what she eats. Everyday menus at Gatcombe Park, her home in Gloucestershire, are plain and must not take up too much of her valuable time. But she is trying more sophisticated dishes, even adding an extra touch to an old royal favourite – scrambled eggs.

Gatcombe Scrambled Eggs

Use two large eggs per person, and for each egg allow ½oz (15g) butter and 1 tablespoon cream. Beat the eggs with a little salt and freshly ground pepper. Melt the butter in a heavy-based pan, pour in the egg mixture and cook over a low heat. As the egg mixture begins to thicken, stir continuously until it is softly set. Remove the pan from the heat and stir in the cream.

As an added attraction serve with lobster, shrimp and tomato in mayonnaise.

Naturally the chefs at all the royal residences have their own favourite dishes and ways of making them. But many of the long established items seen on royal menus have been passed down from generation to generation, and some of the dishes enjoyed by The Queen and her family today are exactly the same as those eaten by Queen Victoria and her family more than a hundred years ago. Modern kitchen appliances may have made the life of the cook a lot easier in the latter part of the twentieth century than in Victorian times, but the individual touch must still be there even if the meals served in the royal palaces and castles today are modest by comparison. There is only one standard when it comes to royal cooking – and that has never changed. It has to be perfect!

9

The Royal Suppliers

—

If The Queen fancies a couple of sausages for breakfast she buys them from Mr Edwin Baxter, a great-great-grandson of the founder of the firm G. G. Baxter Ltd of Birchington in Kent. Their pork sausages are world famous and are made from a recipe that has been in the family for 125 years.

The Queen is the only private customer the company supplies, but if you want to sample the royal sausages, you can buy them from the royal grocers, Fortnum & Mason. The eggs to accompany the sausages will come from Goldenlay Eggs (UK) Ltd from their headquarters at Wakefield in Yorkshire, and the ham or bacon will come from Messrs J. H. Dewhurst Ltd of Smithfield Market in London's East End.

Frank Cooper Ltd of Esher in Surrey make the very special marmalade enjoyed by Her Majesty, and the toast, or at least the bread from which the toast is made, will be provided by Justin De Blank (Provisions) Ltd of Walton St, London SW3. Mr De Blank is one of a select band of bakers remaining in central London who still make bread in the traditional way, baked overnight on a flat-bottomed oven. Her Majesty will have a choice from the 30 to 40 different types of loaf of which he bakes up to 600 every night.

The Queen enjoys honey at breakfast-time, and the man who is entrusted with keeping her supplied is Mr Bruce Gorie who used to run a shop named Kirkness & Gorie in Kirkwall, the capital of the Orkney Islands. The shop has closed down but Mr Gorie has retained his customers through a mail order business and Her Majesty is particularly fond of the crystal-clear honey which is produced only in a tiny area of Orkney farmland.

Her Majesty does not often eat fish for breakfast, but if she does feel like a couple of kippers, they will be delivered fresh to her table by the royal fishmonger Mr Eric Ruffell. Mr Ruffell has a shop at 13 High Road, Chadwell Heath, Romford in Essex from where he sets out in the early hours of the morning to visit Billingsgate fish market to buy his day's supplies. He starts deliveries to his customers as early as 5 am – and has usually finished them by 7 o'clock in the morning.

The Queen is woken every morning at 7.30 by her maid, who brings in the tea. It is a special blend made by R. Twining & Company Ltd, The Strand, London. The firm enjoys the unique distinction of being the oldest ratepayer in the City of Westminster, having occupied its present premises continuously since 1706.

Coffee is served with breakfast and this is also a special blend, made by The Savoy Hotel Coffee Department. Savoy Hotel coffee is famous in many parts of the world; during the Second World War General Eisenhower had a constant supply forwarded to him when he commanded the Allied Armies in Europe.

The coffee will be served in a cup supplied by the Worcester Royal Porcelain Company, which has been providing china and porcelain to the Royal Family since the days of King George III in 1788. The glasses on the table will have come from Thomas Goode & Company (London) Ltd of South Audley Street in Mayfair. The original Thomas Goode, the founder of the company, began supplying royalty in 1863 when the then Prince of Wales, later King Edward VII, became a customer. His Royal Highness was Goode's largest single customer, sometimes ordering £1,000 worth of glass and china in a single day. Much of what he bought is still in use today.

All these individuals and companies who supply The Queen and her family with their everyday requirements, from toothpaste to toilet rolls, are members of an exclusive organisation called The Royal Warrant Holders Association. They are all British, and even though those engaged in commerce in Britain, in either the whole-sale or retail trade, are numbered in their tens of thousands, fewer than one thousand are entitled to display the Royal Arms together with the words 'By Appointment'.

It is a special privilege and one which is highly sought, not only for purely patriotic reasons, but also, of course, in the good, old-fashioned cause of profit; the public knowledge that one is a supplier to the Royal Family is a tremendous boost to trade. Obviously, there is 'snob' appeal in being able to claim that your tablecloths are the same as those used by The Queen or that your dinner service comes from the same shop. Some people like to boast that they drink the same coffee as Her Majesty, write with the same pen, wear the same raincoats and drink the same gin. The Royal Family is very much aware of the prestige attached to the award of a Royal Warrant and jealously guard the privilege by enforcing strict regulations to govern the honour. Of course the appointment's exclusivity only serves to emphasise its value and prestige.

Any individual or company which has supplied goods or services for three years to The Queen, the Duke of Edinburgh, Queen Elizabeth the Queen Mother or the Prince of Wales may apply for a Royal Warrant. These four senior members of the Royal Family are the only ones who grant warrants, so select designers who make dresses for the Princess of Wales and the Duchess of York are not able to display a 'By Appointment' sign over their shop doors. Nor can those who supply the Princess Royal, Prince Edward or Princess Margaret.

Royalty has always known its value as a marketing commodity, and for more than 600 years successive sovereigns have actively encouraged trade by lending their name to commercial undertakings. The official history of The Royal Warrant Holders Association states that royal patronage can be traced as far back as the twelfth century, the first Royal Charter on record being that of the Weavers' Company granted by King Henry II in 1155. When Dick Whittington was Lord Mayor of London in the reign of Richard II (1377–1400), he obtained a Royal Charter for the Mercers' Company.

Henry VIII drew up his own 'Statutes of Eltham' to govern the 'good order of his household'. His Majesty was renowned for his appetite and among those who were commissioned to supply him was:

> Thomas Hewytt who hath bound himself by his deede obliga-
> tory to serve the Court with Swannes and Cranes, price the
> piece two shillings. The said Hewytt shall serve the King with
> all kinds of Wildfoule, in every degree according to the articles
> specified. It is ordeyned that the said Purveyor shall have
> authority by the King's Commission to make his provision of
> Poultry within this Realme.

Henry VIII also gave his official blessing to a lady as Court Laun-dress.

> Anne Harris, the King's Laundresse, shall be delivered, for the
> King's Highness, the washing of the napery which shall serve
> the King's Own Table. The said Anne Harris shall weekly
> wash the pieces as need shall require, and for her paines be paid
> £1 10s. a yeare, without further charge for wood sope, or any
> other thing.

These days the laundry for The Queen, the Duke of Edinburgh, Queen Elizabeth the Queen Mother and the Prince of Wales is all done by Sycamore Laundry of Old Town, London. It is a company which had humble origins in 1865, when the founder, a Mrs Buck-land, began taking in washing for the gentry of South London. She prospered when her daughter married a Mr Lehman and their great-grandchildren are still running the family business. When The Queen holds a State Banquet or official dinner, the napkins are sent to the Sycamore Laundry immediately the function ends – and so far they have never lost a single piece!

Every item that is bought by the Royal Family is entered into the Household Book. These days the operation is computerised, but until fairly recently everything was entered by hand and some of the older books make fascinating reading.

During the reign of Elizabeth I (1558–1603) the Yeoman Purveyors of 'Veales; Beeves & Muttons; Sea & Fresh Water Fish' were listed. The Yeomen were required to attend the Court on a regular basis and were paid as follows:

> Purveyors of Beeves & Muttons to have £13 13s 4d a yeare, and all riding charges. The Purveyors of Veales 100 shillings a yeare, and 20 pence per diem Board Lodging. Purveyor of Fish £10 a yeare entertainment and £22 11s 8d a yeare for losses and necessaries.

In the seventeenth century there was one unusual royal supplier: 'Goffe-club Maker – David Gassiers'. This was during the reign of James I, who is credited with introducing the game of golf into England when he moved south from Scotland in 1603.

The payment of royal accounts hasn't always been as prompt as it might be. In the reign of Charles II (1660–85), his Master of the Great Wardrobe wrote to him explaining as tactfully as possible that some of his bills had been outstanding for two years, and suggested that, as the tradesmen were 'very necessitous persons and their wares contracted for as for ready money' perhaps he should settle up. The amount at the time was £1,348 18s 4d – well over a million pounds in modern terms.

These days the accounts are submitted to the Master of the Household, who scrutinises them minutely before passing them for payment to The Keeper of the Privy Purse, who is also Treasurer to The Queen. Cheques are despatched promptly and advantage taken of any discounts available. The terms under which royal suppliers are awarded contracts are never disclosed, but the House-hold knows only too well that theirs is very much a 'buyer's market' and negotiates accordingly.

One or two companies supply the Royal Family with several different items for which they have been awarded Royal Warrants. J. & J. Colman Ltd was first granted a Royal Warrant by Queen Victoria in the early part of the nineteenth century simply for providing mustard for the royal table. Reckitt & Sons were sole suppliers of metal polish to Victoria's son King Edward VII. The two companies merged and, as Reckitt & Colman, were awarded warrants to supply King George VI with mustard, blacklead, metal polish and antiseptics. They now hold Royal Warrants to Queen Elizabeth II as suppliers of a variety of household products, including the original mustard, floor and furniture polish, air fresheners and OK Fruity Sauce.

Like many people in the western world, The Queen buys Hoover vacuum machines to clean her house, in fact all the royal residences. So does the Queen Mother. Hoover has held a Royal Warrant since 1927, and at the beginning of each year, the Housekeeper at Buckingham Palace informs the Master of the Household how many new cleaners she needs, and which parts will need replacing in the coming months. With literally acres of carpets to be kept spotless, 'hoovering' is a constant occupation for the housemaids and daily cleaning ladies in the palaces. The Royal Mews needs vacuum cleaners of the heavier type. These are bought from the Sturtevant Engineering Company of Brighton, whose machines, all named after large wild cats – Lynx, Tiger and Panther – will pick up anything from old straw to snow and ice.

A great many of the items that are used in the Royal Household are supplied wholesale, such as toilet rolls, light bulbs (the responsibility of the Department of the Environment, not the Master of the Household), soap and cleaning fluids. But some things of this nature are needed only on an occasional basis and then perhaps only one or two. So when, for example, a broken door hinge needs to be replaced or an extra key has to be cut, Buckingham Palace has a friendly neighbourhood ironmonger practically next door. Temple and Cook Ltd has the distinction of being the only ironmonger in Belgravia, London's most exclusive residential area and home to many of the capital's diplomatic corps. They have held a Royal Warrant for more than fifty years and pride themselves on being able to supply from stock all the little things that most other large department stores do not bother to carry.

Among the more unusual items required at Buckingham Palace and Windsor Castle is a patented chewing gum remover. It's called Novafrost and is manufactured by British Nova Works Ltd of Southall in Middlesex. The company has been supplying floor wax and other cleaning products to The Queen since the 1960s but, in common with all the other Royal Warrant Holders, its staff are reluctant to discuss the specific requirements of their royal customers; and nothing will persuade them to disclose the identity of the Head of State after whose visit they were called in to remove chewing gum from the carpets.

Probably the most famous suppliers to The Queen and her family are Fortnum & Mason, who have held a Royal Warrant for more than 150 years. Queen Victoria first recognised their unique qualifications and granted them a warrant in 1836. According to the company's records, they despatched goods all over the world on behalf of The Queen, including beef tea, with all its recuperative powers, to history's most famous nurse, Florence Nightingale, during the Crimean War.

Every sovereign since Victoria has continued to patronise Fortnum's who today are known as 'The Queen's Grocers'. Their salesmen still wear formal morning coats every day and rarely a week goes by without royalty – either British or foreign – being escorted through the renowned food hall on the ground floor or browsing among the magnificent crystal and china in the basement. They also sell fashionable clothes, toys, leather and fancy goods and, indeed, hold a warrant as suppliers of leather and fancy goods to Her Majesty Queen Elizabeth the Queen Mother. Some of the staff at Fortnum's have been serving the Royal Family for so long that they are treated as old friends, and a number find themselves invited to Christmas parties at Clarence House or Kensington Palace with members of the Household. They have also been required in the past to show royal servants (and on occasion even royalty themselves) the correct way to make a cup of tea. The story is told of one young royal being invited to tea by his tutor at university. When he returned to his rooms he was asked how things had gone. He replied: 'Pretty mediocre, Indian, milk in first. The man obviously hadn't been educated at Fortnum's.'

Harrods, arguably the most famous shop in the world, is able to boast warrants from all four senior members of the Royal Family. They supply provisions and household goods to The Queen; china, glass and fancy goods to Queen Elizabeth, the Queen Mother; and are outfitters to both the Duke of Edinburgh and the Prince of

Wales. Not for nothing is their company motto 'Everything for everyone, everywhere'. Harrods claim that if they cannot supply it – it doesn't exist! The Knightsbridge store spans 15 acres (6ha); there are eleven entrances and every day more than 40,000 customers pass through its 125 departments. Not all have come to shop: Harrods is also one of London's premier tourist attractions.

Provisions for Buckingham Palace are supplied direct from the food hall on the ground floor where they stock more than 500 different types of cheese and 200 brands of whisky. When the Princess Royal (then Princess Anne) opened the new food hall in 1983, she insisted on bringing forward the ceremony half an hour to eight thirty in the morning, so that shoppers would not have to wait past the normal opening time of nine o'clock. Her Royal Highness was invited to stay for the traditional Harrods breakfast of fruit juice, scrambled eggs, sausages, bacon, sauté potatoes, toast and tea, and as she cleared her plate she remarked that the enticing smells of the food hall had brought back pleasant childhood memories from when her nanny used to take her shopping. Queen Mary was the first to grant Harrods a Royal Warrant, in 1913, and there is a story (never authenticated) that she once bumped into her mother-in-law, Queen Alexandra, when they were both looking around the same department.

Like Fortnum's Harrods is well used to serving royalty and has supplied every royal family in the world. The Queen used to visit the store privately after closing time, during the weeks before Christmas, in order to choose personal gifts; but security has become such a nightmare that now a Lady-in-Waiting carries out this task. The firm has an elegant mail order catalogue and if occasionally Her Majesty needs to see something for herself a selection of goods is sent to Buckingham Palace for The Queen's attention.

Nobody holds a Royal Warrant for supplying wedding cakes to the Royal Family, but if an Appointment were made it would have to be McVitie and Price Ltd of Harlesden, London. They baked the wedding cakes for The Queen (then Princess Elizabeth) in 1947, The Queen Mother (as Duchess of York) in 1923 and Queen Mary when, as Princess Mary of Teck, she married the then Duke of York in 1893. It all came about by accident. In Queen Victoria's time all food consumed in the royal dining rooms, including that at weddings, was prepared in the palace kitchens by her own staff. But when the wedding of the Duke of York was being planned, The Queen's confectioner found he was unable to manage on his own and McVitie's were invited to make one of the cakes – there is always more than one at royal weddings. The McVitie's cake was considered to be so good that when the next royal wedding came around they were asked to repeat the exercise. They also provided the cake for the christening of Prince Charles in 1948 – with what was left over from his mother's wedding cake the previous year. There was plenty for everybody as the original had been nine feet (2.7m) high with four tiers and weighed over 500 pounds (227kg).

McVitie and Price may not hold a Royal Warrant for their wedding cakes but they do have one as biscuit manufacturers to The Queen and their digestives are particularly liked at tea-time in the royal residences.

Queen Victoria was always attended by two Indian servants when she was eating and her son and heir Edward VII employed an Egyptian servant whose sole duty was to make the special kind of coffee the King preferred. As we have seen, King George V was partial to curry, and although The Queen has rarely included curry on the menu at royal meals – though guests at the Coronation Banquet in 1953 were offered a mild curried dish which became known as Coronation Chicken – the London-based firm of J. A. Sharwood and Company Ltd are holders of a Royal Warrant as manufacturers of chutney and purveyors of Indian curry powder to HM The Queen. Curry is served in the Household dining room and in the staff cafeteria and the Duke of Edinburgh has been known to enjoy this most Indian of dishes on occasion.

Cheese is not regarded as a royal favourite and is rarely included as a course at State Banquets. However, the best-known cheese-mongers in Britain, Paxton and Whitfield of Jermyn Street, London, are holders of a Royal Warrant as suppliers of cheese to Queen Elizabeth the Queen Mother. The shop, which has been in existence since 1797, stocks more than 250 different cheeses – but no one will reveal which one Queen Elizabeth prefers.

An order for wine and spirits for the Royal Family is sought

Queen Victoria with her daughter and son-in-law, Princess Beatrice and Prince Henry of Battenberg, and their children having tea in the Oak Room at Windsor Castle in 1895. Whenever The Queen dined, she always had two Indian servants in attendance and frequently ate off gold plate using solid gold cutlery.

after, not only for the prestige but also because they are among the best customers in the country. The Queen's entertaining is legendary and the royal cellars are among the most extensive in the world. All the major champagne houses supply the palace; Bollinger, Heidsieck, Moët & Chandon, Veuve Clicquot are all holders of Royal Warrants, as are George Sandeman & Company Ltd who were first awarded a Royal Warrant by King Edward VII in 1913 and have been granted warrants by every monarch since. Theirs is a regular order at Buckingham Palace and Windsor Castle, because all royal toasts are traditionally drunk in port. Plenty of whisky is also drunk at Buckingham Palace. Nowadays most of it is consumed by staff and members of the Household but The Queen's grandfather, King George V, used to drink whisky with any food, whether fish, meat or poultry. The finest malt whiskies are supplied by John Dewar & Sons Ltd, who have held a Royal Warrant since Queen Victoria's reign, and John Haig, whose Dimple Haig and twelve-year-old Glenleven have been the favourite tipples of a succession of Private Secretaries.

The most interesting of all Royal Warrants is held by the appropriately named Royal Brewery of Park Street, London. They are the only company to hold a Royal Warrant in perpetuity, which means that they do not have to apply for a fresh warrant from every new monarch. This unusual distinction was awarded by King William IV in the early nineteenth century when the brewery was owned by Sir William Booth, a Sheriff of London. He financed the early polar expeditions and in recognition of his services to his country The King made the unique gesture of allowing him to call the company 'Royal' (even today you cannot add the word royal to a company's name without the Lord Chamberlain's permission) and to display 'in perpetuity' the royal coat of arms. Their beer, now brewed under the name of Courage, is served in all royal residences including the Royal Yacht *Britannia*.

The Queen, together with nearly all the other members of the Royal Family with the exception of Princess Margaret, does not smoke. Nevertheless, cigars and cigarettes are provided for guests through the services of Messrs Alfred Dunhill and Benson and Hedges. The latter company supplied King Edward VII with his cigars and when he was given a gift of Egyptian tobacco made it up into what became Cairo No 1 cigarettes. With that sort of royal patronage they could not fail; indeed the publicity they received as a result helped them to become the leading tobacco company in the country.

Chocolate in all its forms is enjoyed by every member of the Royal Family, and Cadbury's of Bournville near Birmingham is able to boast that it has supplied five English Queens: Victoria, Alexandra, Mary, Elizabeth (Consort of George VI) and Elizabeth II. The firm began business in 1824 as a one-man shop and after the first chocolate factory was founded soon built a reputation which has lasted for more than 160 years. Queen Victoria granted Cadbury's their first Royal Warrant in 1853 and since then they have never looked back. In 1969 they joined with another long-standing royal supplier, Schweppes, whose tonic water is a standard mixer with gin and vodka.

For chocolates with a slightly more sophisticated taste The Queen goes to either Charbonnel et Walker of Old Bond Street, London or Prestat of South Molton Street, just across the road from Claridges. Both hold Royal Warrants, with Charbonnel's bitter chocolates and Prestat's truffles appealing in particular to Her Majesty's sweet tooth.

The Royal Family has always been loyal to the shopkeepers of the towns nearest to their homes. Windsor, Sandringham and Ballater in particular have reason to thank their royal patrons. In the small Scottish town of Ballater, the nearest to Balmoral, almost every other shop doorway seems to display the royal coat of arms. Butchers, grocers, florists, game dealers are all 'By Appointment to'. George Strachan owns the shop which is nearest to any royal residence. It is literally outside the gates of Balmoral Castle in the village of Crathie and no one displays the royal coat of arms more proudly. The Queen and Princess Margaret used to shop there regularly when they were children, and the present generation of younger royals are frequent customers during the summer holidays. There are Strachan shops in Ballater and Braemar, and in their main store in Aboyne they display the largest selection of whiskies in the world – nearly 400 proprietary brands.

H. M. Sheridan of Ballater is the town's only butcher and his
Royal Warrant was granted by the Queen Mother who is very fond
of his speciality, venison sausages. Alistair Cassie is another Ballater
businessman with a 'By Appointment' sign. He runs the local television shop and whenever anything goes wrong with the picture at
Balmoral, it is Alistair who goes along to put it right. The Coun-
trywear shop has been called upon to supply The Queen's guests
with shooting sticks, tweed hats and thick sweaters for long days
on the grouse moors and as a result they too are on the list of royal
suppliers. J. & D. Murray, the Ballater chemists, keep everything a
good local drug store should and don't mind driving the few miles
to Balmoral if there is an emergency call for bandages, ointments
or any one of a hundred other items.

Robin Callander of Finzean is listed in the Supplement to the
London Gazette, which records the names of every Royal Warrant
holder, as a Drystane Dyker. He repairs the uncemented stone walls

on the Balmoral estate. His is an age-old craft and one for which he has been rewarded with royal patronage for many years.

Although no present member of the Royal Family plays the bagpipes, The Queen loves the sound of the Scottish national instrument. Every morning at nine o'clock a piper plays on the terrace outside her window, and no State Banquet would be complete without the music of the pipes. R. G. Hardie & Company of Glasgow are the world's leading makers of bagpipes and as such are suppliers to Her Majesty.

The shopkeepers and craftsmen in the area surrounding Sandringham also have good cause to be grateful to the Royal Family. Everything from Christmas crackers to new thatch for roofing is bought locally, and the thousands of tourists who visit Sandringham every year are delighted to be able to buy a souvenir from one of the shops bearing the royal coat of arms over their doorway.

Tom Smith & Company of Norwich have supplied boxes of Christmas crackers to the Royal Family for a hundred years and have held a Royal Warrant since 1906. K. W. Milton of Dersingham is a general store just a mile from Sandringham House. Its Royal Warrant states that the proprietors are purveyors of meat and poultry to The Queen. In fact their main royal customer is Queen Elizabeth the Queen Mother, who likes to sample their home-made pork sausages when she visits Sandringham. The shop was opened in 1954 and four years later, after supplying Sandringham with virtually all its meat and poultry for the required three years, Mr Milton was awarded his warrant. He no longer has a monopoly in supplying Sandringham; Dewhurst's has the bulk of the business these days; but Milton's still supply enough meat to remain on the royal list.

The Queen likes to spread her patronage around the local businesses so another small butcher's shop, R. F. and J. Scoles of Chapel Road, Dersingham, also gets a share of royal trade when the family is in residence at the 'Big House'. So too does M. D. Bowden, the local newsagent in Dersingham, who delivers *The Times* and *Daily Express* to Sandringham every morning. A number of the cottages at Sandringham are thatched and the Norwich firm of Farman & Son looks after these roofs using reeds grown locally.

Her Majesty's sporting requirements range from pigeon food to her own exclusive racing colours, which come from Gibson Saddlers of Newmarket. The food for the deer on the royal estates is supplied by the old established Scottish mills of the Hamlyn Milling Company of Aberdeen, while her gun dogs at Sandringham are housed in kennels built and sold by A. Neaverson & Sons of Peterborough. The royal kennels are exactly the same as any others, with one addition – they are all built a foot longer than normal. At Sandringham and Windsor, Her Majesty enjoys riding whenever she can, and her jodhpurs and hacking jackets are supplied by no less a figure than the Speaker of the House of Commons, Mr Bernard Weatherill. In his non-political life, he is a very successful retailer, holding Royal Warrants as supplier of sports clothes to both The Queen and The Queen Mother, who remained an active angler well past her eightieth birthday.

The three garden parties in the grounds of Buckingham Palace and the one held at the Palace of Holyroodhouse in Edinburgh are the four largest entertainments that The Queen provides. At Buckingham Palace, the catering is carried out by J. Lyons & Company, who provide everything, from the sandwiches, cakes and iced coffee to the 9,000 cups, saucers, plates and spoons. The tea tents and marquees are erected by Black & Edgington of Tower Bridge, London. They received their first royal order from Queen Victoria and have been supplying tents for royal garden parties ever since. The Master of the Household does not have the same problem as Black & Edgington's other customers, who need to place their orders for tents and marquees at least eighteen months in advance, such is the demand for their services.

The annual garden party at Holyroodhouse is held at the beginning of July when the Court sits in Scotland for a week. It is a much more attractive setting than Buckingham Palace, with the ruins of the medieval monastery alongside the palace and in the shade of Arthur's Seat, the impressive hill which overlooks the city of Edinburgh. Two companies have been entrusted with providing all that is necessary for The Queen to entertain up to 7,000 guests for the afternoon. They are Crawford's Catering of Distillery Lane, Edinburgh, who do for Holyroodhouse what J. Lyons does for Buckingham Palace, and Andrew Wilson & Sons of Abbeyhill, who supply the catering equipment. Between them these two firms reckon they can cope with anything from a children's tea party to a State Banquet, and they will provide everything from the paper napkins to the portable lavatories.

There is one feature of The Queen's public role which no one would envy and that is the number of hands she is required to shake. Her Majesty even has an entry in the *Guinness Book of Records* as having shaken hands with more people in a single day than anyone else in the world. Possibly the only people who welcome this aspect of The Queen's working life are those who work for Cornelia James in Brighton. This is the company responsible for making all The Queen's gloves, and as she can get through as many as five pairs in a single day on an overseas tour, the royal order is obviously very good to have.

The Queen's wardrobe plays a most important part in her public life. Three designers with international reputations look after all Her Majesty's clothing requirements, and each is able to display the Royal Warrant.

Although its founder Norman Hartnell died in 1979, the House of Hartnell continues with the royal patronage which started in 1935, with the marriage of Princess Alice, Duchess of Gloucester, when Hartnell designed the wedding dress and the bridesmaids' outfits, including one for the then Princess Elizabeth. Queen Elizabeth the Queen Mother has been dressed by Hartnell since she became Queen Consort in 1937, and when our present Queen came to the throne in 1952, Norman Hartnell designed practically every coat and dress she wore in the early years of her reign.

Those for which he was not responsible were made by Hardy Amies, who began his professional relationship with The Queen when she was still Princess Elizabeth. It was in 1948 that Hardy Amies was invited to design a wardrobe for the Princess as she set out for the royal tour of Canada, and he has never lost the connection with Buckingham Palace. In the year of The Queen's Silver Jubilee, 1977, Mr Amies was made a Commander of the Royal Victorian Order, the sovereign's personal Order of Chivalry. Today, his Savile Row premises are the headquarters for an international business empire which includes ready-to-wear and ladies' and gentlemen's bespoke tailoring; he has even designed uniforms for the air hostesses of British Airways.

Ian Thomas is the newest designer to join the ranks of Her Majesty's dressmakers, and his creations are often worn by The Queen in private. He works from a small boutique off Lowndes Street in Kensington, London, where the atmosphere is informal and slightly chaotic. Not that The Queen has ever seen it. Her dressmakers all come to her.

The relationship between The Queen and most of her dressmakers is the same – friendly but formal. Her Majesty's programme is worked out at least a year ahead – sometimes two for extended overseas tours – and the proposed schedule is sent to the designers, with a request to submit their suggestions for the coming year with preliminary sketches and swatches of suitable materials. Each receives an identical programme but they are not invited to compete against each other. At home The Queen changes her clothes at least three times every day; abroad it can be as many as five times, so there is plenty of work for them all.

Once the drawings are complete and the materials selected, an appointment is made to see The Queen at Buckingham Palace. There Her Majesty makes her choice and the dresses are made up for the first fitting. There will probably be three or four fittings before everyone is satisfied. They take between two and three hours and are always held in the afternoon. Apart from the designer himself, who is always present to supervise, there will be a small army of attendants, each one vital to the operation. There is a dress fitter, a men's tailor for the woollen fitted clothes, a ladies' tailor for the skirts and a secretary to take notes. The designer enters the palace through the Privy Purse Door, while his assistants go in through the Tradesman's Entrance in Buckingham Palace Road. This is not because of any class distinction – it is simply that goods are not taken through the front entrances of the palace. All the clothes are carried individually on specially covered hangers so that no one gets a glimpse of what The Queen will be wearing.

Most women have a friendly relationship with their dressmaker and The Queen is no different; the only distinction is that Hardy Amies grew up in an age when formality was the accepted thing while Ian Thomas is much more informal with everyone – including Her Majesty. During the fitting nobody sits down in The Queen's presence and the men leave the room while she is changing. After two or three hours they are all ready for a cup of tea, and this is provided in another room once the session is complete.

The Queen's wardrobes are, in fact, large rooms, and she insists that as a professional courtesy each designer's clothes are kept separately. So when Ian Thomas is fitting Her Majesty he is not likely to come across a Hartnell or Hardy Amies dress. The rules governing the choice of clothes for The Queen are simple and inflexible. They must be able to travel without creasing; coats should be light to wear (The Queen never takes her coat off at an official function). Hats should not have large brims because they shade Her Majesty's face from the public who have come to see her; shoes should be 'sensible' and, strange though it may seem, nothing must cost too much. With the price of a simple woollen dress being anything up to £750 and that of an evening dress as much as £3,000, The Queen likes to get good value for her money. Also she does not want anything too fashionable, because she often wears the same outfit on more than just one occasion. There is one other rule – all her clothes must be British. As the leader of Society she has to be seen to support the British fashion industry; so for her the couture houses of Paris and Rome are out.

The Queen's hats are made for her by Freddie Fox of Sloane Street and Simone Mirman of West Halkin Street, who also makes hats for the Queen Mother. Freddie Fox's creations are outstanding, and he has designed hats for the Princess of Wales, the Duchess of York and Mrs Margaret Thatcher. When The Queen wears a Freddie Fox hat it is usually to complement an outfit designed for her by Hardy Amies. Madame Mirman includes Elizabeth Taylor among her distinguished clientele.

Another milliner with a Royal Warrant is the firm of S. Patey (London) Ltd, but although they number several of the Royal Family among their customers, The Queen herself is not one of them. Patey's specialise in riding hats, toppers and mortar boards for academics, so their warrant is for supplying the ceremonial headgear to the coachmen and grooms in the Royal Mews. When

The Queen rides she doesn't wear a hard hat (something for which she has been criticised more than once). The Princess Royal wears a Patey top hat when she takes part in dressage competitions, but as she does not grant Royal Warrants, her custom is valued but cannot be publicly recognised.

No fewer than five shoe shops are holders of Royal Warrants as suppliers to The Queen. Two of them have premises very close to the palace. They are John Lobb of St James's, where the cheapest pair starts at £500, and Henry Maxwell of Savile Row, who makes Her Majesty's riding boots. K Shoes of Cumbria have supplied shoes to the housemaids at Buckingham Palace, Windsor Castle and Clarence House, and outdoor footwear to the staff of the Royal Mews, for more than sixty years, while H. & M. Rayne of Old Bond Street make some of the daytime shoes worn by The Queen and the Queen Mother and nearly all the evening shoes. As a result they work in close cooperation with the royal handbag makers, S. Launer & Co. Finally there is James North & Sons of Hyde in Cheshire. Their speciality is safety footwear, and it is worn by the Royal Household at Buckingham Palace and Windsor.

Jewellery is an important accessory to the royal wardrobe and The Queen has the finest collection in the world. It has been amassed over many years, the most valuable pieces being handed down to her. Six jewellers hold Royal Warrants, but only one, Garrard, are known as The Crown Jewellers. This is because they not only supply Her Majesty with personal and public jewels, but also have the responsibility of looking after the Crown Jewels at the Tower of London. It was to Garrard's that Captain Mark Phillips went to choose Princess Anne's engagement ring in 1973. So too did the Prince of Wales in 1981, and more recently the Duke of York in 1986. Wartski's were the first jewellers to introduce the fabulous Fabergé pieces to Britain, and both The Queen and her mother are still avid collectors.

Collingwood's of Conduit Street has a unique connection with the Royal Family. They fashion all the royal wedding rings out of the single nugget of Welsh gold that has been used for every royal wedding since 1923, when the Duchess of York (now the Queen Mother) was married in Westminster Abbey.

Both Cartier and Asprey, two of the world's leading jewellers, have been supplying royalty for many decades. Asprey received their first Warrant from Queen Victoria in 1862, and Cartier theirs from King Edward VII in 1908, after they had designed and made 27 diadems for his coronation in 1906.

The most recent of the royal jewellers is Andrew Grima of Jermyn Street. In 1970 he was awarded his first Royal Warrant after making a number of spectacular diamond brooches for Her Majesty, one of which was commissioned in 1972 as a present for Madame Pompidou, the wife of the French President.

When The Queen 'puts on the style' for a formal occasion such as a State Banquet, she is ablaze with magnificent jewels. Any other woman would seem overdressed – The Queen looks just right. The diamonds glitter from tiara, necklace, earrings, bracelets and brooches. Only her hands are free of decoration – and that is for a very practical reason. She shakes hands with so many people that she never wears anything on her right hand, and on her left there is only her plain gold wedding band and the diamond solitaire engagement ring given her by Prince Philip, which was reset from stones belonging to his mother, Princess Andrew.

The exchange of gifts is an integral part of royal entertaining. When overseas Heads of State visit Britain, The Queen always presents them with an appropriate memento of the occasion and is given something in return. No one, however, could match the gifts offered by some of the rulers of the Arab countries, whose presents are valued at over a million pounds. This happened when The Queen was a guest of King Khalid of Saudi Arabia, during her State Visit to his country in 1979. He presented her with a solid gold tray and gold falcon studded with amethysts, and two gold goblets. It was an extraordinarily generous gift even between two sovereigns, and it took The Queen completely by surprise. Her gift to him, however, while not in the same league financially – and what did that matter to a man whose annual income was measured in billions of dollars – was quite unique. He received the Royal Victorian Chain, the highest award in the sovereign's personal Order of Chivalry, and a specially framed photograph of himself with The Queen and members of both Royal Families, taken on board the

Royal Yacht *Britannia*, plus a valuable silver salver. Members of his suite said afterwards that His Majesty was more touched by the gift of the photograph, which had been personally chosen by The Queen, than by anything else he had received. When King Fahd of Saudi Arabia paid a State Visit to Britain in 1987, King Khalid's gift was displayed prominently at the State Banquet in his honour, and The Queen took equal pains in selecting a suitable gift for him. He also received the Royal Victorian Chain, and an oil painting by Harold Wood of one of his illustrious ancestors, Faisal al Dowish, after the Battle of Sibillah in 1929. It is today cherished among the many treasures in the royal palace in Riyadh.

Possibly the most unusual present to Her Majesty came during a visit to The Gambia in 1961, when she was given a baby crocodile. It spent the night in the bath being watched over by a member of the royal entourage, before being transported back to Britain, where it was housed in a zoo. Every present received by The Queen and the Duke of Edinburgh is carefully catalogued, and then found a home in one of the royal residences, where it can be located immediately and displayed prominently should the donor come to visit.

Choosing presents is a problem to most people and when you have to select hundreds the problem is multiplied accordingly. The Queen is extremely diligent about making personal selections, and she enlists the help of two small shops for the smaller, more interesting gifts. Halcyon Days of London supply *objets d'art*, such as individually hand-painted jewellery boxes, to The Queen, and she often looks to them when seeking personal gifts for her friends. A selection of their goods is on sale in the gift shop at The Queen's Gallery in Buckingham Palace. The other shop which is very convenient for last minute purchases is The Token House at Windsor. It is directly opposite the King Henry VIII Gate to the castle, and they have supplied The Queen with exquisite Waterford glassware for her to give away.

Throughout the year The Queen hands out hundreds of medals, stars and other insignia. Of course they all have to be made by someone, and Messrs Spink and Son of London have been the royal medallists for many years. Theirs is an age-old craft and one of which they are justifiably proud. They receive enquiries and orders from all over the world, and even when they have to refuse to carry out a commission – as when ex-President Idi Amin of Uganda demanded his own version of the Victoria Cross – manage to do so with such exquisite politeness that nobody takes offence.

The Queen wears ceremonial robes on very few occasions. But every year there is the State Opening of Parliament, usually in November, and in June she joins other members of the Order for the annual Garter Service at Windsor Castle. Her robes are made by Ede and Ravenscroft of Chancery Lane, London, a company which has been carrying on the same trade since 1689. Luckily, they don't have to rely solely on royal ceremonial occasions – they do a thriving trade in judges' robes, barristers' wigs and hiring out academic gowns to impoverished students on graduation days. They also made the robes for the Investitures of both Princes of Wales this century: the late Duke of Windsor in 1911, and Prince Charles in 1969.

The ceremonial side of The Queen's life means that a large number of Royal Warrants is granted to companies and individuals who supply goods and services to the Royal Mews. Swaine, Adeney, Brigg & Sons of Piccadilly provide the whips and gloves worn by the coachmen in the State Processions. Turner-Bridgar of Goring-on-Thames make the harness for the horses. Rolls Royce, Jaguar, Vauxhall, Ford and Austin Rover supply the motor vehicles, and Walter Sturgess of Leicester makes the horse-boxes.

Mr G. C. Francis of North Lancing has the distinction of being the only heraldic artist to hold a Royal Warrant. He is kept busy making sure all the designs on the royal coaches are in perfect condition, and his expertise in the use of gold leaf is greatly appreciated by the Crown Equerry, to whom he works.

As we have mentioned, once a year The Queen distributes The Royal Maundy. It is a ceremony as old as the monarchy itself and takes place in Westminster Abbey and a cathedral outside London, on alternate years. On the day before Good Friday, Her Majesty gives special coins to as many of the 'well-deserving poor' as she has years, plus one for 'the year of Grace'. At least, those were the original recipients. Today, happily, the need for such charity has largely disappeared and the men and women who receive the

Maundy Money now are those who have been nominated because of their own charitable good works. They also are drawn from a much wider area than the immediate parish where the ceremony takes place, and the service is now ecumenical with Anglicans, Roman Catholics and non-conformists all taking part. The coins are contained in special purses made for the occasion by Barrow Hepburn Equipment of London. In return The Queen is presented with sweet-smelling nosegays by the children of the parish, as a reminder of the days when the odours of the poor and unwashed were considered a little too strong for royalty's delicate sensibilities. These days the nosegays are not made by the children, but by a lady who lives at Haslemere in Surrey. Her name is Valerie Bennet-Levy, and for her efforts in this particular royal ceremonial she too has been granted a Royal Warrant.

Nearly every royal occasion is recorded on film. The photographers currently in favour with The Queen are her ex-brother-in-law, Lord Snowdon, who remains a good friend despite his divorce from Princess Margaret; Norman Parkinson, the extrovert fashion photographer who is a particularly close friend of the Duke of York (himself a royal photographer of note); Lord Lichfield, a cousin of The Queen, who took the official photographs at the christenings of both of the Princess Royal's children, and the latest addition to the group, Tim Graham, a red haired, energetic young man, whose photographs of the Princess of Wales in particular have been published all over the world, making him a rich man in the process. But none of these has been granted a Royal Warrant. That sole distinction rests with the firm of the late Peter Grugeon, whose studios are in Reading, not far from Windsor, and who still take official photographs at State Visits.

If Her Majesty wants to watch herself on television, she does so by courtesy of DER, one of Britain's largest television rental companies. Like so many of her subjects, she rents her television sets, but she buys her radio sets – from Roberts Radio, who claim to make the best radios in the world.

The list of Royal Warrant holders stretches into nearly twenty pages, and many of the most famous companies in the world are represented. But the names are not all those of international conglomerates whose trade marks are household names. Some of the smallest one-man companies provide equally important services to The Queen and her Household and they too have been formally recognised: the chimney sweeps and window cleaners; the refuse collectors and newsagents.

Not everyone who supplies The Queen is a warrant holder. Even her bankers, Coutts & Company, who provide the royal chequebook, have not yet been granted a warrant. But they, and all those who enjoy royal patronage, know that so long as they can claim The Queen as a satisfied customer, they may, eventually, be allowed to join the exclusive ranks of the Royal Warrant Holders Association – and that is a privilege money cannot buy!

Appendix

The wide variety of people who are invited to meet The Queen at her informal lunches in Buckingham Palace can be seen in a sample of the guest lists for just four luncheons held in 1988.

On 3 March, Her Majesty and the Duke of Edinburgh invited a nun, Sister Carol of the Convent of the Holy Name, Malvern Link; a golfer, Ian Woosnam, who was the first golfer in the world to win one million dollars in a single tournament; Gervase Jackson-Stops, who is Architectural Adviser to the National Trust; Mrs Lorraine Cole, Headmistress of Queenshill Primary School; Harold Cudmore, a successful yachtsman; and Professor Sir Donald Acheson, who is Chief Medical Officer for the Department of Health and Social Security.

At a similar function on 3 June, the Duke of Edinburgh was abroad, so Princess Alexandra joined Her Majesty, together with the world champion snooker player Steve Davis and Nigel Hawthorne, the actor, whose most famous role is that of the Private Secretary to the Prime Minister in the well known television series *Yes, Prime Minister*. Also included were Dame Elizabeth Butler-Sloss, Lord Justice of Appeal, and Felicity Lott the opera singer; Murray Lawrence, Chairman, Lloyd's of London; Vice-Admiral Sir Anthony Tippet, General Manager of Great Ormond Street Hospital; and Andreas Whittam Smith, the Editor of *The Independent* newspaper.

The following month, on 8 July, another mixed bag of guests was present when the Duchess of York joined The Queen to welcome the Principal of an Oxford College, Mrs Mary Moore; General Eva Burrows, General of the Salvation Army; and Sir Bernard Ashley, head of Laura Ashley Limited. The party was completed by Barry Douglas, the pianist; Sir Robin Butler, Secretary to The Cabinet (and said to be one of the most powerful men in Britain); Anthony Christopher, General Secretary of the Inland Revenue Staff Federation; and Marcus Binney, Editor of *Landscape* magazine.

The final luncheon of the year was held on 30 November, when the guest list included Dr Alan Borg, Director-General of the Imperial War Museum; Adrian Moorhouse, the British Olympic swimmer; Sir Barry Shaw, Director of Public Prosecutions in Northern Ireland; Marina Warner the author; Mrs Ethel Chamberlain, who is Chairman and Managing Director of her own large engineering company; and Peter Grant, Chairman of Sun Alliance Assurance Company. A civil servant, Sir David Hancock, and an eminent surgeon, Professor John Camm of St George's Medical School, completed the list of a typically varied assortment of people from many walks of life who had been entertained to lunch at Buckingham Palace in 1988.

Bibliography

Channon, Sir Henry (Chips), *Diaries*, Weidenfeld & Nicolson, 1967

Churchill, Randolph, *They Serve the Queen*, Hutchinson, 1953

Duff, David, *Alexandra: Princess and Queen*, Sphere, 1981

Duncan, Andrew, *The Reality of Monarchy*, Pan, 1973

Edgar, Donald, *Palace*, Comet, 1983

Edwards, Robb and Anne, *The Queen's Clothes*, Express Books, 1977

Garrett, Richard, *Royal Travel*, Blandford, 1982

Grunfeld, Nina, *The Royal Shopping Guide*, Pan, 1984

Hibbert, Christopher, *The Court of St James's*, Weidenfeld & Nicolson, 1979

Laird, Dorothy, *How the Queen Reigns*, Hodder & Stoughton, 1959

Longford, Elizabeth, *Victoria R. I.*, Hodder & Stoughton, 1964

Longford, Elizabeth, *Elizabeth R.*, Hodder & Stoughton, 1983

Martin, Kingsley, *The Magic of Monarchy*, Nelson, 1973

Morrah, Dermot, *The Work of the Queen*, William Kimber, 1958

Morton, Andrew, *The Royal Yacht Britannia*, Orbis, 1984

Morton, Andrew, *Inside Kensington Palace*, Michael O'Mara, 1987

Nevill, B. St John, *Life at the Court of Queen Victoria*, Webb & Bower, 1984

Nicolson, Sir Harold, *Diaries and Letters 1930–39*, Collins, 1980

Royal Archives, courtesy of the, *The Royal Menu Books*

Tschumi, Gabriel, *Royal Chef*, Kimber, 1957

Whiting, Audrey, *The Kents*, Hutchinson, 1985

Windsor, HRH The Duke of, *A King's Story*, Cassell, 1951

Picture Credits

Index